LOCH NESS MONSTER

And other UNEXPLAINED MYSTERIES

First published in 2013

A catalogue record for this book is available from the British Library

ISBN: 978-0-85733-202-8

Published by Haynes Publishing, Sparkford, Yeovil,
Somerset BA22 7JJ, UK
Tel: 01963 442030 Fax: 01963 440001
Int. tel: +44 1963 442030 Int. fax: +44 1963 440001
E-mail: sales@haynes.co.uk
Website: www.haynes.co.uk

Haynes North America Inc., 861 Lawrence Drive,
Newbury Park, California 91320, USA

Creative Director: Kevin Gardner
Designed for Haynes by BrainWave

Printed and bound in the US

LOCH NESS MONSTER

And other UNEXPLAINED MYSTERIES

J F Derry

HEADQUARTERS
LOCH NESS
EXPEDITION
CAMPBELL
FEED
L.
TAKE UP
R.

Introduction Monsters and Aliens

A member of the Loch Ness Investigation Bureau sets up his camera in 1966.

Monsters and aliens occupy the unseen areas of our universe, lurking within its dark recesses, flitting between the shadows, and stalking the canyons of our minds. They hardly ever allow themselves to be seen or make their presence known, so meeting them is rare, and very few of us have had that personal experience where our paths have actually crossed. Nonetheless, their influence has spread to every one of us, through the stories that they inspire. Our books have captured them at the bottom of the deepest ocean and the top of the highest peaks. Our films pitch battle against them throughout the outer spiral arm of a galaxy we call the Milky Way. What's a monster flick without a marauding monstrosity? Sci-fi *sans* an alien?

Mythical fire-breathing monsters have become ingrained into our cultural psyche over the course of millennia: from stories from ancient India and the Far East, to Greek and Norse mythology, European folklore and the princess-stealer slain by St George, Tolkien's treasure-hoarding Smaug and Ishirō Honda's city-crushing Godzilla, to the tamer, Pete-befriending Disney variety that caused Mickey Rooney to sing, "A dragon! A dragon! I swear I saw a dragon."

Sea monsters have had a similarly ancient history: the Norse Jörmungandr was said to encircle the Earth, the Old Testament's Book of Isaiah speaks of a "wriggling serpent" leviathan, while the goddess Athena sends two serpentine executioners in Virgil's *Aeneid*:

> When, dreadful to behold, from sea we spied
> Two serpents, rank'd abreast, the seas divide,
> And smoothly sweep along the swelling tide.
> Their flaming crests above the waves they show;
> Their bellies seem to burn the seas below . . .

These types of beast could have their origins in less fantastical creatures, for example, dragons could be exaggerations of their Komodo namesakes, or imagined out of crocodile sightings, or recreated from dinosaur fossils. Oarfish, assorted whales, giant squid, basking sharks and the prehistoric-looking frilled shark all bear striking similarities to various reports of sea serpents.

Lake-dwelling monsters may also be more mundane in nature than legends would have us believe. Swimming deer, seals, otters, freshwater fish, floating logs, boat wakes and wind-blown waves have all been proposed to dismiss claimed sightings of mythical beings.

And yet … and yet, there still persists a belief in the mysterious and unexplained.

The technical term for disputed and unsubstantiated animals is "cryptids", and the search and study of them is called "cryptozoology". One of the most famous is, of course, Nessie: immortalized in countless movies, not least, *Loch Ness* (1996) starring Ted Danson, Werner Herzog's *Incident at Loch Ness* (2004) and, most recently, *The Water Horse: Legend of the Deep* (2007) with Emily Watson; put into song by the likes of Judas Priest and Eminem; given its own voice in Edwin Morgan's brilliant sound poem *The Loch Ness Monster's Song* (1973); and captured by Montgomery Burns with assistance from Homer Simpson; etc., etc., etc.

Even so, the Loch Ness Monster is by no means the only lake dweller. There are, in fact, over 250 lakes worldwide where unidentifiable creatures have been sighted. That's a lot of different monsters! For example, the Ogopogo or Naitaka ("lake demon") is the 12 to 15m cryptid lake monster living in Okanagan Lake in Canadian British Columbia. The cryptid in Vermont at Lake Champlain, the sixth largest in the USA, is lizard-like, with four legs and webbed feet, a forked tongue, and is also amphibious.

Nor is Loch Ness the only place in Scotland where there have been reports of large unidentified water creatures. Mòrag is the loch monster of Loch Morar near Lochaber, also in the Highlands of Scotland. The loch is the deepest freshwater body in the British Isles, reaching 310m – plenty of water to hide a brown, 10m-long, rough-skinned, "peculiar serpent-like creature" with three humps.

Are aliens cryptids? Well, yes, insofar as they are also unconfirmed, controversial creatures whose existence has not yet been proven. But what is the likelihood that aliens exist, and will they be similar to us, in the way that they are most often portrayed in our science fiction? Astronomers tend to think about extraterrestrial life at the microbial scale, rather than as highly developed complex organisms. Ogilvy in H G Wells' *War of the Worlds* famously commented, "The chances against anything manlike on Mars are a million to one." In reality, the odds are much, much less, but because there are so many galaxies, the absolute numbers are quite large. Hence, the Drake equation predicts that there are about 6 billion solar systems in the observable universe that could support life, and 10,000 planets in the Milky Way alone that could contain life intelligent enough to communicate with Earth. With such prodigious potential, it would be more a mystery why aliens had not attempted to make contact.

Other cryptids include the Himalayan Yeti and North American Bigfoot, also known by Native Americans as Sasquatch. The first reports of an Abominable Snowman filtered through to the West as the hidden kingdom of Tibet relaxed its foreign policy

to allow Charles Howard-Bury's expedition, which included George Leigh Mallory, access to Mount Everest in 1921. While crossing the "Lhakpa La" pass at 21,000ft Howard-Bury found footprints, "probably caused by a large 'loping' grey wolf", but his Sherpa guides, "at once volunteered that the tracks must be that of 'The Wild Man of the Snows', to which they gave the name 'metoh-kangmi'" (man–bear snowman). The name "abominable" resulted from a mistranslation of "metoh" as "filthy". Since then, the Abominable Snowman has been a fascination for Himalayan climbers.

Around the same time, the first encounters with Bigfoot were taking place. But it wasn't until discovery of footprints and the ape-like creature was captured on 16mm film during the following half-century that the mysterious being was also catapulted from local, indigenous legend to international interest through media coverage. The name "Sasquatch" was coined from the similar-sounding name as spoken in a local dialect.

To appreciate our obsession with the paranormal, just look at the many ways we refer to such phenomenon: apparition, banshee, bodach, Doppelgänger, duppy, eidolon, ghost, hallucination, lemures, manes, phantasm, phantom, presence, poltergeist, revenant, shade, shadow, soul, spectre, spirit, spook, visitant, vision, wight, wraith. The greatest storytellers fed this fascination. Shakespeare transmogrified our concept of ghosts, from adrift will-o'-the-wisps, doomed to an Earth-bound eternity, into full characterizations of their live counterparts. Dickens took this one stage further, using ghosts to investigate his characters' state of mind, and to comment on current social and political conditions.

A Christmas Carol remains a firm seasonal favourite. There have been over 100 film adaptations in the last century, many making it to the big screen, including versions from Disney, the Muppets and the Smurfs. Alternatively, the 1984 film *Ghostbusters* has become cult viewing, while the more recent trend in paranormal television has made reality TV stars out of spiritualists, with fly-on-the-wall film crews following them as they investigate hauntings.

The Beast of Banburyshire, The Creature from Curridge, The Wildcat of the Chilterns, The Cadmore Cat, The Chilterns Lion, The Fen Tiger, The Pulford Panther, The Beast of Bodmin, The Beast of Shap, The Wrangaton Lion, The Dartmoor Lion, The Durham Puma, The Essex Lion, The Wild Cat of Woodchester, The Malmesbury Big Cat, The Sundrum Slasher, The Lochwinnoch Leopard. The list goes on, and on. About 180 names have been coined for the big cats sighted across the United Kingdom. And of all the mysterious creatures in this book, these big cats are the most definite; some have been caught. A puma in Inverness-shire, an Eurasian lynx near Norwich, a leopard on the Isle of Wight. Furthermore, there is an extensive record of video and photographic evidence in support of the sightings, although there have also been the usual hoaxes and misidentifications.

British big cats might seem like a recent phenomenon, however, first reports date back to the mid-18th century. Luckily we can draw on the *Daily Mirror*'s outstanding archives to delve into the historical depths and trace our fascination with all these types of unknown. This book is organized into subject areas, and presented in a chronological sequence that reveals our changing relationships with mystical phenomena.

Despite modern-day doubt and a cornucopia of reasonable explanations, for many people across the world the myths and legends of our past are as real now as they ever were, and continue on as unexplained mysteries.

This book would not have been possible without the invaluable research assistance of Anna Krzak. Thank you, Anna.

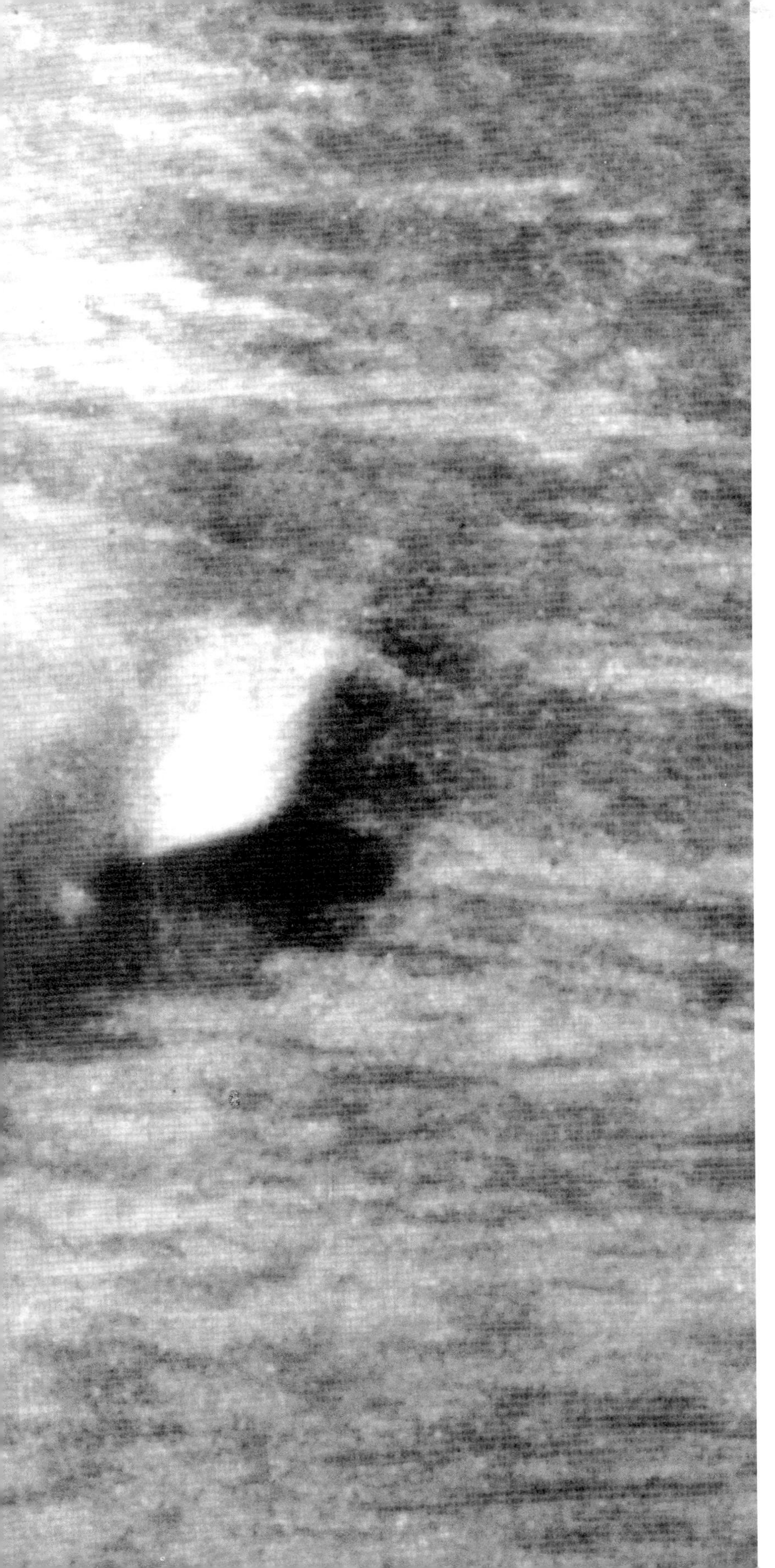

Loch Ness Monster – Enter the Dragon

"Four Sundays ago after church I went for my usual walk near where the river enters the Loch. The Loch was like a mill pond and the sun shining brightly. An object of considerable dimensions rose out of the water not very far from where I was. I immediately got my camera ready and snapped the object which was two or three feet above the surface of the water. I did not see any head, for what I took to be the front parts were under the water, but there was considerable movement from what seemed to be the tail, the part furthest from me. The object only appeared for a few minutes then sank out of sight."

Hugh Gray, 1933.

The Loch Ness Monster ("Niseag" in Scottish Gaelic) lives in the vast, murky waters of Loch Ness in the Scottish Highlands; its water visibility is exceptionally low due to a high peat content in the surrounding soil. The 56.4km-square loch is the second largest Scottish lake in terms of surface area, only surpassed by Loch Lomond. However, due to its great depth – down to 230m, deeper than any other loch except Loch Morar – it is actually the largest by volume, containing more fresh water than all the lakes in England and Wales combined.

Loch Ness follows the Great Glen Fault, a valley excavated by glacial erosion. The Great Glen accommodates Loch Lochy, Loch Oich and the 36.3km-long Loch Ness, which runs from Inverness in the north to Fort William in the south.

At its southwestern end near Fort Augustus is the one and only island, Cherry Island, an artificial crannog built during the Iron Age. The other island, Dog Island, was submerged by the raising of the water to 16m above sea level by Thomas Telford's construction of the Caledonian Canal, which ultimately connects the loch to the Beauly Firth in the northeast, and Loch Linnhe in the southwest.

The first recorded sighting of the Loch Ness monster was in the sixth century AD by the missionary Saint Columba. A handful of anecdotal observations and folktales of kelpie water horses followed until the start of the contemporary era, when we came to know the monstrous dragon as "Nessie". This began in 1933, with an increase in sightings coinciding with construction of a road along the loch's southern shore. Indeed, Londoner George Spicer was driving along the road in that year with his wife when a 12 to 15m creature, "a most extraordinary form of animal", crossed the road ahead of them, lumbering like a seal: "Although I accelerated quickly towards it, it had disappeared into the loch by the time I reached the spot. There was no sign of it in the water. I am a temperate man, but I am willing to take any oath that we saw this Loch Ness beast. I am certain that this creature was of a prehistoric species."

Through the subsequent explosion in publicity, the monster was truly brought to the world's attention. It is now the 80th anniversary of that inauguration, since when there have been over 11,000 sightings, most indicating that the creature has a long slender neck, small head, four flippers or elephant-like legs with webbed feet, and one to four humps.

11th August 1933

TO-DAY'S GOSSIP

AN HISTORIC LOCH

Loch Ness, which is becoming famous as the supposed abode of a dragon, is one of Scotland's most historic lakes.

Surrounded, as it is, by ancient castles and the scenes of many desperate battles, it needs only the legend of a dragon to complete its glamour.

17th August 1933

'DAILY MIRROR' EIGHT IN THE WEST

"Monster" of Loch Ness? – queerly-shaped tree trunk, washed

It's a bad habit to get into. It grows upon one!

ashore at Foyers, may, it is thought, be responsible for reported appearances of a "Monster".

28th October 1933

RE-ENTER THE MONSTER!

A great deal of publicity has been gained by the celebrated monster that is supposed to be lurking in the depths of Loch Ness, and Scotsmen in Inverness are wondering if they really ought to charge entertainment tax to see it!

But the story of this monster of Loch Ness is almost as old as the Scottish hills. There is hardly a household in the Highlands that has not heard the tale during the last hundred years.

The story of the beast, known locally as the water-kelpie or water-horse, goes back to the first century, when St. Columba met it, and vanquished it. At least that is the legend.

Adamnan, the ninth Abbot of lona, wrote the Life of St. Columba in the seventh century and in it he tells us that the saint, in the year 571, on approaching the River Ness, came upon a group of natives in the act of burying a man who had been seized a short time before by the monster as he was swimming across.

This monster, whose size we must imagine ourselves, was given the attractive title of Aquatilis bestia, and the Abbot further relates that St. Columba, wishing to cross to the other side, ordered one of his monks to swim over and obtain the boat moored on the farther bank.

While the monk was crossing the great monster appeared, but the saint saved his disciple by making the sign of the Cross.

The country legends that have been associated with the sight of the barn or white owl at night, or the weird courting night cry of the loon nesting on some Scottish loch, originated many a ghost story that no manner of proof can eradicate from the local beliefs.

The story of the monster in Loch Ness is one of these. No matter what comes to light as the cause of these sensational stories, Scotsmen, crofters and ghillies will still tell their children of the monster that lurks in the bottom of Loch Ness, and when all this bubble has died down someone again will rouse the alarm, as it has been roused time and time again for centuries.

4th November 1933

TO-DAY'S GOSSIP

MONSTROUS

The Loch Ness "monster" has reached the zenith of fame by the bestowal upon it of the nickname. It is now known as King Kong.

28th November 1933

TO-DAY'S GOSSIP

FESTIVAL OF ST. HAGGIS

St. Andrew's Night – festival of Scotland's Patron Saint – will be celebrated in London next Thursday with haggis, bagpipes, Highland dancing and – some new Scots jokes!

One of these, according to a brochure issued by the Savoy about their St. Andrew's Night festivities, is that the Loch Ness monster must be of Sassenach origin because it gives people frights.

Daily Record and Mail.
WEDNESDAY, DECEMBER 6, 1933

MONSTER PHOTOGRAPH OF THE MYSTERIOUS LOCH NESS OBJECT.

The above photograph (details of which are explained on Page One), despite its haziness, reveals the object photographed by Mr. Hugh Gray, of Foyers. This picture is the most mysterious ever published. It will occasion debate wherever it is seen. Everyone will ask, " What is it?" Experts have been unable to identify it.

The picture is reproduced without the slightest retouching. The photographic experts pointed out that the camera which was used was obviously letting in a certain amount of light.

NEW CHURCHES.

Sites Obtained In Glasgow.

It was reported at last night's meeting of Glasgow Presbytery that sites have been obtained for churches at Croftfoot, Newbank, Balmore, Cardonald, and South Carntyne, and negotiations are proceeding for ground at Merrylee, Williamwood and Blawarthill.

In respect of other two churches which it is proposed to build, nothing is being done meantime.

Plans and architects for at least three of the churches will be discussed at an early date.

PORT-GLASGOW LAUNCH.

SCREW STEAMER FOR LONDON OWNERS.

Messrs. Lithgows, Limited, Port-Glasgow, launched yesterday the screw steamer Harpasa, which they have built for Messrs. J. & G. Harrison, Ltd., London.

The vessel, which is a sister ship of the Harealo, launched in October, is designed to carry about 8500 tons deadweight, and superior accommodation has been provided for 12 passengers in single and double staterooms.

The machinery and boilers will be fitted by Messrs. David Rowan & Co., Ltd., Glasgow.

FAMILIES OF FOUR—HEIL!

Berlin, Tuesday.

THE ambition of all good Germans must be to have a family of at least four children, otherwise Germany will share the fate of all decaying nations of being overrun by more populous neighbours, says an official statement.

" Support to the utmost," is promised poor people in recognition of their sacrifices.—Reuter.

MOTORS IN COLLISION.

Two Glasgow Men Injured.

TWO men, Leslie Johnston, of Raeberry Street, Glasgow, and James Alexander, 775 Maryhill Road, Glasgow, were injured when two motor cars collided at the corner of Trongate and Glassford Street, Glasgow, about 11.30 last night.

The men were the occupants of a car travelling west in Trongate.

The other car was being driven south out of Stockwell Street, towards Glassford Street, when the two vehicles met in the centre of the crossing with a terrific impact.

The two cars, locked together, swerved to the west side of the crossing, but fortunately there were no pedestrians or other vehicles on the crossing at the moment.

The injured men were taken to the Royal Infirmary, where Johnston was detained suffering from serious head injuries.

Alexander, who received injuries to the face and leg, was able to go home after receiving treatment.

BRINGING UP FATHER : : : : : : : : : : : BY GEORGE McMANUS.

12th December **1933**

M.P. AND LOCH NESS MONSTER

CALL FOR INVESTIGATION IN INTERESTS OF SCIENCE

Whether the Secretary of State for Scotland, in the interests of science, will cause an investigation to be made into the existence of a monster in Loch Ness.

This question will be asked in the House of Commons to-day by Mr. Anstruther-Gray (Con., North Lanark).

Mr. W. Adamson, Secretary for Scotland in the last Labour Government, said to an interviewer in London yesterday: –

"You Southerners are far too sceptical regarding the Loch Ness monster. In my opinion the monster is real – and I am not joking."

Sir Murdoch MacDonald, Liberal National M.P. for Inverness, suggested, yesterday, that the best method of solving the mystery would be to trawl the loch.

12th December **1933**

A WARNING WORD TO LOCH NESS

It is admitted – is it not ? – that the police have plenty to do – all over the country.

There are the streets and roads and motor-accidents; the bandits; the latest and most modern as well as the oldest and most familiar types of crime. There are also the innumerable regulations about shop hours, closing times, drinks and cigarettes …

Still, they are evidently people who believe that all this is not enough.

For up there, on the shores of Loch Ness, the alleged monster we mentioned on Saturday is fascinating a band of stalwart policemen under the wary surveillance of a Chief Constable.

True, we've nothing to report about the monster itself since we informed you that bits of its back or fragments of its tail (if it has one) had been sighted in the Loch.

But it's best to be on the safe side; and at any moment some canny Scot, as he wanders home along the braes, may be gifted or afflicted with a vision of another bit of the strange beast.

He may see a claw, or a huge molar tooth, jutting like a promontory from the edge of the lake. The creature may be sharpening his dental outfit for a sudden raid upon bonnie bairns thereabouts.

This second sight (known to be a Highland privilege) would mean the drafting of a small army of police from the main cities of Scotland. The traffic and all the other things just noted could look after themselves. Who minds a motor-lorry when there is a dinosaur about? First, or strange things first.

But our Scottish friends may say that their prehistoric peeps and police regulations are their own affair, as indeed Mr. Compton Mackenzie frequently reminds them and us.

Perhaps. But we are sure that this Loch Ness business will not stop in the Loch. It will not be long, according to the immutable laws of imitation, before little Fred and tiny Dot, sailing their boats on the Round Pond, or hoping to skate upon it, will sight a dragon's hump and run howling to mamma, who will of course demand that Kensington Gardens and Hyde Park be patrolled by an army of Metropolitan police lest the awful creature, emerging, may sweep along the grass, consuming infants as hors d'oeuvre before swallowing the Albert Memorial whole.

This is definitely what we fear and why we warn Loch Ness. Terror travels fast and it may not be long before even Lord Trenchard begins to lose his head and sees alligators in Scotland Yard.

14th December **1933**

MONSTROUS!

W.M. might feel very differently if he lived near Loch Ness.

He wouldn't then make fun of a peril that is admitted to be one, not only by the police, but by scientific men who know more of such things than your leader-writer.

E.E.

Coniston-road, Croydon.

DON'T KILL IT!

Let me add a word to the Loch Ness controversy.

I wish to commend your plea that, if there is a curious creature lurking in the Loch, it shouldn't be destroyed by the fools who will shoot or kill any rare animal.

For one thing, there's money in monsters! What would Whipsnade give for a live dinosaur?

Zoologist.

MONEY FOR FUN

The idea of fishing for the Loch Ness monster appeals to me.

If Parliament would spend more public money in amusing the nation, we should feel we had better value for our tobacco and beer.

M. D. Marriott

Northolt-road, Harrow, Middlesex.

OVERHEARD IN THE TUBE

I was travelling in the tube the other day and overheard a talk about the monster.

"The monster has been lying at the bottom of the Loch for hundreds of years and the Loch is very deep.

"The county council has been improving the roads in that district, and there has been a great deal of heavy blasting, which would disturb the monster from its sleep, and it just came up to see what all the noise was about."

Hence its appearance.

D. S.

15th December **1933**

MORE LIGHT ON "IT"

We publish this morning a photograph of an alleged monster which turns out to be of arboreal origin: it is, in fact, a bit of a great tree, shamming as a big peril in the wintry waters.

With extraordinary mimetic skill, this tree has, you will see, simulated a simpering face, not unfriendly in archness of uncouth expression. But it is just a tree, being rather silly in a seasonable or Yule log loutishness of sport ... Simultaneously, we begin to receive monstrous reminiscences from readers who, dazed by the heat of summer in seaside resorts, have seen (in August) serpents and other beasts which disappointingly revealed themselves later as row-boats, dinghies, rafts, beer bottles, and even old boots carelessly discarded by marine litter fiends.

What bearing has all this upon Loch Ness?

Little or none, if you like. One may see a rum barrel. And one may see a jabberwock. Much depends on the seer.

But it will not be considered irrelevant, we hope, if we call attention to something that has now been not only seen but landed at Auckland; and that is, or was, a unicorn ribbon fish with a comb longer than it had any business to be, curling above an abnormal snout.

CAN THIS BE THE MONSTER ?—This tree trunk, which is often brought to the surface of Loch Ness by strong under-currents and carried along at a fair speed, shows how easily people can be deceived into thinking they have seen a "monster."

PIP, SQUEAK AND WILFRED | LOOKING FOR THE MONSTER | THRILLS ON LOCH NESS

1. Returning via Scotland, the 'plane carrying the pets came down near the world-famous Loch Ness.

2. The opportunity was too good to miss. The pets decided to go out and see if they could spot the monster.

3. By great good luck they found a boat lying unattended near the bank.

4. In a few moments, with Pip at the oars, it shot out into the Loch with Wilf and Stan as observers.

5. Suddenly the boat seemed to rise into the air. Something was moving underneath!

6. Then a mist sprang up. Turn which way they would nothing could be seen.

It has at once been claimed by a museum – very properly. Today we want only to suggest that a representative from South Kensington should get ready at Loch Ness to find a home for – whatever may be there.

If it's dead, it can be transported by motor-coach; if living, it can be led on ropes of sufficient thickness to prevent it straying, gobbling, or singing prehistoric carols on the road South.

16th December 1933

'THIS WAY FOR THE MONSTER!'

There's a fortune awaiting the man who can capture the Loch Ness monster.

It could be exhibited in London in some large open space, such as Hyde Park, and a fee charged to view it. Thousands would flock to see it.

The monster could be taken for a tour of Great Britain, and then, when most people had seen it, could perhaps be stuffed and given over to the Natural History Museum.

S. T.

QUITE HARMLESS

If there is a Loch Ness monster it is undoubtedly a harmless one, and the best thing to do would be to leave it alone.

As for this creature being a survival of the prehistoric age, I would point out that such a species could not exist in our present climate.

S.

Forest Gate, E.7.

21st December 1933

THAT LOCH NESS MONSTER

PIP HAS GREAT HOPES OF SEEING IT

My dear boys and girls,–

Pip, Squeak and Wilfred have long had a habit of "getting in the news". If anything interesting happens anywhere it is pretty certain

PIP, SQUEAK AND WILFRED | BAG-PIPE 'MONSTER' SCARE | TERRIFYING VISION IN LOCH NESS

1. Floating about on Loch Ness, surrounded by a thick mist, our five little adventurers were far from happy.

2. Would the celebrated "monster" appear? To their horror they saw a weird object in the distance.

3. It had a most terrifying aspect — three large "horns" seemed to be sticking out of its head.

4. Slowly the "monster" floated towards them—such an object would have frightened me in that eerie place.

5. And then they saw what it was — some absent-minded Scot had dropped his bagpipes in the Loch!

6. Shortly after this they were rescued from the Loch by their airman friend and were flying to London.

we shall find one or other of our happy little family on the spot. What Lord Mayor's Show, for instance, would be complete without Squeak or Wilfred getting hopelessly entangled with the crowd and seeing nothing but boots and legs? What Boat Race would be a Boat Race without antediluvian monster. Over fifty people claim to have seen it. It is said to have a long, thin neck like a swan, and a snake-like body some thirty feet long. One scientist suggests that it may be a sort of "overgrown newt".

So important has this supposed monster become that questions have been asked about it in Parliament, while policemen have been patrolling the loch to prevent any big-game hunters shooting it.

This is the interesting spot where our young adventurers are spending a brief halt on their way back to London. Not only are they at Loch Ness, but they are on it. If there is a monster of any kind they are in a very good position to see it …

Visibility is apparently very bad on the Loch; a thick, Scotch mist has descended on the waters; Pip, Squeak, Wilfred, Stanley and Auntie are, once again, in a very precarious position indeed … I don't think I should like to be there.

Your affectionate
Uncle Dick.

27th December 1933

DART BROTHERS SEE THE LOCH NESS MONSTER

IT KEPT UNDER THE WATER
– BUT THEY DIDN'T

SPOTS – AND 'SPOTS'

LOCH NESS
WE HAVE SEEN THE MONSTER!

Perhaps I ought to start in the orthodox way and describe this extraordinary happening from the beginning.

Doubtless, at this moment the telegraph wires are red-hot with the story of the remarkable experience I am about to relate, while sizzling cables on the ocean-bed flash the almost incredible story of the news-hunting presses of Europe and America.

"The Truth About Loch Ness!" "Overwhelming Evidence

Pip, Squeak and Wilfred

DAILY MIRROR CHILDREN'S SECTION

AUNTIE HOAXES REPORTERS: SHE FINDS LOCH NESS "MONSTER" AND BRINGS IT ASHORE

1. Journalists on the "Loch Ness Monster" story were astonished when Auntie appeared on the scene.

2. While they held a fierce discussion on foot-prints, Auntie and her companion got busy.

3. Obtaining a boat, they pushed off and were soon over the very centre of the loch.

4. While Auntie let down a line, Charles produced a queer, shapeless mass of rubber.

5. He began to blow it up while Auntie let out a wild shout of joy. She pretended to have caught something.

6. See their little game? Unfortunately, at that moment, Auntie did really catch something.

7. The boat was overturned, and Auntie went struggling down into the depths.

8. Then the line broke and she came floundering to the surface. She and Charles made for the rubber monster.

9. The journalists ashore were astounded when this curious trio came paddling towards them.

PIP, SQUEAK AND WILFRED

MERELY HAGGIS 'HORRORS'

1. While wandering around Loch Ness, Auntie was presented with a haggis.

2. The small Scot who gave it to her assured her she would find it "verra good."

3. Without hesitation, Auntie and Charles fell to and had a hearty meal.

4. About half-way through they both began to feel a little bit dizzy.

5. Holding on to each other they walked unsteadily for a moment and then sat down.

6. Before their amazed eyes, dozens of monsters seemed to inhabit the Loch.

of Monster's Existence." "Dart Brothers See Sea-Serpent with Own Eyes." "Irrefutable and Conclusive Testimony of Two Famous Witnesses."

We arrived here, Stephen and myself, in the afternoon. Time being an important factor, we had come all the way from London by road and had completed the difficult and arduous journey in just under five days, having lost our way only twice during the run – the first time we arrived at Blackpool under the impression that it was Carlisle, the second time we found ourselves at Lossiemouth, where the inhabitants turned out to meet us, having mistaken the sound of our engine for Mr. MacDonald's aeroplane.

A LITTLE LATIN

We managed to reverse, however, and make good our escape without suffering any damage.

There was a cold, bleak wind blowing when we arrived on the banks of the loch. The water looked like molten lead and we stood for a few minutes in an atmosphere that came straight off the ice. I swept the dreary landscape with an eager glance.

"Don't see anything," I announced.

"There was one about two miles back," said Stephen. "Just off the main road."

"Why the dickens didn't you tell me?" I shouted. "We may not get the chance of ever seeing it again."

"I did tell you!" he replied, "but you wouldn't pull up. You were getting all worked up about seeing this confounded monster. It was a perfectly good inn with a whisky advertisement outside and …"

You see how hopeless it is travelling with a man with a one track mind like that. Instead of concentrating on the job in hand he spends his time counting the public-houses. I began to wish I'd brought a camera instead. After all, the camera cannot lie, which is more than I would care to say about some people.

"How far back did you say?" I asked. "Couple of miles,"

replied Stephen.

"Well, I'm sure there's no sign of any monster at the moment," I said, glancing hastily along the Loch, "so there doesn't seem much point …"

"Exactly," Stephen answered with some emphasis. "Just what I've been thinking all along. I don't know why you want to waste precious time coming down to this dreary stretch of water when there's a nice warm fire further back. As for this monster – I've said all along that it's merely the figment of some credulous peasant's imagination."

"Don't forget," I warned him, " that we're here in the interests of science – figure to yourself, my dear Stephen, the stir that would be caused in the scientific world if the news got about that this brute had been seen by no less persons than ourselves – they might even call the species after us – *Dracontes frateri saggitae* – for example."

"I'd just hate to be a dragon's godfather," said Stephen, "and in any case, unless your Latin has improved out of all recognition in the last twenty years, that probably doesn't mean a thing when it's translated – if it can be translated."

We went back to the local hostelry. The proprietor greeted us with that spontaneous cordiality which is so typical of the Scots.

"Whaddaye want?" he said, looking at us suspiciously. We told him.

"It's no' time yet," he grunted. I told him we wanted rooms for the night as well. Having put ourselves on the right side of the law and signed the visitors' book, we took a drop of something to keep out the cold.

"So ye're fra London?" he said as he watched the visitors' book with one eye and the inkpot with the other. Nobody was going to fill his fountain-pen at that inkpot while he was around. We admitted we were.

ICY COLD

"We've come about your monster," I told him.

"Ye're newspaper men?" he demanded, with a sudden light in his eye. "Well, well, ye should ha' tellt me taat before. Come into the parlour."

"You've seen it, of course?" Stephen asked.

"Aye," he replied. "I've seen it. An' it's a grand sight."

"What's it like?" I said. "Could you describe it?"

"Aye," he answered. "Yon's a great clipperty-clapperty beastie wi' green een an' a lang snortie snootie."

"Quite," I said. "Most – er – vivid and all that. Had it got a long tail – you know – a lang teelie tailie?"

"Aye."

Mr. MacMunchausen appeared to be feeling the cold as well as ourselves. He said there was nothing like a drop of the right stuff for keeping out the cold.

So we started keeping out the cold like anything. I think we kept out all the cold in Loch Ness by the time the bar opened to the public.

Very soon we were surrounded by ghillies and things and some of the descriptions they gave us of the monster were even better than our host's, although we hardly understood a word.

It sounded like Burns Night at the Caledonian Hotel, but I'm sure it was all terribly Celtic twilight and poetical.

Stephen said it was actually a meeting of the Loch Ness Publicity Club and that we were probably rather *de trop*.

"Let's slip down to the loch now," he suggested, "and see whether our headlights will attract it."

We rose quietly and slipped down. I slipped down the whole flight of stairs but Stephen managed to save himself by grabbing the banisters.

"Hey," shouted Mr. MacMunchausen. "Come out of there. Yon's the cellar."

"It's a bit late to tell us now," I answered. "We've found it out for ourselves."

Down by the loch the wind howled dismally and a ghostly moon shed a pale shuddering light on the water. Fortunately we had brought something with us to keep out the cold.

"Have a spot more," said Stephen.

Suddenly, in the headlights, I saw it. It had great eyes which reflected the lights of our car. It seemed to be swimming towards us at a tremendous speed. It was a curious pale shade of pink with green spots.

"Look!" I cried, grasping Stephen's arm. "See it?"

"Great heavens!" he shouted. "There are three of them."

We put the car into gear and set off flat out for the warm and comfortable parlour of the local inn.

* * *

Looking back on it now I rather think Stephen's imagination played him false and that some trick of the light had trebled the image of the monster. For myself, I'm sure, well, almost sure, that there was only one. According to Stephen, the monsters he saw were playing concert trumpets, while I am prepared to swear that it was a concertina.

Anyway, I expect we're both lucky to have got away with our lives.

6th January 1934

LOCH NESS 'SENSATION': BIG GAME HUNTERS AND JOURNALISTS GET THE SHOCK OF THEIR LIVES

My dear boys and girls,–

Once again – you will remember the pets called there on their way back from Russia – we are transported this morning to the wild waste of waters known as Loch Ness. As all the world knows, a mysterious monster is said to lurk within its depths; Auntie, with a Rag-street friend, has gone up there to find it.

Her little joke yesterday – while on the lake Charlie Higgs blew up a weird-looking indiarubber "monster" – proved very useful as, when their boat overturned, it helped them to reach the shore.

There was consternation in the ranks of the armies of reporters, photographers, "movie-men", zoologists, scientists, big game hunters and others when they saw Auntie and Charlie bringing what appeared to be a strange antediluvian creature to the shore.

They had been searching every inch of the lake for weeks past for any signs of the monster and now – like the small boy angler with a bent pin and a worm – Auntie and a Cockney urchin had caught the big "fish"!

How relieved they all were when they realized that the "monster" was merely a large kind of balloon! Despite this "little joke" Auntie seriously intends to discover the mysterious inhabitant of Loch Ness – if such a creature really exists. All the Press representatives, with their shot-guns, nets, telescopes, microscopes and callipers, will have to redouble their efforts next week or Auntie will "crash" in and win!

PIP, SQUEAK AND WILFRED | **MISTAKEN FOR 'MONSTER'!**

1. The waters of Loch Ness looked so refreshing that Auntie decided to have a swim.

2. Scouting the idea that the monster would catch her, the old bird dived in.

3. Now, two journalists, observing ripples on the surface, thought it was the monster.

4. As Auntie drew near, one seized an enormous net and prepared to catch her.

5. In another moment Auntie was scooped neatly out of the water, a prisoner.

6. The journalists were disgusted to find the "monster" was an old penguin.

PIP, SQUEAK AND WILFRED | **"OCH AYE!—IT'S GRRRAND!"**

1. Auntie and Charlie Higgs opened their "show" yesterday in a little village.

2. Naturally the youngsters were very keen to see the Loch Ness "monster."

3. This little lassie bravely approached the tent where the creature was confined.

4. Charlie, standing outside the tent, assured her there was no danger.

5. And here is a glimpse of the weird Loch Ness "monster" or rather tree trunk.

6. The small children were thrilled but—will the grown-ups be taken in?

12th January **1934**

MONSTROUS IDEA!

IS THE LOCH NESS MONSTER REALLY HENRY'S OLD FRIEND, BILL BLOGGS?

Dear boys and girls,–

There has been a lot of fuss in the newspapers lately about a monster which is supposed to be living in Loch Ness in Scotland. Various expeditions have been fitted out for the purpose of capturing this creature; journalists, cinema-photographers, fishermen, tourists and trippers swarm the banks of this now famous stretch of water, but as yet there has been no absolutely, downright, cast-iron evidence as to what sort of a beast is there.

If you ask my opinion I am certain there is no such thing as the Loch Ness monster. No, I haven't been there to make sure, but my uncle, who is employed in a firm of Scottish window-box weeders, was once sent on a job in this locality, and, being a keen fisherman, took a boat out on the Loch for an hour or so.

He wrote and told me that he hadn't seen a single trace of the supposed monster, and that's sufficient for me. Incidentally, my uncle said that the sight of the sun tipping the hills with gold moved him to tears. He said there was a time when he was as lucky as those hills, but that those good old days disappeared with the withdrawal of the sovereign from circulation.

MY OWN THEORY

Coming back to the monster, it may be my old friend Bill Bloggs, who once accepted a wager to swim the entire length of the Loch clad in a policeman's coat and trousers, top boots, spurs and a tin hat, dived in and hasn't been seen since. For all we know, Bill might have found the water so much to his liking that he has decided to spend the rest of his days there, swimming lazily up and down. On the other hand, he may have – (You needn't go into that side of the

Pip, Squeak and Wilfred

DAILY MIRROR CHILDREN'S SECTION

GOOD-BYE TO "MONSTER"! WTZKOFFSKI, SALMON-FISHING, THOUGHT HE HAD CAUGHT IT!

1. A thrilling adventure with the bogus "monster" today. *While hauling it through Scotland there was a crack—*

2. —and the rope connecting the trailer with the pets' car snapped! *Away went the "monster" down the hill.*

3. Auntie and her Rag-street friend, Charlie Higgs, *thought it wisest to hop off. They did.*

4. All the family joined in the chase down the hill after the trailer, but it was hopeless.

5. Now comes the odd and delightful part of the story. In the stream below, Wtzkoffski—

6. —was indulging in the lordly sport of salmon-fishing. At last he thought he had a "bite."

7. A bigger "bite" than he imagined, for a huge, weird creature crashed on him from above!

8. Of course, the Bolshy thought it was "the" monster. He swam for his life down the swift stream!

9. And the joke was that nobody knew—except us—that Wtzkoffski had been there at all!

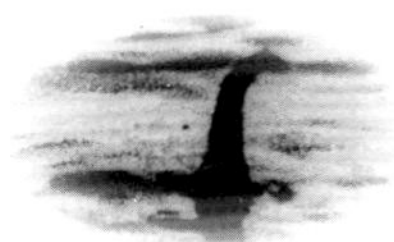

PIP, SQUEAK AND WILFRED

Auntie has already started to make money out of the Whelksea Sea-serpent Sensation—by charging visitors a penny a peep at "the monster"—which (oh, Auntie!) is really a newt!

question, Henry. – The Printer).

Well, that's my theory and you can take it or leave it, but the idea of a prehistoric sort of monster swimming about in Loch Ness in 1934 is – well, monstrous!

17th January 1934

"MONSTER" THEORIES

Henry has some more to say about this absorbing subject.

Further to my letter to you all the other day, I am advancing several more theories regarding the Loch Ness Monster. I said, if you remember, that I was almost certain there was nothing at all in the Loch, but that if there was it might be my old friend, Bill Bloggs, who, for a wager, dived in clad in a policeman's coat and trousers, top boots, spurs and a tin hat. Since writing that I have thought the matter deeply over, and have come to the conclusion that the monster is probably one of the following:–

The wreck of Professor Haughjorlechampmondley's (pronounced Jones) patent flying rocket which was sent up in the early summer of '98 and completely disappeared after travelling at terrific speed for about five miles. An old ghillie, who was stalking tartan near the Loch, said he heard a loud commotion in the middle of the Loch about two minutes after the time the rocket was let off.

* * *

The household effects – notably a brass bedstead – of Baillie Burns who, while crossing the Loch with a couple of bailiffs in full cry, was shipwrecked, losing the entire cargo. Baillie Burns himself managed to swim ashore, but his furniture still remains deep in the Loch.

* * *

The scenery and effects of a theatrical company which were being transported from Land's End to John o' Groat's by air. Over the Loch the bottom of the machine fell out and so did the scenery and effects.

* * *

I offer these theories to journalists, safaris explorers, big-game hunters and museum representatives, etc., for what they are worth.

20th January 1934

UNCLE DICK'S LETTER: A FEW REFLECTIONS ON MONSTER-HUNTING – CAN'T WALES FIND A DRAGON?

My dear boys and girls,–

Very glad to see that Auntie's treetrunk "monster" has disappeared for ever into one of the swift streams or burns of the Highlands and is not likely to be seen again. (It may, of course, turn up in Loch Lomond and create a rival sensation to that of Loch Ness, but that is none of our business.) I am glad to see the bogus "monster" has gone because it was, after all, rather a fraud and it didn't seem quite fair for children to pay their halfpennies to see merely a painted-up piece of wood. Pip and Squeak and all our little party of adventurers are returning at once to town.

Just a few last reflections on the real monster that is supposed to exist in Loch Ness. Those people who have seen it – not one of the hawk-eyed big-game hunters and investigators who have been searching the loch for weeks has had more than a glimpse, by the way – report that it is growing smaller. First of all it was some 20ft. long with several "humps" like a sea serpent; now it is only about 7ft. long with one "hump". In a short time, I am afraid even the "hump" will have disappeared.

It is time that somebody discovered some other oddities in different parts of the country. For instance, surely Wales – the ancient home of dragons – can produce at least one of these monsters from its misty hills and unexplored caverns?

"Weird creatures seen prancing on hillside near Pontypridd," we might read. "Said to breathe fire by startled villagers."

Then indeed we should have another monster-hunt. All the scientists, big-game hunters, etc., would flock to Pontypridd and we might be very sure they would find – nothing at all!

2nd March **1934**

MONSTROUS!

One of our contemporaries reported yesterday the discovery of a marine monster – dead – with a head resembling a camel's.

What of it?

We have nothing to say about it or against it – in itself. But we resent the suggestion (just as the holiday season is being prepared in Scotland) that this is the Loch Ness monster.

We all know, first, that the Loch Ness monster is not dead; and, next, that its face isn't, or wasn't when last seen, a bit like a camel's; but more like a tapir's or a giraffe's – with its length laid sideways, and its body hunched at intervals and fretted with carbuncular hillocks.

Is just any little porpoise, found dead of pneumonia in the stormy seas, to be taken for our monster? Why won't people wait until we've got up to the Loch at Easter and seen what we can do to cajole the superlizard into the hotel lounge?

20th April **1934**

MARGARET ROSE AND THE DRAGON

"WHAT A DARLING LITTLE MONSTER."

The Duke of York, speaking as the Earl of Inverness, told the best Loch Ness monster story of the year last night.

He was the guest of the London Inverness-shire Association – and here is his story:–

"The fame of the Loch Ness monster has reached every part of the earth. It has even entered the nurseries of this country.

"The other day I was in the nursery, and my younger daughter, Margaret Rose, aged three, was looking at a fairy story picture book. She came across a picture of a dragon.

"Pointing at the picture, she said: 'Oh, look, mummy, what a darling little Loch Ness monster.'"

The company greeted the story with laughter and applause.

20th April **1934**

LOCH NESS AGAIN!

LONDON SURGEON SEES DENIZEN WITH SMALL HEAD AND SWAN-LIKE NECK

The Loch Ness "monster" has been seen again!

A London surgeon, Mr. R. K. Wilson, of Queen Anne-street, W.1. who was motoring along the side of Loch Ness, near Invermoriston, says he saw a "monster" with a small head and swan-like neck about 300 yards from the shore.

He saw no body, but there was a considerable commotion in the water.

The famous "Surgeon's photograph".

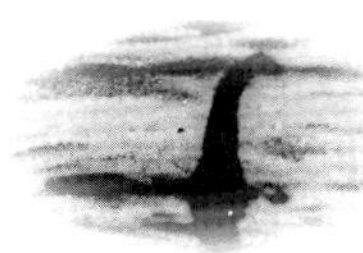

Loch Ness in glorious splendor.

UFOs – The War of the Worlds

UFOs flying over Conisborough, Yorkshire.

While unidentified aerial objects have been recorded for thousands of years, our obsession with alien UFOs arose out of the period following the Second World War, leading up to the Cold War of the 1950s. The paranoia of nuclear conflict between America and the Soviet Union fed both a social fear of anything foreign as well as a desperate look to the stars for salvation from impending doom. The modern era can be dated from mid-1947 when pilot Kenneth Arnold reported a string of nine, shiny UFOs travelling at approximately 1,932km/hr. Arnold's description of the objects led to the coining of the phrase "flying saucer". Two weeks later, the infamous Roswell incident began a controversy that still rages over a US government conspiracy to cover up an alien spacecraft crash. Since then, there have consistently been several sightings reported worldwide each year.

3rd April **1950**

THE LITTLE MEN WITH RED HAIR

A bus conductor saw it first. At 1.20 p.m. He dialled the Air Ministry and said: "They're here. There's a flying saucer in the sky with lots of little men with ginger hair inside."

A housewife saw it next. She left her Yorkshire pudding and roast beef to tell them: "It's a boomerang thing. Swaying. There are some black dots at the bottom …"

"Little men with ginger hair?" the Air Ministry Duty Officer asked. No, she couldn't say; she had left her spectacles in the kitchen.

At 1.29 p.m. a man selling newspapers near Whitestone Pond on Hampstead Heath came through jerkily: "It's round and white and it's high up in the sky."

For three hours the phone in the Air Ministry duty room rang and rang. Then the Assistant Duty Officer answered a call. He said: "It's a parachute training centre at Weston-on-the-Green in Oxfordshire. They say it's urgent …"

It was. They had to report that one 60ft.-long parachute jumping balloon – minus cage – had broken away from moorings.

With no little men with ginger hair on board.

5th April **1950**

FLYING SAUCERS

MR. PENROSE BELIEVES THEY'RE MANNED BY SPACE MEN 10 FEET HIGH

Mr. Peter Penrose, a twenty-nine-year-old London businessman, believes he has the answer to the mysterious Flying Saucers which have been reported over various parts of the world.

When he read a report from California that the bodies of 26in. dwarfs had been found in a wrecked Flying Saucer, he didn't laugh.

He just said indignantly: "It isn't right. The people in the Flying Saucers are about 10ft. tall. And they haven't landed on earth … yet."

For Peter Penrose and his friend, Miss Lee Starling, claim to know all about the Flying Saucers and where they come from.

They have known, they say, since last August – but they have kept quiet. They felt they were "handling dynamite". And, in any case, they needed Fezial's permission to speak.

Now they have his permission. Fezial talks a great deal.

But the first message they had from him – it came at 6.15 on a warm Sunday evening last August – wasn't very encouraging.

It read: addjlgddhgcemmajemel.

Mr. Penrose – who is not a spiritualist – started table rapping as an experiment. A few days after he started, Fezial came through with his mysterious message. It was delivered with the aid of letters stuck round the table-top. An upturned tumbler moved towards each letter in turn when Peter put his fingers on it.

Fezial's first understandable message said "The Threns of Strorp Peta think what you call Saucers are ships. There are a great race of scientists on Strorp. Think this is the first time ever contact made."

Fezial describes himself as "the Planet Master of Strorp", a planet 20,000 light years away from Earth.

And Fezial has told Mr. Penrose and Miss Starling that the Flying Saucers are space ships from another planet. They are carried inside bigger planet-ships.

The Saucers are manned by peaceful beings about 10ft. tall.

After seven months of communication with Fezial, Mr. Penrose is convinced he exists. Penrose has already made a "Kelmic receiver" – under instructions from Fezial. It looks like a plastic salt-cellar packed with wires and parts of radio valves.

This receives telepathic vibrations from Fezial, concentrates them, and projects the vibrations into Penrose's mind.

The spacemen, apparently, are advanced scientists having a look at life on the other planets.

Contacting this earth is just an experiment to them.

Will they land here?

All that Penrose will say is this: "Obeying Fezial's orders, I have cancelled a holiday I planned to spend in Ireland.

"I shall drive into the blue – Fezial's orders again. I do not know what I shall meet."

He thinks it may be a Flying Saucer from Strorp.

Space Captain Jim Stalwart in the "Fantastic Adventures of the Missing S200". Jim Stalwart appeared in the weekly *Junior Mirror* in 1955.

* * *

THE SCIENTISTS SAY THEY'RE SECRET EXPERIMENTAL AIRCRAFT

Ten-feet high men from an unknown planet visiting the earth in Flying Saucers?

Nonsense, say the scientists.

Much more likely to be ordinary men about 5ft. 9in. flying the latest types of research aircraft.

These saucer-like planes are no mystery to the slide-rule experts who plan the shapes of the Things that will be flying as a matter of course five years from now.

Nor are they mysterious to the test pilots, who have the job of proving in fact what the slide-rule boys have worked out on paper.

Listen to the former United States Secretary of Agriculture, Clinton Anderson.

Speaking the other day on this Flying Saucer business, he said: "There is too much going on in the large research establishments in my State of New Mexico to pooh pooh eye-witness stories of Flying Saucers. Official denials are to be expected."

Two years ago, at the top-secret American aircraft proving ground at Lake Muroc, in the Californian desert, an aircraft right out of the pages of fiction zoomed into the sky.

It was the XF6U-1. It was almost circular. It was jet propelled. And it had an estimated top speed of 550 miles an hour.

That was two years ago. And stranger craft have flown since then. I have seen weird-looking shapes in British skies – not space-ships from another planet, but our latest experimental aircraft on a routine proving flight.

The Air Ministry know all about Flying Saucers. A special section of the Intelligence Department deals with all reports, whether they originate in Britain or the United States.

Technical experts sift the details.

"We do not get many reports, but we have received some quite recently," said an Air Ministry spokesman. "We keep an open mind about them."

Against the saucers are the doctors, the psychiatrists – and the Government's Royal Aircraft Establishment.

The doctors always tell you about an experiment carried out by an Australian professor named Cotton.

He took 450 students on to a rooftop, asked them to look at the sky for ten minutes. Then he said: "How many people saw things moving in the sky?"

Up went twenty-two hands. What they "saw" was caused by blood corpuscles moving in the eye.

The psychiatrists put the blame on mass hallucinations. One of Britain's leading experts told me: "Today there is world-wide anxiety about the hydrogen bomb and the threat of invasion from other planets. Perfectly honest people swear they have seen Flying Saucers. In fact, they are looking for something to allay or confirm their fears."

Ronald Bedford

21st October 1950

THIS IS THE 'FLYING SAUCER' FESTIVAL CROWDS WILL SEE

The first "flying saucer" ever to be seen in captivity will puzzle thousands of visitors to the travelling section of the Festival of Britain next year.

It is a milky-coloured plastic disc, measuring six feet across. It has no engine, no working parts and makes no noise.

At the Festival exhibition, its inventors claim, it will fly round in circles at a height of about sixteen feet, and will stay in the air as long as the operators wish.

The flying saucer that will tour Britain next year—an artist's impression.

The "saucer" has been designed and built by Mr. Richard Levin, chief designer of the travelling section of the Festival, in association with Mr. Geoffrey Larkby.

Mr. Levin said last night: "I don't regard this as a contribution to the science of aviation. It is rather a scientific curiosity."

'NO MECHANISM'

"But it is not a toy. It will probably puzzle a good many scientists, as well as the general public. It involved a considerable amount of mathematical calculation."

Mr. Levin would not reveal how the "saucer" was controlled, but he said: "It could be taken completely to pieces, and no mechanism of any kind would be found."

Asked why he had made it, he said: "There have been so many stories of the mysterious flying saucers that we decided to make one of our own. We call it the 'Ectoplat'.

"We have already successfully flown a half-size model. The full-size one will have its maiden flight soon."

An Air Ministry spokesman said last night: "We shall watch its development with interest."

The Ectoplat will be seen only at Manchester, Nottingham, Birmingham and Leeds. It will not appear in London.

13th February **1951**

'WE SENT UP THE FLYING SAUCERS', SAYS ATOM MAN

Flying saucers are real, but there's nobody in them and they are not visitors from another world, says Dr. Urner Liddel, chief of the nuclear physics branch of the U.S. Office of Naval Research.

In the U.S. Magazine *Look*, he gives what is called "the first Government disclosure of what is considered to be the real cause" of the flying saucer stories.

They are, he says, only huge plastic balloons used in cosmic ray studies. The balloons – called "skyhooks" – could be mistaken for flying saucers.

They carry instruments to record what happens when cosmic rays hit atoms.

30th September **1953**

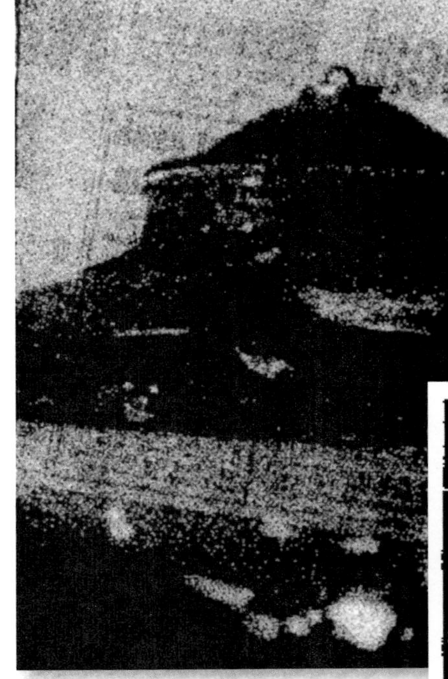

TOP: Venusian flying saucer or "Scout Ship" photographed by George Adamski through his telescope.
CENTRE: George Adamski.
RIGHT: The man from Venus, sketched by a witness.

WHAT DO YOU THINK OF THIS FANTASTIC STORY?

'I MET A FLYING-SAUCER MAN FROM VENUS'

A man named George Adamski announces to the world today that he has talked with a man who pirouetted down to earth from the planet Venus in a Flying Saucer.

Most people laugh at Flying Saucers. But, as Adamski recalls, everyone laughed when Columbus set out to prove the world was round.

Adamski tells his amazing story in *Flying Saucers Have Landed*, of which he is coauthor with Desmond Leslie.

The meeting with the Venusian, claims Adamski, took place "on the California desert 10.2 miles from Desert Center toward Parker, Arizona", at about 13.30 p.m. on November 20 last year.

Adamski, "philosopher, student, teacher", admits to being saucer-crazy since 1946. He lives on Mount Palomar, California.

He had made several unsuccessful trips to nearby desert areas because of reports that Flying Saucers had been landing. But he kept on hoping.

Then, on November 20, it happened … Dare you believe it?

First, he says, a mother-ship, gigantic, cigar-shaped and silvery came into view riding high. It vanished when American planes roared over.

Nevertheless, Adamski sensed that there would be a landing. He instructed his six companions to watch from a distance.

Soon, there was a brilliant flash and "a beautiful, small craft appeared to be drifting between two mountain peaks and settling half a mile away".

BEAUTIFUL

Then, near a ravine, a man with long hair appeared, beckoning, Adamski says: "I was in the presence of a man from space – a human being from another world!"

CAN YOU BELIEVE IT?

The man from space smiled. 'The beauty of his form surpassed anything that I have ever seen …" He extended a hand.

But "instead of grasping hands … he placed the palm of his hand against the palm of my hand just touching it."

His fingers were long and tapering, like an artistic woman's.

Do you believe it yet?

SUN-TAN

He looked about 5ft. 6in. 9lst. and twenty-eight years old.

His forehead was large, his eyes grey-green and slightly aslant. He had high cheekbones, a face as hairless as a child's, and beautiful white teeth, and even a sun-tan.

The long hair, sandy in colour, hung shoulder-length in waves "glistening more beautifully than any woman's". And he wore a chocolate-brown ski-suit, without seams.

When Adamski spoke, the man shook his head. So Adamski tried gestures and telepathy – "I had been teaching this as a fact for thirty years."

In this way, he says, he learned the man had come from Venus. The man even repeated "Venus" after Adamski. And his voice, slightly higher-pitched than an Earth man's, had music in it.

STILL BELIEVE IN IT?

Adamski says he learned that Venusians had come to earth to study its radiation because atom-bombs were affecting outer space. Too many explosions were dangerous for the earth, too, signalled the space-man and said: "Boom! Boom!"

And there, hovering near the ground, was the Flying Saucer, "more like a heavy glass bell than a saucer". He pointed to it, explained that it had come from the mother-ship.

The Venusian, says Adamski, revealed that:

People like us live on other planets;

They visit the earth;

They do not land in populated areas because they fear violence;

There had been many landings and would be many more;

They believe in a Creator;

Their Flying Saucers are operated by the "law of attraction and repulsion".

Is it all possible?

SYMBOLS

Speaking in his own language – "like a mixture of Chinese and an ancient earth language" – the visitor kept pointing to his feet, which left strange footprints from soles embossed with symbols that scientists are trying to interpret.

Adamski walked with the Venusian to his spaceship.

There were port-holes, strange glows, another beautiful long-haired creature looking out.

The space visitor warned Adamski not to get too near. Adamski did; his arm was jerked up and thrown back against his body: "I had no feeling in it."

Feeling returned only three months later.

Adamski wanted a trip in the ship, or just a look inside. But the man from Venus shook his head, and left, taking with him an exposed film – in its holder – that Adamski had taken earlier. He promised to return the holder – some time. Did Adamski snap the space-man? No. The space-man had objected.

Witnesses to this meeting – they have sworn affidavits about it – were a Mr. and Mrs. A. C. Bailey, of Winslow, Arizona, a Dr. and Mrs. George H. Williamson of Prescott, Arizona, Flying Saucer enthusiasts, Mrs. Alice K. Wells, who runs a cafe at Palomar, and Mrs. Lucy McGinhis, Adamski's secretary.

RETURNED

Did the Venusian return the film-holder? "Yes," says Adamski, "twenty-three days later. A Flying Saucer flew low over Mount Palomar and a hand tossed it out from a porthole."

This was when Adamski took the picture of the saucer printed on the previous page.

In the holder, the original picture that Adamski took seemed to have been replaced by a strange photograph and a symbolic message no one has ever deciphered. It looks like shorthand.

This is Adamski's story.

Two Washington officials listened to it without "expressing any doubt".

What do you think?

Vicky cartoon 6th September 1956 – Tomorrow morning Mars will be nearer to the Earth than at any time in the past 30 years. Martians board a space rocket – in the distance is the Earth with Soviet H-test, US H-test and British H-test nuclear explosions.

TO-MORROW MORNING MARS WILL BE NEARER TO THE EARTH THAN AT ANY TIME IN THE PAST THIRTY YEARS.

SUEZ CRISIS

SOVIET H-TESTS

U.S. H-TESTS

BRITISH H-TESTS

MBC

VICKY

"Martians! There is no need for panic—their military preparations are purely precautionary measures . . ."

20th September 1954

FLYING SAUCER DIDN'T KEEP THE 'APPOINTMENT WITH VENUS'

Two coach-loads of men and women spent an hour in a windswept field yesterday waiting for a flying saucer.

They were trying to get in touch with one by telepathy. And they all concentrated their thoughts on the planet Venus.

But no visitors from outer space joined the party, who had driven from London to the field near the Wiltshire village of Avebury.

The trip was the result of a suggestion made at a London lecture by Mr. Foster Forbes.

Mr. Forbes, in white gloves and bow tie, told me: "Flying saucers appear to have a tremendous telepathic range.

"We hoped one of them might pick up our thought vibrations.

"But I'm not disappointed. I think if further experiments are held on the same lines we will get somewhere."

'TELEPATHY'

He added: "If some of the people here have grown sceptical, they are not seriously interested in the subject."

Although no flying saucers appeared, one of the party, Mr. George King, of Clifton-gardens, Maida Vale, said that he got into telepathic communication with Venus.

A dozen people told me that as Mr. King went into his "trance" these words came from his lips:

"Some of you would be frightened if we came today. There is too much difference of opinion here."

Mr. Kenneth Kellar, of Stoneydown-avenue, Walthamstow, said: "I heard the voice 'using' Mr. King quite plainly.

"It seems there were too many of us and conditions were not suitable.

"The Venusians will not come apparently if anyone is going to be frightened of them.

"There must be complete friendship between us and the visitors from outer space."

▲ They've let these UFOs go to their heads – the Flying Saucer hat, July 1955.

Mr. King said: "In earlier communications with Venusians, they have told me they are not out to hurt us.

"But they want to help because they are frightened at the damage we may do to ourselves with atomic research."

THOSE DOGS

A disappointed woman in the party said: "Of course a flying saucer didn't come; if some people will bring their dogs, how can we possibly project our thoughts into space?

"Just think what harm a few yapping dogs would do to such an experiment."

18th May **1959**

IF YOU GO DOWN IN THE WOODS TODAY ...

The Hon. Brinsley le Poer Trench, half-brother of the Earl of Clancarty, spent his Whitsun week-end thinking, in the nicest possible way, about the people of outer space.

Mr. Trench is convinced that if Martians or Venusians received friendly thoughts from anyone on this earth it might encourage them to climb in their flying saucers and pop down to look at us.

Several thousand other people have been radiating friendly thoughts this week-end too.

TELEPATHY

Enthusiastically, Mr. Trench told me yesterday: "It's all part of the International Flying Saucer Contact Weekend.

"All over the world we flying saucer enthusiasts – thousands of us – are trying to contact the men from outer space.

"Some of our members are watching TV sets tuned into unused channels. Or listening on radios to wavelengths not used by radio stations.

Some of us are trying telepathy. The outer space people use it, you know."

NO KNIVES

What happens if you find a flying saucer? "You simply mustn't go near it," said Mr. Trench. They are surrounded by a powerful electricity force. Wait until the spacemen come out. Then you know the electricity is off.

"And don't produce a revolver or a knife. It will scare them off."

Mr. Trench, who is 6ft and forty-seven, will take an optimistic walk with friends in Ashdown Forest today looking for any flying saucers that might be nestling between the trees.

Why Ashdown Forest? Has he got some inside information?

Mr. Trench gave me a down-to-earth reply: "It's a nice place," he said "to spend a Whit-Monday."

18th May **1959**

JULIANA AND A 'SAUCER MAN'

A sixty-eight-year-old "space traveller" who claims to have flown round the Moon in a space-ship from Venus, is to be received in private audience by Queen Juliana of the Netherlands, tomorrow.

The man is George Adamski, former hamburger seller from California.

He has written several books on space travel, and claims to have received a "message" for the Earth from the people of Venus.

The appointment with Queen Juliana, which has been widely criticized in Holland, was arranged by Mr. Peter Lokkers, secretary of U.F.O. – an organization which studies "Unidentified Flying Objects".

Mr. Lokkers said today that the Queen became interested in the subject after a lecture in Holland by Air Chief Marshal Lord Dowding of the RAF, who is a firm believer in "flying saucers".

She was invited to one of Mr. Adamski's lectures, and then notified the secretary that she would like to see him privately, at the Palace.

Typical of Dutch reaction is an editorial in the paper *De Volkskrant*, which says that Adamski is regarded everywhere as a charlatan.

It is suggested that there are too many "floating minds" at the Dutch Court, and that the Queen is too readily influenced by cranks.

Many people here are hinting at a parallel between the flying saucer affair and the rumpus over the Queen's friendship with faith healer Greet Hofmans in 1956.

Miss Hofmans was then said to have caused a temporary rift between Juliana and her husband, Prince Bernhard, and to have used her influence with the Queen to interfere in politics.

1st October **1962**

DON'T LOOK NOW ...

THE INVISIBLE MARTIANS MAY BE HERE ALREADY

There may be a strange little man or woman from Mars

creeping up behind you.

And you won't see a thing because these super-people know the trick of invisibility!

At the third Flying Saucer Convention, attended by 100 people in London at the week-end, members of the Aetherius Society were assured by their chairman, Ray Nielsen, that these weird beings are all about us. He said: "We feel that inhabitants of other worlds, with much greater wisdom than ours, have been watching us for centuries.

"Now they find us pot-shotting with H-bombs and probing into Space and they are afraid of the damage we may cause to the Universe."

In a neat blazer adorned with a motto, in an ancient Eastern language, meaning 'God Is Wisdom', Mr. Nielsen, a 26-year-old sweets-salesman from London's Palmers Green, told me:

"The Aetherius Society – the name is Greek meaning 'one who comes from outer Space' – was started as a religious, non-profit-making organization by George King in 1954.

"Today we have headquarters in London and Los Angeles and branches in many countries.

"Our aim is to provide a liaison between the people from Space and our world so that when the saucer-men become visible people won't go off with the screaming hysterics."

WHIZZ

During the two-day Convention members gave crisp evidence of seeing brightly-lit saucers hovering above Putney Bridge, whizzing down Oxford-street and jinking above the Kent hop fields.

One elderly member claimed to have seen more than a dozen in one glorious night.

One of the highlights was provided by a member who had made a tape recording of a flying saucer. It sounded just like a vacuum-cleaner.

A spokesman for the Air Ministry told me: "Most of these sightings can be accounted for and explained: the odd 5 per cent, can't because of insufficient details."

And the American Air Force, which investigated 483 "flying saucer" sightings last year, reported:

"All but ninety-nine were accounted for … as birds, balloons, aircraft and atmospheric conditions. The ninety nine could not be checked for lack of details."

POOH!

These findings were pooh-poohed at the Convention.

Over lunch one of the organisers told me:

"We are up against suppression from the governments – and the Press of the world.

"They know we are right that they dare not tell the people the truth for fear of riotings."

8th November 1962

➡ Unidentified flying objects seen and photographed by a Sheffield schoolboy in 1962.

LIVE LETTERS … CONDUCTED BY THE OLD CODGERS

ALERTED BY UFOS

A Manchester reader, "Realist", claimed here that recent Space flights disproved previous theories about flying saucers. Now saucer fans retaliate. David Ireland, of Bury Old-road, Prestwich, Lancs, writes:

"I hasten to point out that we now have more evidence than ever before that such Spacecraft do exist.

"I cannot imagine how 'Realist' can be so narrow minded as to believe that we, inhabitants of one small planet among so many millions, are the only intelligent life form in the Universe."

And "Convinced," Worthing, Sussex, writes: "Flying saucers are still being reported. In May, the pilot and co-pilot of a Viscount airliner reported a 'flying saucer – round, brown, with antennae – flying at 14,000ft.' south-west of Bristol."

One theory is that these "saucers" come from Tau Ceti and Epsilon Eridani, two stars in the Milky Way.

Be all this as it may, folks, there is currently a boom in UFO – "unidentified flying objects".

In September, the British UFO Association was formed in London to co-ordinate the efforts of the eight or so provincial UFO Groups with some 1,000 alert observer members. A comparable organization in the United States has no fewer than 20,000 members.

Every year there are approximately 1,000 reports of "flying saucers" from all over the world – about 100 from the British Isles. Eighty per cent of them can be explained away as natural phenomena or hoaxes.

And the other 200 genuine "saucers"? We won't stick our old necks out until we've seen one.

12th December 1963

A 'MARTIAN' VISITS LOVERS' LANE …

Courting couples in a Kent village are convinced that there are THINGS hovering in the sky …

Their reports of glowing red and white lights have intrigued the flying-saucer experts. The couples have even talked of a headless "ghost" with webbed feet.

First to report seeing weird objects at Saltwood, near Hythe, were John Flaxton, 17, and his 16-year-old girl friend Jenny Holloway, of Lenham, near Ashford.

"I was walking Jenny to the station when we saw this white cloud come towards us," said John yesterday.

FAINTED

"Then it changed to a red-glow, and we just ran."

Said Jenny: "It was terribly frightening."

Sixteen-year-old Annette Baxter, of Hythe, saw the white cloud. "But I can't remember anything after that because I fainted," she said.

London family doctor Dr. Bernard Finch, of Finchley, is to spend this weekend at Saltwood to see if a flying saucer has been calling. He has done some saucer-watching on Hampstead Heath.

5th June 1965

'THING' IN ORBIT – NEW RIDDLE

'IT HAD ARMS' SAYS ASTRONAUT JIM

America's orbiting astronauts tonight spotted a mystery object in Space – an object described as having "big arms".

Spaceman James McDivitt spoke these dramatic words from the Gemini 4 Spacecraft as it hurtled round the globe in a marathon that will last until Monday:

"I just saw something else up here with me. It had big arms sticking out of it."

He said he had taken some movie-camera pictures of it before it moved into the light of the Sun and he lost sight of it.

The object was also seen by McDivitt's partner, Ed White.

The discovery started frantic efforts by US Space experts to track the object – and to guess its origin.

Computers at Cape Kennedy were fed with information on the whereabouts of all known artificial satellites – American and Russian.

But later a top official said that none of them was on a collision course with Gemini 4.

Earlier the two astronauts, orbiting about 100 miles above the Earth spoke to their wives in the most expensively-organized phone conversation in history.

'GREAT'

Their wives, both named Patricia, were at Space control centre in Houston, Texas.

This is how the conversations went:

Mrs. McDivitt said to her husband: You are going great.

McDivitt replied: Yeah. We seem to be covering a lot of territory out here. How are you?

Mrs. McDivitt: I am fine. How are you?

McDivitt: Pretty good. I am over California right now.

Mrs. McDivitt: Get yourself over Texas.

McDivitt: Behaving yourself?

Mrs. McDivitt: I am always good.

Then Patricia White spoke to her husband.

Mrs. White: It looks like you were having a wonderful time yesterday.

White: Quite a time … We had quite a time.

… AND A TOWN SEES A SAUCER

The market town of "mysterious vibrations" had a new visitor last night – a "flying saucer".

Scores of people said they saw a cigar-shaped, fiery object hovering in the sky over Warminster, Wilts., from 2.30 until 9 p.m.

Scientist David Holton, of Crockerton has been investigating "vibrations" heard by a dozen Warminster people since Christmas.

Said Mr. Holton last night: "Here is a series of happenings which cannot be explained."

He is sure that Wiltshire will soon be invaded by craft from Outer Space.

11th September **1965**

High above a road not far from London … the strange, fast-moving Thing in the sky that Ray Coombs saw.

… AND FOR THE SECOND TIME A CAMERA CATCHES A MYSTERY IN THE SKY

THE RETURN OF THE THING

Amateur photographer Roy Coombs, 33, was out cycling when he saw it … the strange Thing in the sky.

He jumped off his bike, quickly focused the camera he was carrying and took four pictures.

Roy, a servicing engineer, of Musjid-road, Battersea, London, saw the mysterious flying object at 3.30 on Monday afternoon while he was riding along the Portsmouth road, just south of Surbiton, Surrey.

He was on his way to Kingston upon Thames to take pictures of the boats on the river.

Roy said yesterday: "Suddenly I saw a glint in the sky. At first I thought it was a shooting star – or perhaps an aircraft crashing.

"Then I saw this shape, moving very fast, which seemed to skim across the sky from the East."

Roy, who has a £30 second-hand camera, added: "I don't claim that this is a flying saucer. I have an open mind on this subject. But what is it?"

3rd March **1966**

BEG TO REPORT, SIR, ONE FLYING SAUCER

I was proceeding along the High Street on duty when I observed …

That's the time-honoured way policemen begin reports of incidents on the beat.

But Police Constable 136 Colin Perks's report was right out of

the ordinary.

Out of this world, in fact:

For it was headed: "Unidentified Flying Object".

The thing he observed, as he proceeded through the streets of Wilmslow, Cheshire, at four a.m., was a flying saucer.

He described it as being as long as a bus – about 30ft.

It hovered 20ft. above a field, making a peculiar humming sound.

It shot over the rooftops at a fantastic speed.

PARALYSED

Police Constable Perks handed his report to the sergeant, who gave it to the superintendent, who passed it on to the chief constable, who sent it to the Ministry of Defence (Air).

The 38-year-old constable lives at Northward-road, Wilmslow, with his wife and baby daughter.

He said there last night: "I was paralysed. I couldn't believe what I was seeing."

Mirror science reporter Arthur Smith says: "Strange electrical conditions of the atmosphere sometimes lead to sightings of this sort."

PC Perks' sketch of the UFO.

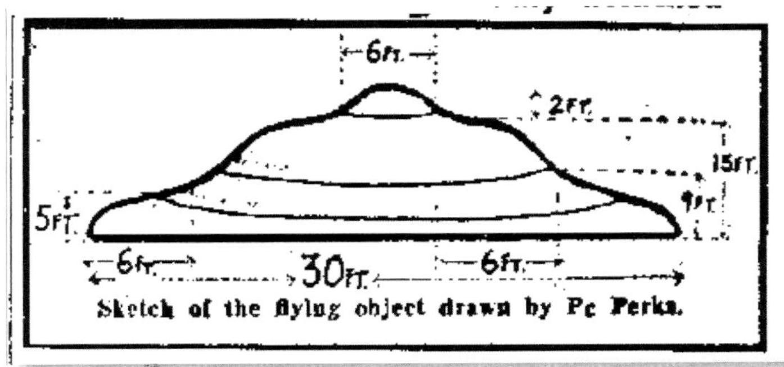

7th July 1967

SPOTLIGHT ON THE START OF THE SAUCER SEASON

UFO

UNIDENTIFIED FLYING OBJECTS

The saucer spotting season really got into orbit yesterday when two policemen were ordered to make out a full report of a mystery object they saw flashing across the sky.

The policemen were eye witnesses to the sighting since the "season" opened on June 24.

That was the twentieth anniversary of the first-ever recorded appearance of what is now called UFO – Unidentified Flying Objects.

In that time thousands of people have claimed to have seen mysterious objects in the sky.

NOTEBOOK

The latest report went into a policeman's notebook.

Police-Constable David Holloway and a fellow officer sped in their radio car to Stoney Cross in the New Forest after receiving a 999 call from a motorist.

Eight minutes later they sent this radio report to police headquarters at Winchester, Hants:

"We can see it. It is a circle with an orange glow round it and it's doing strange aerobatics."

With the policemen were two pilot officials, Graham Pestridge, 23, and Mike Gallagher, 24, from the 130 Bournemouth Squadron, RAF Volunteer Reserve Training.

Graham, a car salesman, said last night:

"You can call it a flying saucer if you like.

"All I know is that it wasn't a star, it wasn't a weather balloon and it wasn't a satellite. It was all very eerie."

And so the season is upon us. Hundreds of people in Britain, and hundreds more around the world, firmly believe in flying saucers.

I am not one of them.

The last one I saw – in fact a whole squadron of them – was from a plane on a winter evening year.

They whipped past my window in perfect formation, slowed, hovered, wheeled – and vanished.

They were the reflection of the runaway lights as the plane banked and turned for its stomach.

That I believe to be as good as a saucer sighting as any in the books.

The RAF department at the Ministry of Defence gets some 1,000 reports a year. Time was when they were all investigated. But they fell into a pattern and today they are just filed away. No investigation, no action.

DEBRIS

In fact, 95 per cent of sightings can be explained naturally. Satellites, rocket, debris, weather balloons, odd cloud formations and the like. The odd 5 per cent?

Some are pure hoax, some plain fraud. The others … unreliable or unsupported witnesses, differing versions of the same sighting, or hallucinations.

Photographic evidence?

It is too easily faked to be convincing. And it has been faked, time and again.

Even so, there are hundreds of honest genuine people all over the world who are convinced of the existence of unidentified flying objects.

I know a lot of people are going to be furious with me.

Or perhaps shake their heads in pity for my hidebound, unimaginative rejection of the whole shooting match.

All right – convince me. So long as it doesn't mean keeping me up all night.

▲ Police Constable Roger Willey (left) and Constable Clifford Waycott chased an apparent UFO in their patrol car along country lanes at up to 90mph in the early hours of this morning, 24th October 1967.

A UFO being inspected by Farmer Jennings after landing in his field, whilst a police officer keeps a safe distance.

Yeti – You Know What They Say About Big Feet

News of the Yeti first came home via British Everest expeditions.

The first British expeditions to Everest reported seeing curious footprints, alerting the West to the existence of a large ape-like biped.

The Himalayan locals interpreted them as belonging to a man-eating beast that they feared greatly, because just seeing one would prove fatal.

Thirty years later, another British expedition managed to photograph more footprints. Within the same decade, big footprints of another upright-walking creature were discovered in the American continent, and Bigfoot, also known as Sasquatch, garnered international interest.

Roger Patterson's footage, known as the Patterson–Gimlin film is the most famous piece of evidence, so much so that Bigfoot has even been given the nickname "Patty".

4th December **1951**

TRACK OF THE SNOW MONSTER

The British Mount Everest expedition has found and photographed footprints of the legendary "Abominable Snowman" – said to be a semi-human gorilla-like monster according to Reuter reports from New Delhi.

Mr. Eric Shipton, forty-four-year-old leader of the expedition, is also reported to have talked to a hillman who said he had seen the monster, which is supposed to inhabit the icy regions of the Himalayas where no other living thing can go.

Mr. Shipton, who is due to leave today by air for London after a three-month expedition to Everest, is understood to be bringing the photographs of the footprints. The footprints are said to be triangular in shape and larger even than the snow-shoes worn by members of the exhibition.

It is expected that the photographs will be examined in London by leading zoologists in an attempt to find out what kind of animal caused them.

According to legend anyone who sees the "Abominable Snowman" will immediately drop dead. Nothing will induce local hillmen to trail the tracks to their source.

British climber Frank Smythe during a climb in the Himalayas in 1937 reported finding an "imprint of a huge naked foot, apparently of a biped", about thirteen inches in length with five toes in front and two at the back.

6th December **1951**

THE TRIANGULAR FOOTPRINTS OF THE ABOMINABLE SNOWMAN

DOES HE REALLY EXIST?

Sixty days from today – on February 4 – further fantastic evidence of the existence of a mountain monster which wanders among the peaks of the Himalayas will be heard by explorers and scientists in London.

For on that day, in an oak-panelled lecture room in Kensington, 850 travelled Fellows of the Royal Geographical Society will study the lantern slides of Eric Shipton, a forty-four-year-old explorer and fellow member, who has just returned from an expedition to the icy wastes of 29,000ft Mount Everest.

But those slides which will make the members lean forward in their green striped tip-up seats will show – the footprints of the Abominable Snowman.

Last night, Shipton, one of the most famous mountaineers in the world, was flying back to London with photographs of the giant, triangular-shaped footprints in the Himalayan snows. These may prove that the dreaded Abominable Snowman, the fabled terror of every tiny Tibetan village clinging to the high Himalayan hillsides, does really exist. For the photographs show footprints larger even than the snowshoes worn by Shipton and his men on Everest.

Once again these photographs will set scientific men in Britain arguing over a mystery which has baffled scientists and mountaineers for thirty years.

Did a monster make the footprints?

The Tibetans who live on the snowline have always believed that there is a giant gorilla-like monster who roams the inaccessible peaks of the Himalayas.

They call it the Abominable Snowman. They say the Abominable Snowmen have their feet turned backwards to enable them to climb easily. Their hair is so long that when they go downhill it falls over their eyes. They eat yaks, the buffaloes of Tibet – and men.

What evidence is there that these monsters exist?

Shipton is reported to have talked with a Tibetan hillman who claims to have seen a half-man half-beast high on the snowy peaks of the high Himalayas.

Time and again, Tibetans who live in the valley beneath the mountain have warned British mountaineers against the "evil spirits" on Everest.

What was the truth of their warnings?

Seventeen years ago, the learned abbot of the Tang-tra Monastery, on the trade route which leads to Lhasa, came across the snowbound passes into Kalimpong, in India. Before he left he called on David Macdonald, who lived for twenty years in Tibet.

The abbot had come to warn the British against trying to climb Mount Everest. He stood dressed in a red woollen monk's habit and told him: "A race of wild men lives there, covered with hair. Their feet are turned backwards."

Last year in a letter to *The Times*, Lieutenant-Colonel M. Sinclair, who was formerly a British trade agent in Tibet, reported that in the village of Phari, where the inhabitants are more educated than the average peasant, the people accept the existence of snow giants without question.

So strongly do they believe in the hairy monster that flounders along the icy wilderness of the highest mountains in the world that the Tibetans recount, round their smoky yak-dung fires, the detailed legends of the life of the Abominable Snowman.

They say the female is larger and more savage than the male. In hushed, lilting voices, they tell how the Snow-woman woos her mate and kills him if he refuses. And sometimes she kills him if he does not refuse.

That is the legend of the Tibetan peasants.

But civilized Western explorers have reported the footprints for thirty years.

In 1921 Colonel Howard Bury, leader of the first Mount Everest party, came upon strange footprints 22,000ft. high on the mountainside.

Again, in the second Everest expedition in the same year, British mountaineers saw strange tracks far above the snowline long after signs of animal life had disappeared.

In 1937 Prank Smythe, the famous British climber, discovered marks of 12in. paws with five toes in the Garhwal Himalayas which lie between India and Everest.

Smythe's porters signed this statement: "We were accompanying Mr. Smythe over a pass when we saw tracks which we know to be those of a mirka or 'wild man'. We have never seen a mirka because anyone who sees one dies or is killed. There are drawings of the same footprints in Tibetan monasteries."

In the same period, Mr. Ronald Kaulback reported five sets of tracks at 16,000ft. which, in his words, "looked exactly as though made by a barefooted man". And six years before, an explorer named A. N. Tombazi had seen something very strange … something which might have been the Snowman.

He said: "Intense glare prevented me seeing anything for the first few seconds, but I soon saw a figure in outline exactly like a human being, walking upright and stooping to uproot some rhododendrons. The figure showed dark against the snow and wore no clothing. Within the next minute or so it disappeared.

"From inquiries I gathered that no man had gone in this direction since the beginning of the year. My coolies trotted out fantastic legends of Snowmen, I can only reiterate that the silhouette of the mysterious being was identical with the outline of a human figure."

Sceptical scientists said that the footprints may have been made by a huge bear. But Mr. Kaulback pointed out that there were no bears in that part of the world. Large monkeys were suggested, but Kaulback replied that he had neither seen nor heard of any monkeys there – and the strange tracks were 3,000ft. above the snowline.

Is it beast or man that wanders in the rarefied air of the Himalayan snow desert?

An official of the Royal Geographical Society, who helped finance the trip, said yesterday:

"Do we believe the Snowman exists? We're keeping an open mind until the fourth of February."

30th December 1952

AN ABOMINABLE SNOWMAN SEIZED ME, HE SAYS

A porter with the unsuccessful Swiss Mount Everest expedition claims that he was attacked by an Abominable Snowman during the climb.

He told the Swiss climbers, now back in New Delhi, that a Snowman seized him, but it ran away when fourteen other porters came to the rescue.

The Swiss themselves said they had heard "padding and shuffling" outside their tents at heights where there were no animals. The attack was said to have taken place below the Lhotse glacier, about 27,000ft. up the mountain.

Swiss comment was: "It might have been the Snowman. It might have been a bear. It might have been a freak of the imagination."

The Abominable Snowman is a legendary creature, half-man, half-beast, which the Tibetans believe to be a man-eater.

Photographs taken by a British Everest expedition, led by Mr. Eric Shipton, the explorer, published early this year, showed footprints in the snow, which were said to be those of the Snowman.

Mr. Shipton said that he placed a "great deal of reliance" on the report of a porter who said he had identified footprints on the slopes of Everest as those of the Abominable Snowman.

23rd December 1960

Khumjo Chumbi and Sir Edmund Hillary with a Yeti scalp.

HEADMAN!

Village headman Khumjo Chumbi, 48, from the slopes of Mount Everest, is pointing to a scalp which he believes to be that of a Yeti – an Abominable Snowman.

Holding the scalp is Everest conqueror Sir Edmund Hillary, who arrived with Chumbi – and The Scalp – at London Airport yesterday.

Sir Edmund has been back to Everest, in Nepal, to search for the Abominable Snowman, a creature reputed to live in the area.

Sir Edmund did not find a Snowman but in Khumjo's village he was shown The Scalp – said to have been revered by the Sherpa villagers for 240 years.

The villagers would not let Sir Edmund take The Scalp away to show it to a British expert unless headman Khumjo went, too … to guard it. And unless The Scalp is returned by January 5, three tribesmen who stood as "guarantors" will forfeit their lands.

On location filming *Dr Who*. Actor Patrick Troughton filming in Snowdonia with Yeti monsters, 15th September 1967.

Bigfoot in the woods, northern California, 1967

THIS cine-camera footage is the most startling evidence yet of the existence of Bigfoot – the Abominable Snowman's North American cousin.

It was shot by Bigfoot hunters Roger Patterson and Bob Gimlin at Bluff Creek, Northern California, on October 20, 1967.

Patterson spotted the creature striding across a sandbar 90ft away and tore after it – until it turned and froze him with a glare.

Sadly, Patterson died in 1972 having failed to convince scientists that his film showed a real beast.

19th May 1973

➧ Setting out to search for Bigfoot, and a cast of one of the discovered footprints.

BLIND DATE WITH BIGFOOT

The great Yeti hunt is on again. This time the quarry is a hairy giant called Bigfoot.

Sightings have been reported in remote parts of America and Canada since 1811.

Leading the search for the 9ft. tall, 64 stone "monsters" is Peter Byrne, 47, a former RAF pilot.

Dublin-born Peter, who hunted big game in Africa for fifteen years, became fascinated by the giants after tracking the Abominable Snowman in the Himalayas.

BREAK

His big break came when he heard that a rancher in Washington State had filmed a hairy monster which left 14-inch footprints.

The rancher, Roger Patterson, shot 28ft. of Bigfoot film in a wooded area near his home. The film shows a well-endowed hairy female squatting beside a stream.

From a distance of about 30 feet the camera shows the figure stand and calmly walk into surrounding trees.

Peter says: "This is the most vital piece of evidence I have come across since I started the search three years ago."

He has organized the Wildlife Conservation Society to track down the mysterious giant which was given the name Omagh in American Indian mythology.

CLAIM

In the last three years Peter and his 1,000 members have covered thousands of miles of the Pacific North West and studied reports going back over 100 years from people who claim to have seen Bigfoot.

As well as two Land-Rovers Peter's giant-hunters have infra-red camera equipment for night sightings, a helicopter on 24-hour standby and tranquilliser darts.

"I suppose some people think I'm a bit nutty but the evidence is too convincing and sustained for it all to be a hoax," said Peter who now lives in a caravan near Portland, Oregon, the centre of the recent sightings.

Among his bulging files is a report of huge footprints, 25 miles from any road, which were tracked by his investigators for seven miles across rough mountain areas before fading out.

PAGE 18 DAILY MIRROR, *Saturday, May 19, 1973*

Blind date with Bigfoo

THE GREAT Yeti hunt is on again. This time the quarry is a hairy giant called Bigfoot.

Sightings have been reported in remote parts of America and Canada since 1811.

Leading the search for the 9ft. tall, 64 stone "monsters" is Peter Byrne, 47, a former R A F pilot.

Dublin-born Peter, who hunted big game in Africa for fifteen years, became fascinated by the giants after tracking the Abominable Snowman in the Himalayas.

Break

His big break came when he heard that a rancher in Washington State had filmed a hairy monster which left 14-inch footprints.

The rancher, Roger Patterson, shot 28ft. of Bigfoot film in a wooded area near his home. The film shows a well-endowed hairy female squatting beside a stream.

From a distance of about 30 feet the camera shows the figure stand and calmly walk into surrounding trees.

Peter says: "This is the most vital piece of evidence I have come across since I started the search three years ago."

SHE'S 9ft TALL AND WEIGHS 64st

He has organised Wildlife Conserva Society to track down mysterious giant wh was given the na Omagh in American dian mythology.

Claim

In the last three ye Peter and his 1, members have cove thousands of miles of Pacific North West a studied reports goi back over 100 years fr people who claim to ha seen Bigfoot.

As well as two Lar Rovers, Peter's gia hunters have infra-r camera equipment night sightings, a he copter on 24-hour star

Another series of footprints, measuring 17½ in. by 7in., were found in Washington State in October 1969.

Dr. Grover Krantz, an expert in anthropology at Washington State University, studied casts made from some of the prints in

Peter Byrne sets out with his team to search for the shy giants. Inset: A cast of one of their monster footprints.

DNEY YOUNG reports from NEW YORK

and tranquilliser s.

suppose some people k I'm a bit nutty the evidence is too ·incing and sustained it all to be a hoax," Peter who now lives caravan near Port- , Oregon, the centre ne recent sightings.

nong his bulging is a report of huge prints, 25 miles from road, which were ed by his investiga- for seven miles ss rough mountain s before fading out.

other series of foot- ts, measuring 17½in. 7in., were found in Washington State in October 1969.

Dr. Grover Krantz, an expert in anthropology at Washington State University, studied casts made from some of the prints in which the right foot appears to be twisted inwards.

He concluded that if they were a hoax the fakers were absolute experts in human anatomy.

Old Indians Peter has interviewed say their grandfathers told them of seeing as many as twenty giants catching salmon in the Columbia river, but in the 1850s the creatures caught "white man's disease" and died off.

The existence of the American Yeti has some doubters of course.

John Napier, director of the Smithsonian Museum's Primate Biology Department, who is now visiting professor at the University of London, is one.

Male

After studying Roger Patterson's film he said the stride of the figure was essentially that of a male, not a female. Other characteristics, he said, were human aids and out of place in an ape-like being.

But Mr. Napier would not positively say it was a hoax.

Peter says: "The evidence is strong and I intend to continue the search. I will not give up until I find Bigfoot."

If his dream comes true, the shy giant will be released after being examined and photographed.

But Peter has rivals for his "girlfriend's" affections—Tom Biscardi, 24, and Gene Findlay, 25, from San Jose, California, are also on her trail.

They have perfected a monitoring system—similar to the Army's enemy night spotter—which detects objects on the ground from their body heat.

Biscardi says: "We've everything going for us. Every angle is covered.

"We've been ridiculed already. But they ridiculed the Wright Brothers, too."

which the right foot appears to be twisted inwards.

He concluded that if they were a hoax the fakers were absolute experts in human anatomy.

Old Indians Peter has interviewed say their grandfathers told them of seeing as many as twenty giants catching salmon in the Columbia river, but in the 1850s the creatures caught "white man's disease" and died off.

The existence of the American Yeti has some doubters of course. John Napier, director of the Smithsonian Museum's Primate Biology Department, who is now visiting professor at the University of London, is one.

MALE

After studying Roger Patterson's film he said the stride of the figure was essentially that of a male, not a female. Other characteristics, he said, were human aids and out of place in an apelike being.

But Mr. Napier would not positively say it was a hoax.

Peter says: "The evidence is strong and I intend to continue the search. I will not give up until I find Bigfoot."

If his dream comes true, the shy giant will be released after being examined and photographed.

But Peter has rivals for his "girlfriend's" affections – Tom Biscardi, 24, and Gene Pindlay, 25, from San Jose, California, are also on her trail.

They have perfected a monitoring system – similar to the Army's enemy night spotter – which detects objects on the ground from their body heat.

Biscardi says: "We've everything going for us. Every angle is covered.

"We've been ridiculed already. But they ridiculed the Wright Brothers, too."

12th December 1974

BIGFEET FIRST

Launching a campaign to hunt down a world monster mystery is Odette Tchernine, one of Britain's most formidable monster hunters.

She is out to track down the Abominable Snowman, known in

the Himalayas as the Yeti and in North America as Bigfoot.

"Too many have been seen in too many parts of the world for this phenomenon to be a hoax," Odette insisted.

So she is off to Canada in pursuit.

Bigfeet are said to be 7ft. tall, with pointed scalps, receding foreheads and large jaws and teeth.

"Some are harmless vegetarians," Odette said, "but, others eat flesh and there have been reports of them chasing people." Even so she will arm herself only with a camera.

She is not scared.

"I am more frightened," she said, "of being bitten by insects."

31st May 1979

YETI 'MAY BE AN APE'

The legendary Abominable Snowman is probably an ape.

This was suggested yesterday by Everest pioneer Lord Hunt, who has taken fresh photographs of giant footprints in the Himalayas.

The snow covered region where the latest pictures were taken includes forests and Lord Hunt believes the mysterious Yeti could resemble an orang-utan.

Lord Hunt, whose pictures appear in the *Geographical Magazine* wants an expedition mounted to discover the truth about the Yeti.

19th September 1979

DAY ONE OF THE MONSTER BUSINESS

ON THE TRAIL OF BIGFOOT!

After the discovery of huge footprints, thousands of Russian soldiers are now searching for the legendary Abominable Snowman in Soviet Central Asia. In the West, meanwhile, another monster disturbs the peace …

It is hairy and perhaps as much as 10ft. tall. It gallops with a 6ft. stride, moans like the devil and smells like a rotting carcass.

They call it Bigfoot – a name it gets from footprints up to 19in. long and 7in. wide.

Nothing like Bigfoot has been seen here, in the heart of the Sioux country, before.

And the creature is frightening the life out of the tribe that defeated General Custer.

Little Eagle is a cluster of huts on South Dakota's Standing Rock Reservation. The road cuts through rolling plains on its way to McLaughlin, the big city (pop. 1,500) fifteen miles away.

The Indians talk shyly of their simple lives and of what little they know of the outside world.

But Bigfoot is bad medicine, and few will even acknowledge its name.

There is one way to gauge fear and that is to share it and set out on the Bigfoot trail.

DARK

Lemar Bare Ribs made the first sighting here twenty-one months ago. He was seventeen and was walking down a dark track after an evening with friends at the home of Jim Chasing Hawks.

Now in the Army, Bare Ribs recalled: "I had just left the house when some bushes rustled. I thought maybe it was a dog. Suddenly this creature stepped out and just stood there looking at me.

"Its head and shoulders were taller than those trees over there," he said, pointing at 8ft. cottonwood trees.

"Its head was big and round but it had no neck. It growled at me, kind of low and deep."

Bare Ribs took to his heels, raced home and had nightmares for a week.

He recalled how, once home, it took him five minutes to blurt out to his aunt, Adele Antelope: "There's something big out there."

HAIR

Adele and others immediately drove to the scene and picked up in the headlights "this big thing with lots of dark brown hair".

Adele has not been out at night since.

Esther Thundershield, who also saw the beast, refused to talk, "In case it comes back and hurts me."

After more sightings the law was called in.

Verdell Veo, a lieutenant with the Bureau of Indian Affairs and Windy Village Thunder formed a five-man posse and rode to the banks of the Grand River, shortly before it enters the mighty Missouri.

There, they found four sets of tracks and footprints.

Said Veo: "When I saw them, I had a feeling of being spellbound, hypnotized.

"I had another feeling that no weapons we were carrying would have made any difference. So we got out and left the thing alone."

TWICE

Gary Alexander, manager of the trading post, has also seen the

beast. So have his sons Todd, 14, and Chad, 11 – twice in daylight.

All swear they are telling the truth. Gary produced a huge plaster-cast of an imprint to back up his claim.

The United States Government has ruled that Bigfoot must not be shot, giving two reasons – that the beast should be preserved for study and that hunters might shoot at each other in night-time shadows.

19th September **1979**

BEAST FROM THE FOREST

Indian tribes in the Pacific North-West told the first European settlers of a hairy, oversize man-like creature living deep in the forests. They called it Sasquash [*sic*], meaning "The Big Man". It was not until the early 1800s that a white man first saw it and dubbed it "Bigfoot".

By 1880 newspapers were printing stories of Bigfoot. And since then more than 1,000 people have sworn they have seen it.

Enormous footprints have been found in many remote parts, ranging from the Canadian border to Mexico.

By Indian tradition, Bigfoot kidnaps humans and several Americans claim to have been victims.

• In 1924 a lumberman named Albert Ostman was camping in British Columbia, Canada, when, he reported, he was lifted up in his sleeping bag and carried twenty-five miles to a Bigfoot lair.

The Bigfoot father was 8ft. tall, the mother a foot shorter, and there were two children.

Ostman was treated kindly, but escaped after six days in the confusion caused when one Bigfoot swallowed a tin of his snuff.

Fearing mockery, the lumberman kept his kidnapping a secret for thirty years.

• In 1958 roadbuilders in the North-West California wilderness repeatedly found giant footprints around their camp.

• In 1967 came the most striking evidence of the creature's existence – film shot by rancher Roger Patterson while on a Bigfoot hunt in Washington State.

The film shows, at a distance of about 109ft, a hairy female beast walking upright and looking straight at the camera. It then turns and walks calmly into the surrounding trees.

• In 1976 two loggers working in the Hood River National Forest in Oregon disturbed a Bigfoot. When it ran away on two legs, they chased it, throwing rocks. Investigators later found huge footprints, with those of the loggers running alongside.

A distinguished American anthropologist, John Napier, has written a book about Bigfoot. Although sceptical of its existence, Napier was impressed by a trail of footprints, 17in. long and 7in. wide, found at Bossborough, Washington State.

Another anthropologist, Professor Grover Krantz, of Washington State University, is a firm believer in Bigfoot.

"But if you photographed a Bigfoot down to its tonsils, it would never convince the scientific community," he says.

24th December **1979**

THE YETI LIVES, SAY CLIMBERS

New evidence that there is an Abominable Snowman in the Himalayas has been found by British climbers.

The climbers, who include a doctor, a lawyer and an RAF officer, say they found distinct footprints of the Yeti and heard its scream-like calls.

Their leader, Squadron Leader John Edwards, said yesterday after his return from Nepal: "This has changed me from a sceptic into realising that there is firm evidence of a strange creature in the Himalayas."

The expedition, which was in the Himalayas for eight weeks, conquered a 19,840ft. peak which had never been climbed before.

8th February **1985**

CHINESE CATCH A 3FT 'YETI'

A legendary "wild man" 3ft 8in tall and covered in hair has been captured in China, according to reports in Peking.

The ape-like "yeti" creature was trapped as he teased a woman in a mountain region. Reports of such a beast have cropped up throughout China's history.

7th May **1987**

THE YETI IS SNOW JOKE SAYS CHRIS

Climber Chris Bonington gave his backing to the legend of the Abominable Snowman yesterday.

"You can't discount it," he said. "There's more reason to believe it exists than not."

He was back in Britain after an expedition to the Tibetan Himalayas, where "Yeti footprints" were photographed on the slopes of the unconquered 23,327ft. peak Menlungtse.

26th September 1987

YETI WITH A YEN FOR MEN

She's big, she's busty and she's hungry for love … but don't all rush, chaps.

For she is a lady yeti said to roam the frozen Himalayan wastes searching for lovers to warm her up.

Explorer Chris Frost is there now hoping to catch a glimpse of the sexy snowwoman. But so far he is out of luck.

In a letter to his parents in Highnam, near Gloucester, he writes: "One account says that a furry, large-breasted, wild woman entered a Chinese official's bedroom at midnight with amorous intentions."

Chris, 31, is halfway through a six-week expedition to track down the creature. He says he would be lucky to make just one sighting – preferably from a long distance.

Doctor Jim Dodson, a zoologist at Bristol University, said yesterday that he had not heard of the sex-mad monster, but added: "I wouldn't fancy being out in Tibet if this yeti really is a nympho."

LEGEND: Yeti

YETI FIND BY BRITS

THREE British explorers claim to have found proof of a Yeti-like creature living on an Indonesian island.

The 5ft tall Orang Pendek – Little Man of the Forest – is legendary in Sumatra.

Andrew Sanderson, 30, of Newcastle upon Tyne, said: "We didn't see the creature but we tracked it for weeks and made a cast of one of its footprints."

31st October 2001

YETI FIND BY BRITS

Three British explorers claim to have found proof of a Yeti-like creature living on an Indonesian island.

The 5ft tall Orang Pendek – Little Man of the Forest – is legendary in Sumatra.

Andrew Sanderson, 30, of Newcastle upon Tyne, said: "We didn't see the creature but we tracked it for weeks and made a cast of one of its footprints."

7th December 2002

BIGFOOT LAID TO REST

Bigfoot – an apelike creature filmed in an American wood – was a hoax, it was revealed yesterday.

The family of Ray L Wallace, who fuelled the Bigfoot legend, said footage of the creature was his wife in fancy dress.

They decided to come clean after Ray died. His son Michael said: "Ray L Wallace was Bigfoot. He made a lot of people laugh. It was a fun family."

In 1958 Ray put down fake tracks and the local paper in Humboldt County, California, dubbed it Bigfoot. Then in 1967 a grainy film was released of the beast.

3rd June 2008

YETI … THE FIRST EVER 'PHOTOFIT'

IS THIS THE YETI? A BRITISH ARTIST THINKS IT COULD BE

Polyanna Pickering drew the "photofit" helped by scores of people who say it is their neighbour.

And she was shown what was claimed to be a "genuine" 100-year old Yeti scalp.

Ms Pickering, 65, of Oaker, Derbyshire, said: "It was bigger than any human or ape scalp I have ever seen", and "had tufts of reddish black fur".

It was at a remote monastery in Bhutan in the Himalayas which bans photos so she sketched it. Then she drew this picture helped by locals "all sitting round telling me to alter this or how that should look.

"They describe it as a very shy, apelike creature about 8ft tall. They told me of regular sightings, close encounters and even people being carried off."

Jonathan Downes, of the Centre of Fortean Zoology, which studies mystery animals, said: "If true, it is the most important zoological discovery in 70 years."

But other Yeti scalps had "turned out to be manmade".

6th November 2008

SO WE'VE NOT FOUND IT YETI

An Oxford scientist admits he is annoyed after DNA tests showed

Yeti.. the first ever 'photofit'

IS this the Yeti? A British artist thinks it could be.

Polyanna Pickering drew the "photofit" helped by scores of people who say it is their neighbour.

And she was shown what was claimed to be a "genuine" 100-year-old Yeti scalp.

Ms Pickering, 65, of Oaker, Derbys, said: "It was bigger than any human or ape scalp I have ever seen," and "had tufts of reddish black fur".

It was at a remote monastery in Bhutan in the Himalayas which bans photos so she sketched it. Then she drew this picture helped by locals "all sitting round telling me to alter this or how that should look.

"They describe it as a very shy, apelike creature about 8ft tall. They told me of regular sightings, close encounters and even people being carried off."

Jonathan Downes, of the Centre of Fortean Zoology, which studies mystery animals, said: "If true, it is the most important zoological discovery in 70 years."

But other Yeti scalps had "turned out to be manmade".

▸ **ARTIST** Polyanna

hairs thought to be from a yeti came from a Himalayan goral goat.

Ian Redmond OBE, 54, found the hairs near sightings of Bigfoot in India. He said: "The search goes on."

28th December **2011**

YETI MYTH *DNA*ILED

A mummified finger smuggled out of Nepal 50 years ago and revered as a yeti's has been revealed to be human after all.

The relic was taken from a monastery by a US explorer in the 1950s, who replaced it with a human finger to fool the monks. Then film star James Stewart helped to smuggle it out of India by hiding it in his wife's lingerie case and it ended up in the Royal College of Surgeons' museum in London.

But yesterday, scientists at Edinburgh Zoo said DNA sample analysis found it to be human. The zoo's genetics expert Dr Rob Ogden said: "It was obviously slightly disappointing."

23rd May **2012**

BIGFOOT NOT FOUND … YETI

Organic remains found by an explorer are being retested to try to prove the existence of the mythical yeti.

Bernard Heuvelmans investigated sightings from 1950 until his death in 2001 and saved a collection of samples, including hair.

Some were found to be human but Oxford University's Bryan Sykes said tests may have been contaminated, so British and Swiss scientists are checking DNA again.

He said: "Testing techniques, particularly on hair, have improved a lot due to forensic science advances."

29th August **2012**

BIGFOOT BLUNDER

A hoaxer trying to start a Bigfoot scare was run over and killed as he stood in the road attempting to terrify drivers.

Randy Lee Tenley, 44, was wearing a ghillie suit – a straggly full-body camouflage outfit resembling the mysterious ape-like creature also known as Sasquatch – hoping it would lead to reports of sightings. But because he was camouflaged he was hit by one car then run over by another as he lay in the road. "The suit made it difficult for people to see him," said police in Kalispell, Montana.

They suspected Tenley had been drinking and added: "He was trying to make drivers think he was Sasquatch so people would report a sighting. You can't make it up."

Loch Ness Monster – Who Wants to be a Millionaire?

Urquhart Castle on the shore of Loch Ness, Scotland.

Nessie sightings are predominantly at either ends of the loch, or midway around Urquhart Bay, especially on the side of the loch opposite the famous castle. Here there is a six-mile stretch of southern shore, between the villages of Foyers and Whitefield, along which about a third of the sightings have been logged. While the sightings appear in clusters, their locations do not reflect any obvious properties of the lake, such as its geography, nor do they readily correspond to human habitation.

The road on the north shore of Loch Ness leading to Urquhart Castle, c.1960.

19th September **1967**

NEW SIGHTING OF OLD NESSIE

Top engineer John Mathieson said that he saw the Loch Ness monster yesterday.

Mr. Mathieson, communications engineer with the North of Scotland Hydro-Electric Board, at Fort Augustus, Inverness-shire said that he saw it swimming in the loch.

Three huge dark-coloured humps, each as big as the back of a rhinoceros, were showing above the water, he said.

What staggered him most was a terrific wash from the monster, which threw waves up on the shore.

2nd June **1969**

LOOK OUT NESSIE, DESPERATE DAN'S AFTER YOUR HIDE

In this era of time and space, the existence of an alleged monster of unknown shape, texture, quantity and temperament, dwelling on the peat stained bottom of a loch, comes down to pretty small potatoes.

But when a stocky, chubby-cheeked, blue-eyed skipper from Georgia, USA, Dan Taylor, 28, comes bucketing up to this slumbering village riding a highly-personalized yellow submarine, equipped with what looks like four Black and Decker drills fastened by jubilee clips to both blunt ends, and swearing to skin the hide off the Loch Ness monster, the tale lives again.

Snorts, forsooth.

The captain trails the 20ft. two-ton home-made fibre glass sub

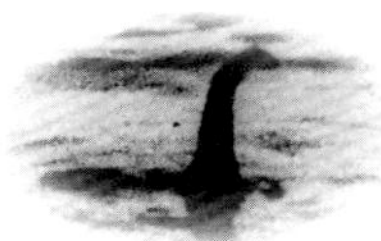

up past the bus shelter, which claims that Edith Duncan loves Billie McLeod, and parks it at the rear of the Glen Lodge Hotel.

He wears a three-quarter length green corduroy coat and tight white pants and he has the dedicated, cool look of a loner.

Loch Ness is 754ft. deep, roughly twenty miles long and one mile wide.

PLUNGING

They once used to use it to test naval mine casings because if Loch Ness didn't crush them nothing would.

There are stories of divers having gone mad after plunging into its depths.

Down there, I'm told, visibility is nil, and if you can imagine slurping about in a gigantic bowl of Scotch broth, that's it.

None of which bugs Captain Taylor.

He said at a conference in the cosy bar of the Glen Lodge Hotel: "What's so big about what I'm doing? We'll be on the Moon soon, won't we?"

But while the indomitable little chap was saying this outside, the locals were tapping the somewhat primitive looking gadgets in the car park and saying: "What a way to get your trousers pressed." Which indicated that they had fears of what could happen in the notorious depths of the loch.

Captain Taylor said that he had simulated depths up to 1,000ft. in the States, and that he would be using sonar equipment and searchlights to find Nessie.

I pointed out that visibility was zero after a certain depth, and why couldn't the job be done better by sonar equipment used from a surface vessel. "I think mine is the ideal way of doing it," he replied. "I am an experienced submariner, formerly of the US Navy, and I assure you this is not just a publicity stunt. I aim to get close enough to fire a sort of dart into Nessie's side and pull off a piece of skin so that the scientists can examine it."

At both ends of the captain's yellow submarine are pairs of electric fans with plastic blades with which to manoeuvre the hull.

The main motor is electrically driven and the 600 layers of fibre glass give an odd sound when you drum your fingers along its flanks.

As many people are doing at this very moment.

Captain Taylor says: "Man, if anything goes wrong down there, like the monster coming into the attack, I'll just press my little red button and blow myself out at forty to fifty knots with my ejection equipment. I don't want to tangle with that thing."

The captain is being helped, for want of a better word, by the Loch Ness Phenomena Investigation Bureau Limited, which is run

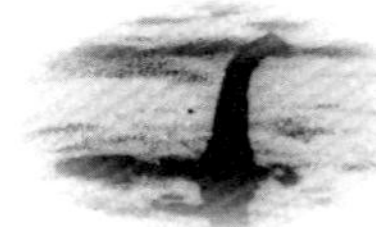

largely on subscriptions and donations.

Students, male and female, take part in the Bureau's work and get a subsistence allowance. Posses of them ring the sombre, brooding loch, now and then peering intently through binoculars and cameras out to where Nessie awaits the forthcoming attractions.

PARKING

The landlord of a lochside pub said: ""We would like the monster to be established as a living thing, or for the myth to be destroyed."

The local bobbies have been up to the hotel to make sure that there has been no vandalism to Captain Taylor's submarine.

But protection for Nessie?

"Och, no – we'll just make sure that there are no parking problems when the operation starts."

Which leaves Nessie entirely vulnerable, I suppose.

Whether or not the monster exists is another matter, but one of the researchers has told me in strict confidence that he was out rowing on the loch just recently, filling in time I guess, when up it popped.

What did you do, said I. Said he: "Do? Nothing. I have seen it seven times in all and it knows me. After a while it went down again and I rowed on."

Ah yes, I said. Ah yes.

Preparing a mini-submarine before a dive.

A mini-submarine on Loch Ness, searching for signs of the Loch Ness monster in July 1969.

17th July 1969

DON'T BE CRUEL TO THE LOCH NESS MONSTER

The Loch Ness Monster hunters have promised that they won't be beastly to Nessie.

It's a relief for Tory Peer Lord Kilmany.

He is so worried about the monster being ill-treated by the scientists who are searching for her with submarines that he brought the matter up in the House of Lords yesterday.

He was told that even if she is found, Nessie won't feel a thing … except a small pinprick.

Lord Hughes, Joint Parliamentary Under-Secretary at the Scottish Office, explained that the scientists were planning to use a retrievable dart to obtain a small bit of Nessie for study.

But Lord Hughes added that Nessie could not count on the protection of the law.

The Cruelty to Animals Act of 1876 might not cover her.

Though it all depends what sort of monster Nessie is.

Lord Hughes said: "Unless and until the monster is found, we cannot say if the provisions of the Act would apply."

29th August 1969

A PLAIN MAN'S GUIDE TO NESSIE-SPOTTING

This week, slap in the middle of the busiest ever monster-hunting season, a photograph that could have been the latest rival to the notorious Nessie arrived in the Mirrorscope office.

The picture was taken by an Essex couple on holiday on the Isle of Skye. And, on the face of it, it is as realistically monstrous as the elusive Nessie.

But the far more critical eye of Mirrorscope's cameras, "blowing up" the holidaymakers' 8 m.m. cine-film, unmasks the newest mysterious humpback as nothing more unworldly than a dolphin or possibly a whale.

This exposure of the Monster of Skye casts fresh doubts on the existence of Nessie.

For the high season of monster-spotting coincides with the annual visits to these shores of both dolphin and whale.

As, apparently, in the case of the sea-serpent of Skye, whales often swim up the narrow entrance to Scottish lochs, and then,

HUNTING

IT LOOKS LIKE A MONSTER …

BUT IT'S ONLY A DIVING OTTER …

A plain man's guide to Nessie-spotting

THIS week, slap in the middle of the busiest-ever monster-hunting season, a photograph that could have been the latest rival to the now-notorious Nessie arrived in the Mirrorscope office.

The picture (bottom left) was taken by an Essex couple on holiday on the Isle of Skye. And, on the face of it, it is as realistically monstrous as the elusive Nessie.

But the far more critical eye of Mirrorscope's cameras, "blowing up" the holiday-makers' 8 m.m. cine-film, unmasks the newest mysterious humpback as nothing more unworldly than a dolphin or possibly a whale.

This exposure of the Monster of Skye casts fresh doubts on the existence of Nessie.

For the high season of monster-spotting coincides with the annual visits to these shores of both dolphin and whale.

As, apparently, in the case of the sea-serpent of Skye, whales often swim up the narrow entrance to Scottish lochs, and then, bewildered, thresh up and down, looking for the route back to the sea.

The Skye visitor "kept jumping out of the water and churning it up as it thrashed like mad with its tail," according to the holiday-makers.

Unfortunately, for would-be monster spotters, this behaviour fits perfectly that of dolphins and whales.

A similar unromantic assessment of the Loch Ness mythology reveals, also, that the original monster is a trick of the eye.

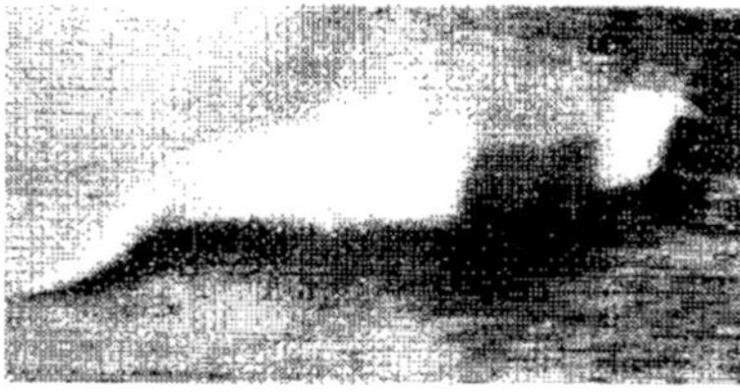

OR A SWIMMING OTTER …

The most-published picture of Nessie (above, left) is one such spoof. The "monster" is almost always shown in close-up. But when one sees the whole photograph (above, right) the "monster" takes on the less terrifying proportions of an otter — showing its tail as it dives.

Otters, in fact, at a fair distance or on an unfair day, are ideally cast for the role of monster.

They roll on the surface and splash about in a manner most monster-like. And a mother otter will swim along with her back humped above the water, followed by a line of smaller bumps—her babies. Instant sea-serpent!

It is thirty-five years since it was first strongly rumoured that Loch Ness housed a monster. But even the first photograph of the later-christened Nessie (centre) also proved to be an otter.

It does not even need a real animal to usurp a monster, however.

"A monster! A monster!" exclaimed the photographer who snapped the picture bottom right. (Had it not a hump?)

But when he paddled his boat up to it, he found it was only a floating stick about an inch thick.

But, despite all evidence to its discredit, scientists show increasing interest in the possibility of a monster. After a survey by Birmingham University scientists, others from Chicago University have arrived for a lochside investigation.

An American educational firm is helping to subsidise a submarine search for the monster (with overall operations run by a body known as the Loch Ness Phenomena Research Bureau).

Questions about the monster were asked last month in the House of Lords, and commercial television is believed to be spending around £50,000 on an underwater hunt by camera.

MARTIN JONES

OR A DOLPHIN …

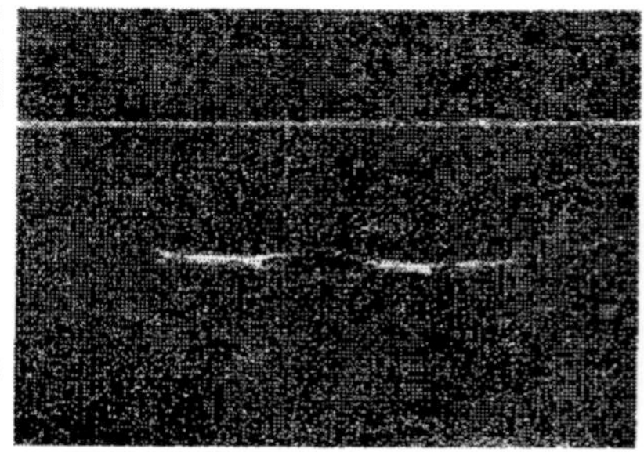

OR EVEN A HARMLESS STICK.

bewildered, thresh up and down, looking for the route back to the sea.

The Skye visitor "kept jumping out of the water and churning it up as it thrashed like mad with its tail", according to the holidaymakers.

Unfortunately, for would-be monster spotters, this behaviour fits perfectly that of dolphins and whales.

A similar unromantic assessment of the Loch Ness mythology reveals, also, that the original monster is a trick of the eye.

The most-published picture of Nessie is one such spoof. The "monster" is almost always shown in close-up. But when one sees the whole photograph the "monster" takes on the less terrifying proportions of an otter – showing its tail as it dives.

Otters, in fact, at a fair distance or on an unfair day, are ideally cast for the role of monster.

They roll on the surface and splash about in a manner most monster-like. And a mother otter will swim along with her back humped above the water, followed by a line of smaller bumps – her babies. Instant sea-serpent!

It is thirty-five years since it was first strongly rumoured that Loch Ness housed a monster. But even the first photograph of the later-christened Nessie also proved to be an otter.

It does not even need a real animal to usurp a monster, however. "A monster! A monster!" exclaimed one photographer who snapped a picture. But when he paddled his boat up to it, he found it was only a floating stick about an inch thick.

But, despite all evidence to its discredit, scientists show increasing interest in the possibility of a monster. After a survey by Birmingham University scientists, others from Chicago University have arrived for a loch-side investigation.

An American educational firm is helping to subsidise a submarine search for the monster (with overall operations run by a body known as the Loch Ness Phenomena Research Bureau).

Questions about the monster were asked last month in the House of Lords, and commercial television is believed to be spending around £50,000 on an underwater hunt by camera.

16th September 1969

A MONSTER HUNT IS ON FOR MONSTER NESSIE

Something really big disturbed the calm of Loch Ness yesterday.

Nothing like it has been seen before.

The monster Monster Hunt was on the move.

An army of searchers, scores of scientists and technicians, a fleet of boats, a mountain of machinery …

They'll be spending the next two weeks looking for Nessie.

Everyone is exasperated with waiting for the monster to show up.

Now they're going down to get her …

CRUDE

It could be rather frightening … for Nessie.

They're going to battle her with science. A pretty crude kind of science, but then Nessie is supposed to be pretty crude herself.

The Navy has lent the searchers special noisemaking machines, which will be dragged through the water from each end of the loch.

The idea is to scare Nessie into the middle. Then electronic detectors will try to pinpoint her exact position.

Divers will be ready to go down the minute anything unusual crops up, carrying cameras which can take pictures in almost total darkness.

Nothing has been left to chance … unless by some chance Nessie doesn't exist.

An official of the Loch Ness Phenomena Investigation Bureau, which is masterminding the monster hunt, said after the first day's search:

"There has been absolutely nothing."

27th July 1970

DOOMWATCH

EVEN THE LOCH NESS MONSTER IS THREATENED, CLAIMS SCIENTIST

The growing menace of pollution may be threatening one of Britain's most famous institutions … the Loch Ness Monster.

A scientist claimed yesterday that the loch is so badly contaminated that the monster, even if it exists, cannot survive for more than about six months.

The Doomwatch warning came from Mr. Drysdale, a lecturer at the British College of Naturopathy and Osteopathy in London. He fears that Nessie may even be dead already.

SAMPLES

Mr. Drysdale said that during a recent holiday in Scotland, he analysed samples of water from rivers and streams which run into the loch.

He found the water polluted to the point where it must reduce the production of plankton … the small organisms which provide the basic food for loch life.

Mr. Drysdale, 49, said: "I am a firm believer in the existence of the Loch Ness Monster, but I don't think it could survive the level of pollution going into the loch. Even a casual inspection revealed surface scum on all the tributaries.

"Suspended matter was considerable, and samples from one of the tributaries showed a high level of acidity.

"If this is common to the other sources, it will slowly turn the loch into a sterile mass of water."

Mr. Drysdale added: "For more than forty years there has been a need for conservation at the loch. Now, by our lack of concern, I believe we must have lost our greatest natural asset – the Loch Ness Monster.

"With so much evidence to show that the monster existed, I feel more care should have been taken."

Mr. Drysdale admitted that he had not actually taken samples from the loch itself, but said that he was hoping to return next year to carry out more detailed sampling to substantiate his claim.

He said: "If I'm wrong at the moment, I hope that Scotland will do something to stop this pollution at once."

Up at Loch Ness yesterday, the locals were insisting that Nessie is alive and well.

'NONSENSE'

Mr. Peter Davies, a member of the Loch Ness Phenomena Investigation Bureau, said: "Mr. Drysdale's allegation is nonsense.

"The incidence of pollution is negligible. In any case, the creatures do not feed solely on plankton. Their principal diet is eels, of which there is a plentiful supply in the loch.

"If the pollution content is as high as he suggests, why have the fish not died? The rivers are filled with big salmon."

10th September 1970

SEXY BAIT – TO TRAP THE LOCH NESS MONSTER

Scientists are hoping to entice the Loch Ness Monster into the open with a tempting new bait … sex.

They plan to dose the loch with the "sex essences" of practically every creature they can think of that might be the least bit alluring to a monster.

The latest search for Nessie is being conducted by four Americans who will fly to Scotland next month for a two-week stay.

They will take with them the freeze-dried "love smells" of such creatures as eels, sea cows, sea lions and other fish and animals that might be related to Nessie.

If the monster exists, and its passions are aroused enough to bring it out of its lair, a battery of more scientific monster-hunting devices – underwater cameras, sonar detectors and powerful arc lights – will be waiting to beam on to it.

The scientists have other temptations to try on Nessie if the smells don't work.

They include tape-recordings of the noises made by various underwater creatures while eating, mating, fighting and communicating.

Finally, the team will drop salmon oil in the water, just in case Nessie likes salmon.

The expedition's leader, Mr. Robert Rines, president of the Academy of Applied Science in Belmont, Massachusetts, said yesterday: "We plan to appeal to Nessie's sensory organs whatever they may be … smell, taste, sex, sound, vibration or sight."

1st October 1970

SOMETHING FISHY IN THE LOCH – IS NESSIE AN EEL?

Some of the intrepid monster-hunters of Loch Ness are certain they are on to something big – a huge eel.

It could be anything up to 48ft. long, and it is probably lurking somewhere in the loch's murky and mysterious depths. If only they can find it.

The monster-hunters – including a team of Americans – say that their eel theory isn't just a piece of scientific fishing.

It's backed up by radar evidence, American scientist Dr. Robert Love told a Press conference in London yesterday.

Another scientist, Dr. Robert Rines, said at the conference that the investigators had found in the loch a "trench" which fish seemed to keep away from.

This "trench" he described as a "vertical indentation in the border of the lake".

Dr. Rines, president of the Academy of Applied Science in Massachusetts, said that divers working in the loch once stood on something they thought was a sunken mast.

But was it a mast – or a creature?

For, two minutes later, fish disappeared from the area.

And on the other side of the loch, a woman who claims many sightings said she had seen a wake in the water.

BREED

Dr. Love said that if the Loch Ness monster IS an eel, this poses a further question: Does it leave the loch and make its way to the Sargasso Sea – part of the North Atlantic – to breed?

Every other known eel in the world leaves its home, and makes an incredible journey – sometimes over land – to the Sargasso to breed.

If the Loch Ness "eel" does not make this journey all the knowledge that scientists have of eels could be affected.

Dr. Love said it was intended to use more sophisticated investigation methods next year.

A submarine might be brought from Hawaii, and an unmanned vehicle equipped with underwater radar and a computer would be used.

The unmanned vehicle would stalk the monster, using its underwater radar, and would be equipped to get a sample of its skin.

30th March **1971**

NESSIE GIVES LLOYD'S THE JITTERS

Nessie, the legendary Loch Ness monster, has given the Lloyd's insurance men an attack of the jitters.

They have a sneaking feeling that there really is something lurking down there in the depths.

And they have refused to back a £1,000,000 prize for Nessie's capture.

A whisky firm wanted to offer the money to anyone who could land the monster alive.

They asked underwriters at Lloyd's to insure them against having to pay out.

But the hard-headed insurance men – whose last refusal was to a Sicilian father who wanted to insure his daughter's virginity – regretfully said "No".

They decided that £1,000,000 was enough bait to tempt some wealthy investigator, or perhaps even the Navy, to start a fantastically serious hunt.

Instead, they offered to cover the whisky firm for a mere £50,000 … at a very high premium.

So the whisky firm Cutty Sark, have called off the contest.

A Lloyd's spokesman said: "There have been some pretty serious investigations in recent years, and they have produced evidence that something does exist in the loch.

"If a prize of £1,000,000 is awarded, more and better-equipped people are likely to go in search of it.

"And if the Navy went dropping depth charges and things, there's no telling what they might bring up."

The whisky firm, Cutty Sark, said:

"We thought that if we put up a £1,000,000 prize there would a proper investigation."

Now the firm, who wanted Nessie brought up alive in a net, have called off the contest.

Instead they are offering a free double whisky a day for twelve months to the first person to take an authenticated picture of the monster.

21st April **1971**

FIND THE MONSTER AND BE A LOCH NESS MILLIONAIRE

Nessie, the Loch Ness monster, is about to discover how precious she really is. For she now has a price of £1,000,000 on her mysterious head.

That is the prize for her capture in a "Net Nessie" contest announced yesterday.

But the offer has four important conditions:

Nessie must be alive and unharmed. She must also be more than 20ft. long.

She must not be disturbed in any way that would endanger her survival.

And she must be accepted by the Natural History Museum as the genuine Loch Ness monster.

And – heartening news for Nessie – no competitor may use a toxic substance or electric device to catch her.

SCOTCH

If the monster is caught, it will remain the property of Lloyd's underwriters.

The "special offer" lasts from May 1, 1971 to May 1, 1972.

The £1,000,000 prize is being offered by the Cutty Sark Scotch Whisky Company Ltd.

The prize is backed by an insurance policy with Lloyd's underwriters. Two other prizes are also being offered.

A large Scotch every day for a year for anyone who can produce an authenticated colour photograph of Nessie.

And a case of Scotch every month for a year for a colour movie film of the monster lasting 12 seconds.

Mr. Russ Taylor, of Cutty Sark, said yesterday: "We are hoping the monster will be netted.

"The contest is open to anyone anywhere in the world and we would expect that the Navy would have the best chance of catching it."

The risk of Nessie being caught has been covered by Cutty Sark in an insurance policy with Bond Insurance Ltd., of New Cross, London, who specialise in unusual risks.

The firm have persuaded a group of Lloyd's underwriters to back the prize.

22nd April **1971**

PUBLIC OPINION

A whisky company is giving £1,000,000 to the person who captures the Loch Ness Monster.

Surely she should have a more glamorous name than Nessie?

I think she should be called something like Jezebel or Salome – good names for a wicked lady.

(Mrs.) G. Sinclair, London, S.W.I5.

Do you agree? If so, what would you rechristen Nessie?

4th May **1971**

A SPRAT TO CATCH A MONSTER

The scene is Loch Ness. A strange figure looms up, disturbing the calm of the water.

Is this the monster of the deep – the legendary beast hunted by countless adventurers?

Unfortunately not. It's just an inflatable walrus.

The jolly little toy was floated on the water by five-year-old David Grant, who lives beside the loch in Invermoriston.

It has been suggested that Nessie might be lured out of hiding by the sight of a fellow monster. David's walrus, alas, did not do the trick.

But it did provide the first ripple of excitement for fortune hunters aiming for the £1,000,000 prize in the competition to capture Nessie.

More than 100 people from many parts of the world have asked for details of how to enter the search. Some plan to fly over from America to track the monster down.

"The inquiries all seem genuine," said a slightly surprised spokesman for the competition organisers, the Cutty Sark Whisky firm.

STRICT

"People aren't saying how they intend to capture the monster, but we've laid down very strict rules.

"Competitors cannot use any explosives, poisons or electrical devices whatsoever."

Inflatable walruses, however, are quite permissible. And they're cute-looking with it.

3rd September **1971**

FOUND! A MONSTER IN LOCH NESS

Scientists were told yesterday that there really is a monster in Loch Ness.

It is about 100ft. high, and travels up and down the loch at a steady 1 m.p.h.

But "Nessie" is never likely to cause any trouble, the scientists at the British Association meeting in Swansea were told.

For the monster is a huge wave, not an animal. And it stays deep below the surface of the loch.

Dr. Steve Thorpe, of the National Institute of Oceanography, said the Monster Internal Wave of Loch Ness was caused by temperature differences in the 800 ft. deep water and the wind which blows along it.

SURGE

The monster takes fifty-six hours to surge from one end of the loch to the other and back again.

"The waves are truly monsters compared with those on the surface of the water," Dr. Thorpe said. "But there is no relation that I can see between them and any animate monster in the lake."

1st April **1972**

NESSIE, IS THIS REALLY YOU?

Nessie herself, or maybe, since there's a mere 15ft. of carcass, a diminutive daughter of Nessie.

It was found stone dead on the shores of Loch Ness yesterday – April Fool's Eve – by Mr. Terence O'Brien, leader of a

DAILY MIRROR, *Saturday, April 1, 1972* PAGE 5

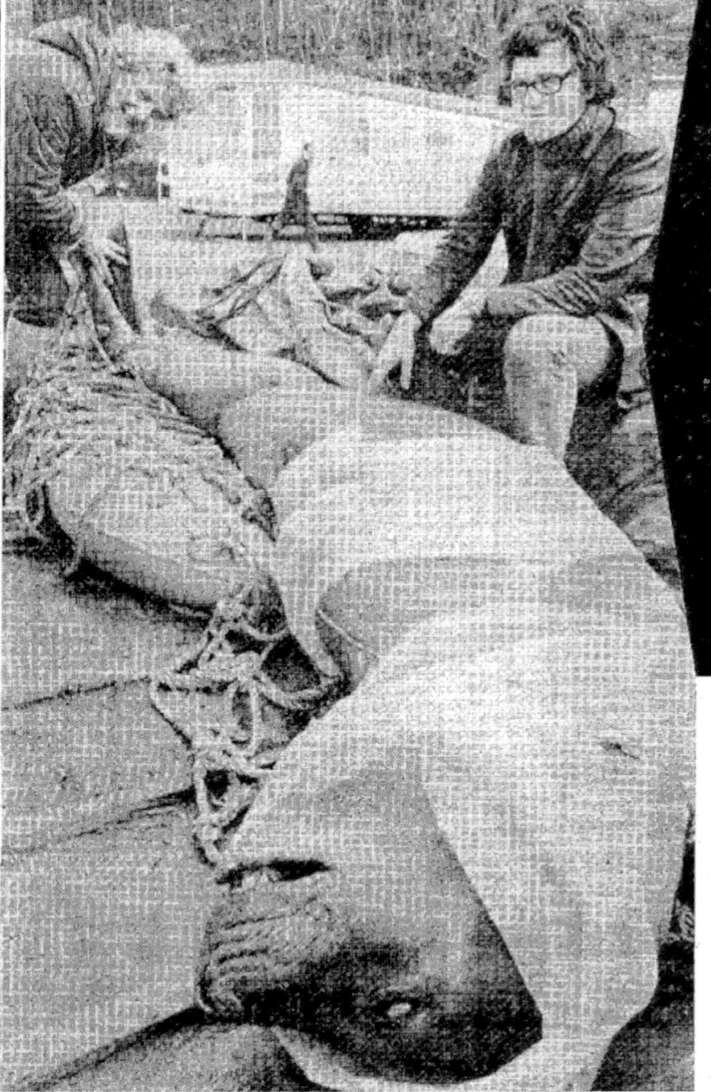

NESSIE, IS THIS REALLY YOU?

THIS could be the face that has launched what seems like a thousand monster hunts.

The face of Nessie herself, or maybe, since there's a mere 15ft. of carcass to go with it, a diminutive daughter of Nessie.

By MIRROR REPORTER

It was found stone dead on the shores of Loch Ness yesterday—April Fool's Eve—by Mr. Terence O'Brien, leader of a monster-hunting expedition from Flamingo Park Zoo in Yorkshire.

Last night the corpse was languishing in a Perthshire police station while the argument raged: Is it genuine, or is it just a bad joke that is rapidly going right off?

The monster fell foul of the law when zoo officials tried to spirit it back to Yorkshire packed in ice.

Arrested

A police patrol, which had got wind of the mysterious goings-on, stopped the party and arrested the carcass under a 1933 by-law.

A police spokesman said: "If the monster—I mean the creature—has been removed from Loch Ness, an offence has been committed.

"I have not seen the creature myself, and I do not know what it is like. But I am remembering it is very near April 1, and I think this might have some bearing on the matter."

The scepticism of the law was shared by a Glasgow University zoologist. He said that the creature looked like an elephant seal.

"But it is highly mysterious how it came to be at Loch Ness," he said.

Mr. Don Robinson, the zoo's 35-year-old managing director, said: "I thought I was having my leg pulled at first—but this is no hoax.

"I am convinced it is a genuine find."

He added: "I am amazed the police have taken it into their custody . . . but I shall certainly be asking for it back.

"It could be a rare and important find."

Mr. O'Brien said: "If my find does turn out to be a hoax, I have been as much fooled as anyone else.

"I found the creature on the shore after receiving an anonymous telephone call."

Last night police said they would be calling in experts today to try to identify the creature.

Monster hunters Duncan Barclay (left) and Jock Shields . . . with the 15ft. mystery.

Monster hunters with the 15ft mystery carcass.

monster-hunting expedition from Flamingo Park Zoo in Yorkshire.

Last night the corpse was languishing in a Perthshire police station while the argument raged: Is it genuine, or is it just a bad joke that is rapidly going right off?

The monster fell foul of the law when zoo officials tried to spirit it back to Yorkshire packed in ice.

ARRESTED

A police patrol, which had got wind of the mysterious goings-on, stopped the party and arrested the carcass under a 1933 by-law.

A police spokesman said: "If the monster – I mean the creature – has been removed from Loch Ness, an offence has been committed.

"I have not seen the creature myself, and I do not know what it is like. But I am remembering it is very near April 1, and I think this might have some bearing on the matter."

The scepticism of the law was shared by a Glasgow University zoologist. He said that the creature looked like an elephant seal.

"But it is highly mysterious how it came to be at Loch Ness," he said.

Mr. Don Robinson, the zoo's 35-year-old managing director, said: "I thought I was having my leg pulled at first – but this is no hoax.

"I am convinced it is a genuine find."

He added: "I am amazed the police have taken it into their custody … but I shall certainly be asking for it back.

"It could be a rare and important find."

Mr. O'Brien said: "If my find does turn out to be a hoax, I have been as much fooled as anyone else.

"I found the creature on the shore after receiving an anonymous telephone call."

Last night police said they would be calling in experts today to try to identify the creature.

30th May **1972**

NESSIE HUNT IS CALLED OFF

Nessie can sleep safely from now on. For the Loch Ness monster-hunters are to shut shop.

The decision to close the Loch Ness Phenomena Investigation Bureau was taken yesterday by the bureau's boss, Tory MP David James.

Planning permission for its lochside caravan HQ is due to run out. Planning authorities have turned down a scheme for a new £100,000 permanent HQ.

1st June **1972**

TAKE A LESSON FROM NESSIE

After ten fruitless years, the Loch Ness Phenomena Investigation Bureau is to shut up shop and leave the legendary monster in peace.

What a laugh! This body should have faded away years ago. There never was a monster.

But now might be the moment to pay tribute to the handful of canny Scots who dreamed up the whole idea to boost tourist trade.

If all commercial ideas in this country were as successful, Britain would have been at the top of the international business league for decades.

Admiring Sassenach (name and address supplied).

The Goodies, filming *The Loch Ness Monster*, on the Lido at Ruislip, 3rd June 1971.

UFOs – He's Got an "Ology"

Elisabeth Sladen, with Jon Pertwee, standing in the courtyard of BBC Television Centre after it was announced that she will play Sarah Jane Smith, a bright young journalist on a woman's magazine who becomes the Doctor's assistant in the new *Doctor Who* series, 26th June 1973.

The term UFO for Unidentified Flying Object was first introduced in 1951 by the United States Air Force. At the other end of the decade, in 1959, the *Times Literary Supplement* invented a term for the study of UFOs, "Ufology". However, the field lacks sufficient scientific approach for it to have been widely accepted as an academic discipline. Carl Sagan thought the subject ought to be studied, in recognition of public interest, but commented, on UFO sightings, that, "the reliable cases are uninteresting and the interesting cases are unreliable. Unfortunately there are no cases that are both reliable and interesting."

A UFO over Warminster, Wiltshire, September 1965.

1st November **1967**

'I OFTEN REGRET GIVING CHASE TO THAT OBJECT IN THE SKY'

Once, in the far north of Scotland, I saw an Unidentified Flying Object. High in the sky, it looked most peculiar, shining brightly in the sunlight. No one had the slightest idea of what it was, how far up it was, or whether it was moving or not. It looked not remotely like a balloon.

It so happened that a photographer and myself had a plane with us, and half an hour to spare. The pilot, who was as mystified as we were, agreed to chase the Object. We flew as high as the plane would go, and as we were climbing the pilot talked to various RAF stations and the like asking if they knew what the Object was.

None did.

When the plane could fly no higher the Object appeared no nearer than it had done from the ground. Fortunately the photographer had a powerful telephoto lens with him. Only when we looked at the Object through his lens, thousands of feet up, in perfect visibility, did we realise that the Object was indeed a monstrous balloon, floating very high indeed, moving pretty fast in a windstream, looking half-deflated, and made of a fabric which reflected the sunlight in a metallic fashion.

Its half-deflated and elongated shape, together with the incidence of the sun's rays on it, made this particular object look long and thin. I have no doubt that in different atmospheric conditions and with different angles of light shining on it, the balloon could have looked wide and flat and circular and to be moving fast.

A flying saucer would presumably look wide and flat and circular and to be moving fast.

SCEPTIC

Since this traumatic experience, I have not only been a sceptic on the subject of flying saucers (I was already that), but a confirmed sceptic. If, however I had not been lucky enough to have a plane and a telephoto lens handy during conditions of perfect visibility, it is possible that my scepticism far from being confirmed would have been shaken.

After all, I had seen this Object from the ground when I was extremely sober through my excellent naked eyes, and it looked like nothing I had ever seen before, and it certainly didn't look like Venus or American aircraft refuelling or come to that, like the balloon it undoubtedly was.

I have many times regretted giving chase to that Object in the sky, for it would undoubtedly have been pleasant in idle moments to fancy that we were being visited by shy little leprechauns from, say, Venus who appeared to do us no harm, and who flitted around our fields at night observing the oddities of our behaviour and playing tag with our policemen.

So I also regret that the Russians have apparently discovered that Venus, likeliest of our satellite neighbours to support some kind of intelligent life, is a pretty terrible place to live in, hellish hot and nothing much to breathe.

But if some sort of life has established itself up there and has evolved the capacity for intelligent contemplation, what, I wonder, will they be thinking now they can observe with their naked eyes, or whatever they've got to observe things with, that a Russian flying saucer has actually landed?

Perhaps they are, right now, squeaking agitatedly to themselves, "It cannot be from Earth. It is far too cold down there to support life, and think of all that dreadful oxygen in its atmosphere. Could it be from Mars after all? Or is it some damn piece of nonsense our secret scientists are playing with?"

7th November **1967**

DRIVER MET A UFO AT MIDNIGHT

Lorry driver Karl Farlow, 25, yesterday told how he came across a "flying saucer".

He sat petrified in his Leyland lorry, he said, as "The Thing" hovered 10 ft. above the road in front of him between Fordingbridge and Ringwood, Hants, just before midnight on Sunday.

"It was egg-shaped and about 15 ft. long and 8 ft. or 10 ft.

high," said Karl, of Madeley, Shropshire.

Suddenly, the "saucer" rose to about 30 ft., and went off "at a fantastic speed".

The green, glowing object turned his lorry's lights out. Two people in a Jaguar car also saw it, Karl said.

14th May 1968

PRIVATE FILE ON FLYING SAUCERS

SIX WAYS A MYTH IS BORN

Did a flying saucer land in fields at Bentilee, Staffordshire, on the evening of September 2, 1967?

Inevitably the question invites a mixed reaction of amusement and cynicism. For this reason alone it is asked, and to an extent answered, by two young amateur astronomers in their "Flying Saucer Report" out tomorrow.

Flying saucer studies are usually stereotyped in one respect: they are biased. The new report by Roger Stanway and Anthony Pace is written from a standpoint of complete neutrality. Neither believes in the existence of UFOs (Unidentified Flying Objects).

Nonetheless the outcome of their investigations into the Bentilee landing and a series of supposed sightings in and around Stoke-on-Trent and other parts of Staffordshire last year is that the idea cannot be dismissed entirely.

Stanway goes further: "We believe there is a *prima facie* case for investigation. Scientists say they will not believe until they have a flying saucer in their laboratories, or until they can prove its existence physically – but most human issues are decided on eye witness evidence and that is what we have gathered together. That evidence warrants serious scientific study."

Stanway and Pace have considerable criticism for the way the Ministry of Defence handles the reports of UFO sightings.

Perhaps the casual attitude of the Whitehall Civil Servants they interviewed was healthily sceptical. Nevertheless it half-convinced the two young sleuths that the Ministry has something to hide.

This suspicion is crystallized in the recommendation they make in the book: that the British Government sets up a permanent, independent scientific commission, possibly based at a university, to investigate the whole field of UFOs.

The idea, of course, is not new. The Soviet Government set up such a commission. Its final report was unequivocal: "Anti-scientific sensations with no scientific basis."

For devotees of flying saucers and critics in general of the Russian way of doing things, there is fresh hope in the study being made now in Colorado by Dr. Edward Condon.

Not only is he a distinguished scientist and therefore an eminently respectable newcomer to the game, but he has been voted £250,000 to investigate officially for the US Air Force.

Condon works in the university city of Boulder. On a news stand not far from his office are no fewer than eighteen lurid paperbacks about UFOs, their subject matter ranging from the purely fantastic "The Horror of Flying Saucers" to the curiously contentious "Flying Saucers are Hostile".

A blood-curdling industry has grown up around the myth and, faced with a complete lack of reliable evidence for reported extra-terrestrial visitations, American authors invented The Great Conspiracy. They suggest that the Air Force, which has studied UFO sightings, and the Government are conspiring to keep the public in the dark in an attempt to avoid panic.

After ten years of this sort of attack, the Air Force gave Condon a contract to examine the issue scientifically.

Condon, 65, is, surprisingly, quite neutral. "Before I was given this contract I had never thought about UFOs," he said, "so I had no opinions."

He should have opinions aplenty by this mid-summer, when he expects to submit his report to the Scientific Advisory Board of the US Air Force. It is doubtful if even the Russians attempted quite so detailed an assault on the UFO myth.

Condon has a team of twenty – astronomers, physicists, engineers, and (perhaps most important of all) psychologists. They have studied thousands of reported sightings, attempted to deduce a pattern and sifted the many photographs submitted.

The project co-ordinator, Robert Low, says they will apply all the techniques of modern science. Some emphasis will be given to the sociological side and particularly the psychological aspects of the problem.

For many years the US Air Force has been running Project Blue Book, which has filed and studied reports; but this was never staffed by scientists and scientific questions have never been answered.

For instance: How do the people who report seeing flying saucers differ from other people? Do they fall into a distinct group of psychological types? These questions need to be asked.

Already facts about some of the sightings have been run through a computer to decide if they have a common factor. The Condon Committee are not talking about the results but they are believed to show a complete lack of consistency.

The Russian inquiry – which lasted a bare two months – was staffed by eighteen scientists and air force officers, and totally ruled out any possibility of extraterrestrial craft.

Perhaps the one real phenomenon involved is the tacit disbelief shared by the public of any country in government denials.

No amount of rational research and argument will disenchant the believers, or the waverers for that matter, from their views.

In fact even the cool analysis of Stanway and Pace is likely to do no more than encourage the idea of little green men from Mars.

PAGE 16 DAILY MIRROR, *Wednesday, October 9, 1968*

UFO

DISCARDED —THE SECRET CRAFT OF WHITE SANDS

COULD this discarded piece of Spaceware be the answer to one of the most intriguing mysteries of the post war years?

The picture was taken by Paul Massa, a columnist and military correspondent for the Columbus (Ohio) Dispatch, during a visit to the White Sands missile range in New Mexico. He found the strange craft in the "missile graveyard" where most experimental vehicles end their days.

At first no one wanted to talk about it officially. But Massa learned enough to support his guess that here could be the explanation for many of the flying saucer reports over the mid-west of the United States.

This particular Unidentified Flying Object was designed for the now-shelved Voyager programme. The object of the operation was to soft-land instruments on Mars for the first close-up study of the Red Planet.

In 1967 the White Sands spacecraft made five flights after being lifted to about 130,000 feet by a balloon. There, in a rarefied atmosphere similar to that of Mars, its eight rockets were ignited and it roared into a trajectory 10,000 feet higher.

After dropping a pack of recording instruments it was lowered back to earth by a giant balloon. The shape and construction of the craft—it is 15 feet in diameter and made of unpainted aluminium—helped it make a point-down landing without damage.

When Massa began his inquiries, officials of the National Aeronautics and Space Agency took several days to come up with the information and the craft was moved out of sight.

But the Martin Marietta company of Denver, where it was built, acknowledged designing several models, some with ten and twelve engines.

Did it not occur to anyone in N A S A that it could have been taken for a spinning disc? Well, yes, a N A S A man said. "Actually the engineers used to call it 'The Flying Saucer'"

TONY DELANO

9th October 1968

The secret of White Sands.

UFO

DISCARDED – THE SECRET CRAFT OF WHITE SANDS

Could a discarded piece of Spaceware be the answer to one of the most intriguing mysteries of the post-war years?

During a visit to the White Sands missile range in New Mexico, Paul Massa, a columnist and military correspondent for the *Columbus Dispatch* (Ohio), found a strange craft in the "missile graveyard" where most experimental vehicles end their days.

At first no one wanted to talk about it officially. But Massa learned enough to support his guess that here could be the explanation for many of the flying saucer reports over the midwest of the United States.

This particular Unidentified Flying Object was designed for the now-shelved Voyager programme. The object of the operation was to soft-land instruments on Mars for the first close-up study of the Red Planet.

In 1967 the White Sands spacecraft made five flights after being lifted to about 130,000 feet by a balloon. There, in a rarefied atmosphere similar to that of Mars, its eight rockets were ignited and it roared into a trajectory 10,000 feet higher.

After dropping a pack of recording instruments it was lowered back to earth by a giant balloon. The shape and construction of the craft – it is 15 feet in diameter and made of unpainted aluminium – helped it make a point-down landing without damage.

When Massa began his inquiries, officials of the National Aeronautics and Space Agency took several days to come up with the information and the craft was moved out of sight.

But the Martin Marietta Company of Denver, where it was built, acknowledged designing several models, some with ten and twelve engines.

Did it not occur to anyone in NASA that it could have been taken for a spinning disc? Well, yes, a NASA man said. "Actually the engineers used to call it 'The Flying Saucer.'"

11th November 1970

MEN WHO SEE FLYING SAUCERS …

The man who reports seeing a flying saucer is often highly intelligent and well educated.

But his job, a leading social scientist says today, often doesn't pay what his brain power should command.

He has a four cylinder brain running on a two cylinder pay packet. His saucer sighting report gives him added status.

The findings, reported in the international journal *Science*, are by Dr. Donald Warren of Michigan University.

➧ The fourth Doctor with assistant Leela and robot pet dog, K-9, 6th October 1977.

23rd November 1970

FLYING SAUCER IS BACK

Those flying saucers are back again. Three sightings were reported yesterday – along with a thing that went bump in the night.

Defence Ministry experts are investigating one saucer report, from writer Douglas Lockhart and his wife, who live in Hackney.

The couple say they saw a "pulsating" flying object over Hackney on Saturday night. It was yellow, black and red.

Student Phillip Morris claims he saw a similar object over Hyde Park an hour earlier. It was changing from white to red.

Taxi driver Stanley Simmonds and his wife spotted something in the sky from their home at Clapton, yesterday morning. It was silver.

The thing that went bump in the night was just a piece of stone which two schoolboys say came out of the sky at Walthamstow.

2nd December 1970

OTHER WORLDS

Mr. Shuttlewood ridicules the idea of flying saucers.

I have no doubt that I saw a flying saucer in 1947.

How anyone can doubt the existence of "saucers" when we ourselves send craft into Outer Space is beyond me.

Intelligent thought admits that life in an advanced form must exist somewhere in Space.

A. Huggins, Bath, Somerset.

27th October 1972

AN EYE ON THE SKY

A man with his eyes fixed firmly on the skies is Professor J. Allen Hynek. He is the world's top expert on flying saucers, or UFOs (Unidentified Flying Objects).

Hynek, 62, is trying to persuade the United Nations to study UFOs.

He is one of the few top scientists technically qualified to comment on flying saucers. He has spent more than twenty years as scientific consultant to the US Air Force on this subject.

Has he actually seen a flying saucer? "I have seen things which

I still refuse to say are UFOs because there is still an outside possibility that there is a natural explanation for them," he said carefully.

There are about 100,000 UFO sightings on record since the famous day in 1947 when an American businessman reported seeing nine gleaming discs skipping like saucers across water.

And Hynek's view is that there is no doubt that enough evidence exists to warrant further serious study.

10th September 1973

TROOPS FLEE AS 'SAUCER' DIVES

Two American military policemen saw a "flying saucer" swoop down on their car in Savannah, Georgia – then it chased them as they fled back to base.

The UFO had flashing lights and dived to treetop level, said the patrolmen. Later police in nearby Manchester also said they saw it.

5th April 1975

A picture of a mysterious silver UFO flying over Warminster in 1965.

SEEKING THE SOURCE OF THE SAUCERS

On June 24, 1947, a new science was born. That was the day a Seattle businessman, Kenneth Arnold, saw a series of shining, fast-moving discs in the sky.

They were Unidentified Flying Objects – UFOs – which created the name Ufology, the study of those objects. These flying saucers, as they were called, suddenly began to appear all over the place.

There have been many thousands of sightings ever since and societies have been set up to investigate the mysterious lights and shapes in the sky.

The reason for all the interest, as Ufologists are quick to point out, is that the universe is so big that there is a good chance of there being other planets with life on them; intelligent life; life capable of creating Spaceships.

Their theory is that UFOs are really Spacecraft manned by observers watching Earth.

The trouble is the Ufologists have not been able to produce much evidence.

Seeking the source of the saucers

ON June 24, 1947, a new science was born. That was the day a Seattle businessman, Kenneth Arnold, saw a series of shining, fast-moving discs in the sky.

They were Unidentified Flying Objects — UFOs — which created the name Ufology, the study of those objects. These flying saucers, as they were called, suddenly began to appear all over the place.

There have been many thousands of sightings ever since and societies have been set up to investigate mysterious lights and shapes in the sky.

The reason for all the interest, as Ufologists are quick to point out, is that the universe is so big that there is a good chance of there being other planets with life on them; intelligent life; life capable of creating Space ships.

Their theory is that U F Os are really Spacecraft manned by observers watching Earth

The trouble is the Ufologists have not been able to produce much evidence.

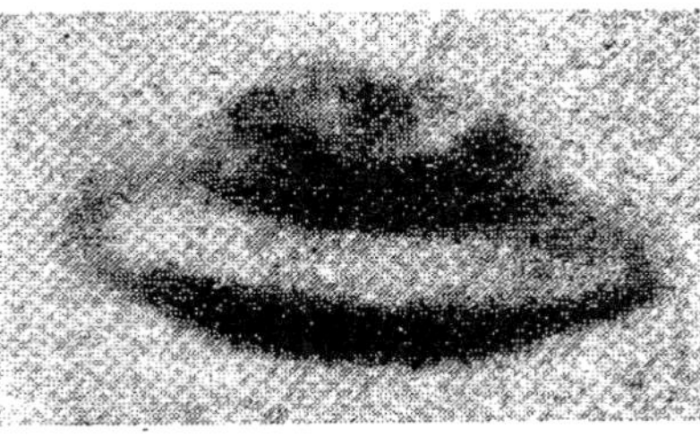

FROM ANOTHER WORLD? Gordon Faulkner took this picture of a mysterious silver U F O flying over his Warminster, Wilts, home in 1965.

Kites

But when American officials investigated flying saucer reports, they found lots of everyday explanations.

The U F Os turned out to be everything from the reflections on aeroplane windows to kites, dust storms, street lamps, and even cigarette-ends seen by short-sighted people.

In one French village, after some lights appeared in the night sky, a rumour spread that Spacemen had landed. So the villagers armed themselves and set off to do battle.

When they arrived at the "landing site" what they found was a garden full of giant chrysanthemums, whose flower-heads had been wrapped in white cloth to protect them from frost.

Another time, in Colorado, there was a rush of flying saucer reports. All the objects had been seen near a small town called Castle Rock. The reports talked about an object which was "about 50ft. long, 20ft. wide and 20ft. deep" and looked like "an egg-shaped bubble."

It turned out that what the people had seen was a scientific experiment by two small boys.

They had taken a small, clear plastic bag, filled it with hydrogen, and then sent it, blazing, into the sky.

Panic

And an American radio company broadcast a dramatised version of The War of the Worlds, by H. G. Wells, the programme began with a mock news programme announcing an invasion by Martians.

Thousands of people in New York panicked, and tried to run away, because they believed it — and that wasn't anything they had seen, just something they had heard.

That fright was soon explained. But what the Ufologists point out, in the quest for contact with other worlds, is that some things are much more difficult to explain.

They ask: what about the five per cent. of UFO sightings which appear to have no explanation at all? They include objects which have not only been seen, but have been tracked on radar at fantastic speeds.

Well, I don't know but I'm pretty sceptical. But if I'm wrong I just hope that they're friendly.

Whatever they are.

HA! HA!

WHAT is cold and cowardly? Frozen chicken.

HA! HA!

WHAT is round, green and a star at Kung Fu? Bruce Pea.

KITES

But when American officials investigated flying saucer reports, they found lots of everyday explanations.

The UFOs turned out to be everything from the reflections on aeroplane windows to kites, dust storms, street lamps, and even cigarette-ends seen by short-sighted people.

In one French village, after some lights appeared in the night sky, a rumour spread that Spacemen had landed. So the villagers armed themselves and set off to do battle.

When they arrived at the "landing site" what they found was a garden full of giant chrysanthemums, whose flower-heads had been

wrapped in white cloth to protect them from frost.

Another time, in Colorado, there was a rush of flying saucer reports. All the objects had been seen near a small town called Castle Rock. The reports talked about an object which was "about 50ft. long, 20ft. wide and 20ft. deep" and looked like "an egg-shaped bubble."

It turned out that what the people had seen was a scientific experiment by two small boys.

They had taken a small, clear plastic bag, filled it with hydrogen, and then sent it, blazing, into the sky.

PANIC

And when an American radio company broadcast a dramatized version of *The War of the Worlds*, by H. G. Wells, the programme began with a mock news programme announcing an invasion by Martians.

Thousands of people in New York panicked, and tried to run away, because they believed it – and that wasn't anything they had seen, just something they had heard.

That fright was soon explained. But what the Ufologists point out, in the quest for contact with other worlds, is that some things are much more difficult to explain.

They ask: what about the five per cent of UFO sightings which appear to have no explanation at all? They include objects which have not only been seen, but have been tracked on radar at fantastic speeds.

Well. I don't know but I'm pretty sceptical. But if I'm wrong I just hope that they're friendly.

Whatever they are.

◀ *War of the Worlds* director Orson Welles fondles an Unidentified Furry Object.

3rd May 1977

HOVERING

THE UFOS FLY FOR CARTER

President Jimmy Carter has joined the ranks of UFO spotters. He sent in two written reports stating he had seen a flying saucer when he was the Governor of Georgia.

The president has shrugged off the incident since then, perhaps fearing that electors might be wary of a flying saucer freak.

But he was reported as saying after the "sighting": "I don't laugh at people any more when they say they've seen UFOs, because I've seen one myself."

Carter described his UFO like this: "Luminous, not solid, at first bluish, then reddish … It seemed to move towards us from a distance, stopped, then moved partially away."

Carter filed two reports on the sighting in 1973, one to the International UFO Bureau and the other to the National Investigations Committee on Aerial Phenomena.

Heydon Hewes, who directs the International UFO Bureau from his home in Oklahoma City, is making speeches praising the president's "open-mindedness".

But during his presidential campaign last year Carter was cautious.

He admitted he had seen a light in the sky but declined to call it a UFO.

He joked: "I think it was a light beckoning me to run in the California primary election."

27th May 1977

SAUCERS IN A SPIN

Two "flying saucers" making a noise like a whirlwind were spotted over the River Trent in South Humberside yesterday.

Roy Thompson, who saw them from his caravan, told police they were 20ft. long and revolving like spinning tops.

The whirlwind noise built up to "a tremendous volume" as the saucers flew from north to south, he said.

The sighting was the second in the area within twenty-four hours.

Earlier schoolboys fifteen miles away at Bransholme, Hull, reported a silent, silver cone-shaped object in the sky.

28th October 1977

COPS SIGHT A UFO

Two police officers yesterday put in a startling report to their station: We've seen a UFO.

The claim was made by PC Chris Bazire, 20, and policewoman Vivienne White, 22, who were on panda patrol duty at dawn in Salisbury, Wilts.

They spotted "what appeared to be a flying saucer" at a height of 500–700 feet over Salisbury Plain, scene of several reported UFO sightings.

Chris said: "It was oblong with a domed top and flat bottom. It was travelling very slowly at first. Suddenly it shot off at tremendous speed, leaving a vapour trail."

A spokesman at the Boscombe Down secret experimental station on the Plain said that it was none of their apparatus. And the Army could shed no light on the mystery.

14th November 1978

A UFO HITS THE DESERT

Reports of a giant UFO – the size of a jumbo jet – are being investigated in the Middle East.

The inquiry was ordered by the Kuwaiti government after the mysterious object was said to have landed at a satellite tracking station.

Two Kuwaiti newspapers said technicians looked on in amazement as it descended on the station.

The report said that seven men, including an American, walked within 250 yards of the UFO, which was dish-shaped.

The men said – they were "frozen with horror" and were certain no humans were inside the flying saucer.

After a few minutes, the object took off vertically at high speed.

3rd January 1979

THAT'S NOT A UFO … IT'S VENUS

The mystery of the Unidentified Flying Object has been solved.

Astronomers yesterday identified the "UFO" encountered by a TV film crew as … the planet Venus. The Object was spotted and filmed by the TV men as they flew between the North and South Islands of New Zealand on Saturday night.

Another sighting of the "flying saucer" was reported from the east coast of Australia early yesterday.

But last night, David Mabin, head of New Zealand's Mount John observatory, ruled out the possibility that the objects were UFOs.

He said both sightings were "almost certainly" the planet Venus.

Dr. Mabin said Venus is currently at its brightest and can be seen for about twelve hours a day in the Southern Hemisphere.

He added: "From a moving aircraft or from a car, it could appear to be moving at the same speed because of the great distance."

American UFO expert Phillip Klass agreed that was "a celestial body – perhaps Venus".

Mirror photographer Alasdair MacDonald believes that the weird image of the UFO, reproduced in newspapers all over the world, resulted from an error by the cameraman.

He thinks that the 200mm lens was so badly out of focus that the image took on the shape of the camera's iris.

The "blips" which appeared on radar screens in New Zealand could have been caused by flocks of high-flying birds, say experts.

The classic silver UFO.

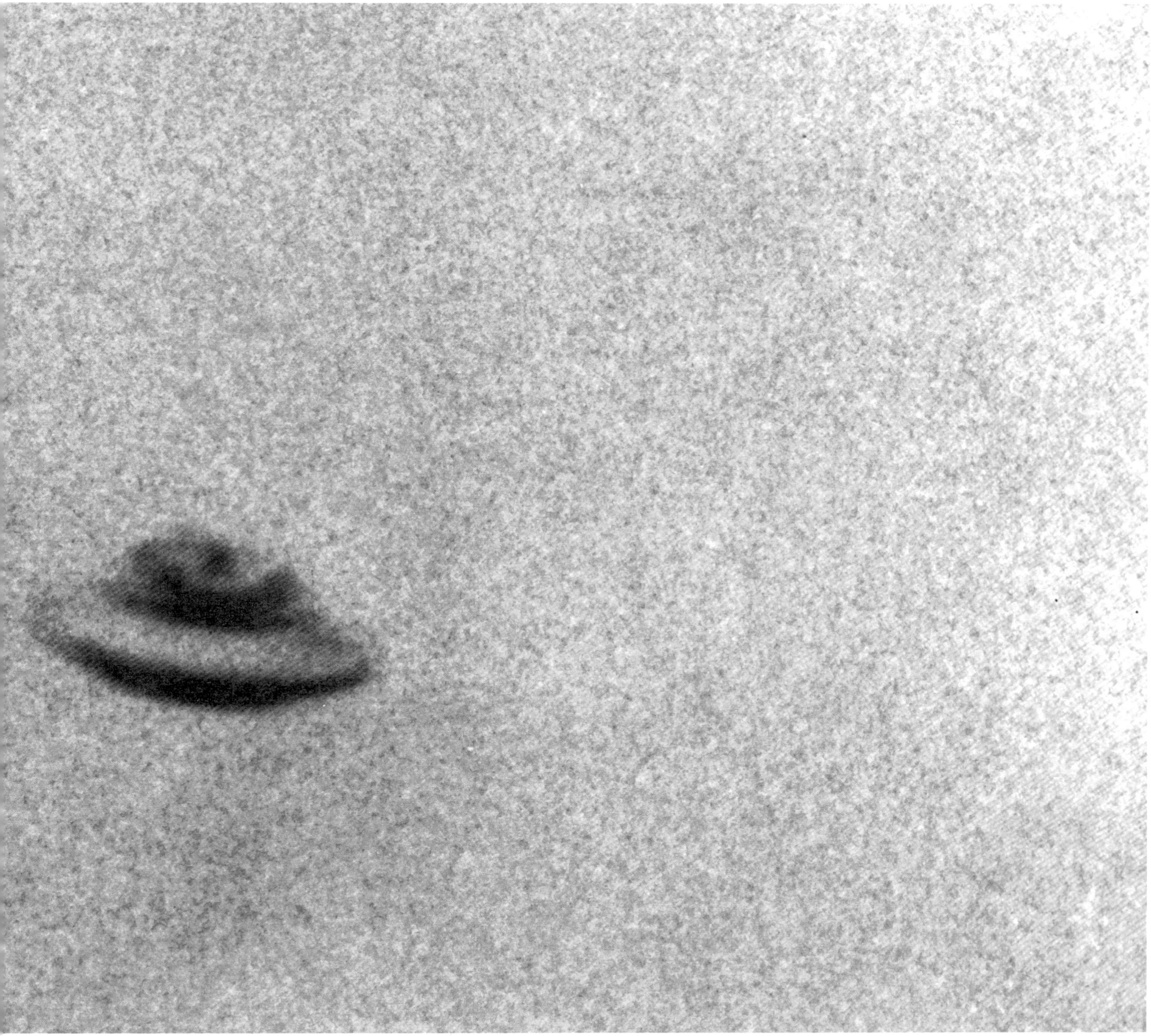

Ghosts – Who You Gonna Call?

Renowned spiritualist Sir Arthur Conan Doyle with Lady Conan Doyle.

There is no doubt that there is money to be made from the afterlife. Despite the debunking efforts of people like James Randi and Simon Singh, exposing dubious practices that would end the career of most other professionals, spiritualists such as Sally Morgan and Derek Acorah continue to be highly successful. From a previous era, one of the most famous sceptics and investigators of paranormal phenomena was Harry Price. Schooled in conjuring tricks and sleight of hand ("legerdemain"), and fascinated by psychical phenomena, Price founded the National Laboratory of Psychical Research in 1925. This existed until 1934, when it was replaced by the University of London Council for Psychical Investigation, its library being transferred to the university in 1938. A high-profile case that Price investigated was the paranormal activity at Borley Rectory, "The Most Haunted House in England".

28th December **1903**

THE KING AND THE DOMESTIC SERVANTS MATTER

The late Mrs. Elliot (a daughter-in-law of the first Lord Minto) used to tell a story of a country house where she was staying once in Scotland at Christmas, and one day, when the wind and rain made everything look very desolate outside, Sir Walter Scott, who was one of the guests, proposed they should all in turn tell a ghost story. He arranged that the room should be dark except for two candles on a little table by the door. The guests all sat round the fire, which cast a fitful glare on the different pieces of old tapestry which hung round the room, and Sir Walter began to tell a weird story. At the critical point, when the ghost was about to appear, both candles fell down suddenly and went out. Great consternation ensued, when Sir Walter spoilt it all by giving way to fits of laughter, as he had prepared for the surprise by tying a black thread round each candlestick, which he pulled at the proper moment when all were thrilled to the utmost.

1st January **1904**

HOW PEASANTS EXORCIZED A GHOST

Another case of strange superstition in Hungary is reported by our Vienna correspondent.

At the village of Terpest-Bihar, a Roumanian landowner named Vigyikan was recently buried, and a few days afterwards the report spread – vouched for by many landowners – that his ghost was seen every night running around, and that he was practising magic on the cows.

To remedy the state of affairs some of the superstitious peasants went at night and opened the grave, burst open the coffin, and cut out the heart of the deceased, which they nailed to a cross in the cemetery.

7th January **1904**

SEASIDE GHOST

BRIGHTON HAS A SPECTRE WHICH MAY LEAD TO A LIBEL ACTION

Brighton is the last place in the world one would associate with ghosts, but residents there have been disturbed during the past month by the visitations of a spectre whose fighting proclivities are very pronounced. Its principal residence is outside a nunnery on the old Shoreham-road.

It was first seen in December by a cyclist, who, riding past the nunnery wall, was horrified to find a filmy shape in nimble pursuit. He put on speed; the film responded; the cyclist rang his bell and shouted, but the spectral pursuer was not annoyed, and went on until a more populous road was reached.

Since then the ghost has been seen in many guises. Once, while sprinting after a pedestrian, it was turned upon, and immediately vanished into a solid brick wall.

One cyclist saw the spectre near Patcham, with attendant scenery in the shape of an ivy-clad tower. Sceptics asked what the cyclist had had for supper. Some members of a local golf club volunteered to probe the mystery with niblicks. If the niblicks went through the ghost they decided it would be time to run. The raid has not come off yet, and the ghost still sprints.

It is even making a libel action imminent. Some well-meaning "ghost-layer" suggested that the spirit came from Cottesmore, a neighbouring boys' school, and proposed an enquiry among the boys. The headmaster of the school has written to the papers, is searching for the libeller and threatens proceedings on sight.

12th February **1904**

NORFOLK GHOST

MYSTERIOUS VANISHING LADY IN AN OLD WORLD VILLAGE

The picturesque old-world village of Castleacre in Norfolk hitherto

has relied on the attractions provided by the remains of an ancient priory and the ruins of the castle, once the seat of the Earls of Warren, for any claims. But now our Norwich correspondent telegraphs: Castleacre has a ghost, and anticipates a visit from the Psychical Research Society. The hair-raising story which is thrilling Castleacre is that the other day a young villager, who had been detained late at business, returned home about midnight. Upon entering the house he locked the outer door as usual and walked into the sitting-room.

This apartment was unlighted except for the half-light from the windows. Directly he entered he became aware of the presence of a female figure at the other end of the room. Suddenly the figure passed swiftly across the room to the accompaniment of a strange "whizzing" sound.

The young man immediately struck a light, but only to find that the figure had vanished. The rest is mystery.

9th March **1904**

A SCOTCH BANSHEE

This month a very desirable town house comes into the market. This is 17, Park-lane, the property of Blanche Lady Rosslyn, who bought it after the death of Mr. Henry Petre.

Blanche Lady Rosslyn is the widow of the fourth Lord Rosslyn, and, herself an extremely handsome woman, is mother of a bevy of beautiful daughters, who are Lady Warwick, Lady Algernon Gordon-Lennox – the smartest woman in London – the Duchess of Sutherland, Lady Westmorland, and Lady Angela Forbes. Her eldest son, the present Lord Rosslyn, is head of an ancient Scotch family.

Until the reign of James VII of Scotland the Earls of Rosslyn were always buried standing upright in full armour, and without coffins.

Their deaths, so it is said, are always heralded by the, illumination of a certain pillar, in Rosslyn Chapel, which becomes, a few days beforehand, surrounded with a halo of mysterious white light.

6th February **1905**

CYCLIST GHOST

"SCORCHES" WITHOUT A LIGHT, AND HAS A TRANSPARENT BODY

Brighton has again been troubled by the visitation of a phantom cyclist – A Hove Corporation official, whose veracity has hitherto been beyond impeachment, says: "I was cycling along the lonely road from Shoreharn to Brighton late the other night when I heard another machine coming up behind me.

"I looked over my shoulder and, noticing that the stranger's lamp was not burning, was about to draw his attention to the fact, when to my horror – I found that his body was transparent. I could clearly see through him the trees bordering the road. Entirely losing my nerve, I scorched my hardest, but the thing overtook me, and when some yards ahead vanished."

This is not the first time the ghost is said to have been seen on the road.

11th February **1905**

SALVATION GHOST

BARRACKS VISITED BY YELLOW-CLAD LADY WITH A MALIGNANT EYE

The Salvation Army barracks at Rhymney are said to be in possession of a really first-class ghost.

The apparition is that of a tall, stoutly-built lady clad in yellow. Her haggard face is of a ghostly hue and distorted by a terrorising expression of hate.

The ghost was first seen by an "Army" officer. At his invitation six friends sat up with him one night to await its reappearance

The vigil was maintained until 4.30, when the wraith floated into the room bestowed glances of malignity upon the terrified watchers, and glided silently away.

8th November 1907

GHOSTS AND WHAT THEY WEIGHED

REMARKABLE EXPERIENCES WITH "SPOOKS" DESCRIBED TO LONDON SPIRITUALISTS

It is something to have seen a real ghost and to have its appearance well authenticated. A greater distinction is to have been present and assisted at the weighing of a ghostly visitant.

Some remarkable stories, which included both these experiences, were told to the London Spiritualist Alliance last night, at the rooms of the Royal Society, Suffolk-street, W. The teller of the tales was Mr. George Spriggs, at one time a well-known spiritualistic medium and now the president of the Psycho-Therapeutic Society.

His narratives embraced experiences both in this country and Australia, and were, he said, easily verifiable by those who cared to look up the official records, signed by competent eye-witnesses.

Mr. Spriggs described how, at a seance held in Cardiff, one of their regularly attending spirit friends, of erect soldierly bearing, who exceeded by some 6in. the stature of the medium, appeared in a long white robe. He left the room, went downstairs, returning in a few minutes with a dish of fruit, which he handed round, and took some of the fruit himself. The ghost's greatest effort, however, consisted in his quitting the house entirely through a back door, and presently returning bearing in his arms bunches of a fuchsia bush.

SPIRITS THAT GREW LIGHTER

Describing some of his experiences in Melbourne, he remarked that at one seance a spirit form, pressed in a white gown and red girdle, drank half a tumbler of water and ate a biscuit.

Then Mr. Spriggs went on to give some particulars about the weight of spirit forms. Weighing machines, he said, were used to ascertain the distinguishing features between the medium and the materialized spirit forms. "My clothes were taken off before the sitting commenced and weighed, and I also was weighed," said Mr. Spriggs. "The same procedure took place after the sitting, and I always found that as a result of the stance I had lost about three pounds in weight, which it took me three days to recover."

The first spirit form who stepped on the scales turned the beam at 100lb., but subsided rapidly in weight. Indeed, failing to turn the scale at 80lb. he hurriedly retreated. Returning again, his weight was registered at 104lb., then 102lb., and then under 100lb. The 20lb. weight being then removed, he failed to turn the beam at 80lb., losing at least 24lb. in about thirty seconds. Another spirit form weighed 139½lb. at first, and then subsided to 117lb.

Dr. Motherwell, who was present, distinctly felt the pulsation of the forms, the medium being shown sitting on his chair immediately afterwards. Dr. Motherwell also found the beating of the heart to be quite natural.

17th May 1909

GHOSTLY HAPPENINGS

WOMAN'S MYSTERIOUS VISITOR WHO LOOKED AT HER LONG AND VANISHED

A ghost is said to have made an unwelcome appearance at Reading.

Mrs. Barker, of Barnstaple-street, states that one morning she saw what she describes as a "creature" enter her room, gaze steadily at her, and then vanish near the window. Her son claims that he was awakened one morning by the ghost touching his hand.

A neighbour also says she has seen the mysterious visitor, whose appearance in other houses is awaited with fear.

24th August 1910

GIRL AS GHOST

STRANGE PRANKS OF YOUNG SERVANT TERRIFY FARMER'S HOUSEHOLD

Hanley, Tuesday. – The Staffordshire police succeeded to-day in solving a haunted house mystery which for a number of days has utterly perplexed people living in the neighbourhood of Uttoxeter. The "ghost", it transpires, is a girl.

On Thursday last week a series of remarkable happenings began at Loxley Hall Farm, near Uttoxeter, occupied by Mr. Wilson, bailiff to Mr. Richardson, a well-known local farmer.

About ten o'clock at night Mr. and Mrs. Wilson were having supper, when they were startled by hearing strange noises, and presently boots and bottles came falling down the stairs, thrown by some invisible hand.

They rushed upstairs to find the place in a state of wild confusion. Their bedroom had been completely ransacked, mattresses had been carried from one room to another, ornaments had disappeared, and the place was in a condition of chaos.

Several farmhands were called in and the premises were systematically searched, without result. Mr. and Mrs. Wilson then retired to rest, but scarcely had they extinguished the light when all sorts of pranks were commenced by what seemed to be a supernatural visitant.

A table was spirited out of the room, all sorts of articles flew in through the door, and when Mr. Wilson got up to investigate, he was assailed with bottles and other missiles. Weird noises were heard in different parts of the house, but search again, proved unavailing.

This was merely the beginning of a series of remarkable incidents during the following days. Mrs. Wilson while at work was made the target for knives, forks and bottles.

Twenty-seven window-panes were smashed by flying stones.

Rigorous police investigations were set on foot, and as a result it was to-day announced that a girl aged fourteen, employed at the farm, had confessed that she is the mysterious spook.

HAUNTED FARMHOUSE: "PULLED DOWN BY GHOST."

The Hermitage. Bedroom window (x) where Mrs. Fallows was pulled down to the floor. *Sitting-room (x) is where screams were heard.*

Miss Botham.

Mr. Large.

Miss Burston.

Miss J. Fallows.

Mr. and Mrs. Bennett Fallows, the tenants of the farm for thirteen years:

Repute says that the Hermitage, a farmhouse at Ipstones (Staffs) is haunted. The ghost has made its presence felt in various ways, and above are some of those who have "met" it in one way or another.

14th November 1913

HAUNTED FARMHOUSE: "PULLED DOWN BY GHOST"

Repute says that the Hermitage, a farmhouse at Ipstones (Staffs) is haunted. The Ghost has made its presence felt in various ways.

4th August 1915

TALE OF A GENERAL'S SPOOK

Paris, August 3. – In a telegram from Petrograd to the France de Demain it is stated that many Russian sentinels declare that they have seen the famous ghost of General Skobelif in a white uniform riding on a white horse.

The apparition, according to tradition, always marks a critical moment for the armies of the Tsar, and invariably causes a terrific panic in the enemy's ranks.

31st December 1918

HAUNTED HOUSE WANTED

BUT HOUSE AGENTS CANNOT SUPPLY ADVERTISER WITH "THE GOODS"

There has appeared an advertisement which runs:–

"Haunted house wanted to rent or purchase, freehold, with five to ten acres of land, within fifty miles of London."

At the offices of Messrs, May and Rowden a representative of the firm said with a smile:

"We do not deal in haunted houses, and I do not know of any."

At Messrs, Waring and Gillow's house and estate agency a similar reply was given.

A representative of the firm said that many years ago he knew of a country house in one of the Home Counties in which, according to the local wiseacres, strange noises had been periodically heard, and uncanny manifestations experienced.

At the headquarters of the London Spiritualist Alliance, publishers of the organ of psychic research, in Queen's-square, no information was forthcoming as to any ghost-tenanted residences, and an official of the organization said:

"One has to be very careful nowadays in stating that a house is haunted in view of the strictness of the law of libel."

23rd February 1921

GHOSTS WHO KNOCK FURNITURE ABOUT

THE POLTERGEIST AND HIS METHODS OF WORK

What is a poltergeist? Have you ever heard one or seen one?

Since there's been so much talk about the bewitched house in

Hornsey I've heard this German word used by dozens of people who probably don't in the least know what it means.

But it's a very old name for a very old sort of ghost; and it is easy to explain.

"Polter", in German, means a noisy, mischievous, clodhopping sort of fellow, and "geist" means spirit or ghost. So a poltergeist is a noisy, upsetting, schoolboyish sort of ghost, such as the ghosts at Hornsey, who seem to be sending lumps of coal mad and upsetting teacups all over the rooms.

I say that this sort of ghost is quite an old sort. And, in fact, in 1883 I remember that a leading London newspaper gave a circumstantial account of the happenings at Wood's Farm, near Wem, Shropshire.

In this case, as in the Hornsey one, coal was mysteriously indued with the power of motion.

It jumped off the fire and set a baby's clothing ablaze. Saucepans followed, teacups were smashed, a grandfather clock ruined, and an American clock flung off the mantelpiece.

All attempts to elucidate the mystery failed, whilst seven eye-witnesses were able to testify to these uncanny facts.

Such phenomena are not to be explained, nor do there, in most of the cases recorded, exist grounds for suspecting human agency.

Poltergeists are the irresponsible low comedians of the Unseen, elemental spirits in the same category as brownies and boggarts.

The Drummer of Tedworth, who beat drums all over the house, was a poltergeist, and made himself apparent to the sense of smell as well as of hearing.

Early in the nineteenth century a poltergeist manifested itself in a house in Sampford Peverell, near Tiverton, Devon.

This elemental being filled the house with thunderous noises and dust, beat the maids black and blue, banged doors, tore curtains, flung a folio Bible across the room, and in many other unpleasant ways attracted attention in a manner to puzzle the materialism of a Hume.

There used to be a poltergeist in a certain aristocratic square in London.

That house is at present in the hands of decorators, and I was interested lately to see, in the freshly-glazed window of the "haunted room" a broken pane of glass – but whether broken by the poltergeist or the workmen I had no means of finding out at the time. I am not going to give the square or the number of the house, for to state that another man's house is haunted is a legal offence known as "slander of title", as any rumour of this sort of reputation is apt to reduce the rental value.

Medieval castles may with advantage harbour their Faceless Monks and Grey Ladies shuddering in the moonlight; but such gauds are out of place in the villas of Peckham or of Balham. These, like Caesar's wife, must be above suspicion.

It seems a pity.

The Inexplicably Uncanny, seated by the fireside, would purely confer the cachet of long descent on the family circle even of a profiteer.

15th December 1922

HUNT FOR SPECTRE

SHY YORKSHIRE SPIRITS THAT ELUDED STRANGER

SPOOKS' ROUTE MARCH

All East Yorkshire, and in particular the village of Long Drax, is busy gossiping about the supposed ghost of Baxter Hall Farm.

Now that the morning has come and the mellow December sunlight is flooding the countryside the ghost story of Baxter Hall Farm seems unworthy of belief.

Last night, however, when the wind was whining down the dark lanes and the bats were in the belfry of the village church, it seemed possible to believe anything – even the story of a local raconteur, who says he has seen fifty spectres marching in columns of fours towards Drax Abbey.

I am thankful that I am unable to corroborate this story.

Apparently Baxter Hall Farm, where "ghostly" monks clank chains and shadows walk out of cupboards, is not the only place in Drax which is visited by "apparitions".

The whole district is "haunted". Transparent owls hoot at the children, medieval women laugh in the faces of old men and headless spectres lounge about the hedgerows in their nightshirts.

If I were more familiar with the Yorkshire dialect there is no doubt that I should be able to recount many more such happenings, for Mr. Livesay, of Drax, told me several.

Unfortunately, I was unable to understand a word he said, though I gathered from his general manner, that they were extremely funny ghost stories.

Although I waited about draughty corners for any other demonstration of a spiritual presence, I saw nothing but the ghosts of trees, heard nothing but the howl of the wind, and felt nothing until I fell into a ditch.

This inability on my part to discover the local ghosts was solemnly explained by a resident.

"Hast thee seen nowt?" he asked.
"No, not even a goat," I answered.
"Then that's because they be Yorkshire ghosts," he said, "and Yorkshire folk were always scared of strangers."
It was then that I thought I felt my leg being gently pulled.

22nd February **1923**

Author Sir Arthur Conan Doyle, creator of Sherlock Holmes, 15th December 1921.

SIR A. CONAN DOYLE AND FEN GHOST

THEORY OF PLAYFUL 'CHILD' OF THE SPIRIT WORLD

FRESH AIR CURE

"VENTILATE WELL AND SAY PRAYER IN EACH ROOM"

Sir A. Conan Doyle has intervened by letter in the remarkable happenings at Mr. Joseph Scrimshaw's farm at Gorefield.

This evening Mr. Scrimshaw received the following letter from the famous author regarding the ghost or furniture-removing hand, who is held responsible for the damage done at New Barn Farm:–

"Dear Sir, I am sorry to read of your troubles and as I have made a study of such cases, many of which have been recorded I will advise you what to do.

"You should send your daughter for a rest and change. Then open all your windows. Ventilate well and you will find the phenomena, after a day or two, will cease altogether.

"If your vicar said a prayer in each room it would be well.

"It is not that your daughter plays any conscious part in this, but it is that at certain times some persons draw out an atmosphere or vapour which can be used in a material way by intelligent forces outside of ourselves. These forces have no power to harm mankind, but they do break more material objects."

"MISCHIEVOUS CHILDREN"

"They can be described as mischievous material children of the physical world.

'Poltergeist' is the name given to each one of these.

"I have asked a friend in London to send you an account of a recent case kept under his observation.

"The medium who throws out this atmosphere is nearly always a child from ten to sixteen years of age, and generally a girl.

"Let me know how my cure works. I shall be here at the Victoria and Albert Hotel, Torquay, till Friday. Then I shall be at Cromer. – Yours faithfully. A, Conan Doyle."

FIEND'S "NIGHT OFF"

NO MOVING TRICKS FOR DISAPPOINTED BAND OF WATCHERS

Whether the ghost has decided that there is nothing else worth breaking at the farm, or whether it is abashed at the excitement it has created, is not quite clear, but last night nothing happened.

Despite the presence of several newspaper representatives, Mr. Joseph Scrimshaw, his aged mother, his daughter, seven cats and a newborn lamb, the furniture in the farm remained unmoved.

Olive, Mr. Scrimshaw's sixteen-year-old daughter, has told me that she slept peacefully throughout the night.

This evening I interviewed a Mr. Langley, who said he had seen the ghost of Mr. Scrimshaw's father.

Mrs. Langley told me to-night that when her husband called at the farm the pianola began to move towards him.

Shortly after he distinctly saw the ghost. He had known Mr. Scrimshaw's father for many years, and could not mistake him.

26th February **1923**

VICAR AND APPARITIONS

The vicar, the Rev. C. L. Tweedale, says that apparitions have appeared at his vicarage, especially that of his aunt with her dog.

22nd February **1924**

BEWARE THE BANSHEE!

FAIRIES, GOOD AND BAD, ALL THE WORLD OVER!

Whether you are boy or girl, young or old, clever or stupid, you know what fairies are – even if you don't believe in them. But it may surprise you to hear that there are several hundred different kinds! Like dogs, which can be terriers, whippets, hounds or what you like, but are still just dogs, fairies have various different names in different parts of the world – but they are always fairies.

You all know our old friend the Dwarf. He is a very familiar figure of fairyland, and generally he is an unpleasant character, although he can also be "faithful and friendly, but hideously ugly".

Then the Pixie is often seen frisking gaily through the pages of a fairy tale. He is a Devonshire sprite, sometimes called Puck, or Robin Goodfellow. I have always liked the Pixie, in spite of the mischievous tricks which he delights in playing.

Ogres, I expect, have often made your hair stand on end. They came from France many, many years ago, but I think they must have all gone back again, as they are not generally seen about nowadays.

MISCHIEVOUS FAIRIES

A Banshee is a rather mournful chap, who howls round houses in Ireland. He is supposed to foretell bad luck, so the best thing to do is to go out and shoot him with an air-gun before he starts howling.

Our old friend the Brownie (a kind of cousin to Puck, I believe) is a Scots laddie, and as naughty as can be. He is very friendly to servants, if they treat him well; and sometimes he does all the work for them – such as cleaning the boots, polishing the grate or the windows – while they are asleep in bed.

The Will-o'-the-wisp is a fairy of quite a different sort, I fear. He also is very mischievous, but he never has his nice moments. His favourite trick is to lead poor travellers into bogs and ditches on wet, stormy nights.

HAY FOR THE KELPIE

In the pages of the *Arabian Nights* and other Eastern stories we meet that dreadful figure, the Genie. Generally he is an evil spirit, and even when he happens to be friendly he proves rather a hard master. It is best not to have anything to do with him. I remember a poor man having a very bad time just because he happened to

throw a few date-stones at a genie's son!

If you live in Scotland you might find a Kelpie one day. He is a kind of horse fairy, found in lakes and rivers, he will be very grateful if you give him a lump of hay.

There are hundreds of other kinds – elves, kobolds, gnomes, goblins, mermaids, leprechauns, imps and peris – but there isn't room for me to describe them all.

26th September **1925**

A DOUBLE BANSHEE

Mr. Elliott O'Donnell's latest book entitled *Ghostland* will shortly be published. It deals with his personal psycho experiences. Appropriately enough, the author has a banshee as an appendage to both sides of his very definitely Celtic ancestry, and his literary connections include the mystic poet Edgar Allan Poe and Frederic Harrison, essayist and positivist.

HAUNTED ANTLERS

During his residence in Cornwall a relative sent him a pair of giant elk antlers taken from an Irish bog. He told me that his old housekeeper, whom he described as an original character gifted with the second sight, could not endure the noise of the padding feet of some invisible animal which moved about the place at night. Nor was the commotion at all acceptable to Mr. O'Donnell himself. His housekeeper insisted that the spirit of the elk came every night and they would get no rest till he got rid of the antlers. The present was passed on and peace ensued.

9th October **1926**

RACKETY GHOST QUIET

POLTERGEIST GIRL STILL SHOWS NO SIGN OF "SPIRIT" MANIFESTATION

Eleonore Zugun, the thirteen-year-old Rumanian poltergeist girl, has been under strict observation by doctors since Thursday at the National Laboratory of Psychical Research.

As yet there has been no manifestation of the "rackety ghost", of which she is supposed to be the medium.

Neither the public nor the Press are allowed to see the girl while she is under observation.

An official at the laboratory stated yesterday that the doctors were making no statement at present, but would furnish a full report to the Research Council.

29th February **1928**

POLTERGEIST TEST

Douglas Dew, an eight-year-old London boy, who is said to be possessed of a poltergeist or unruly spirit, at the National Laboratory of Psychical Research, where he is being kept under observation every afternoon.

5th March 1928

RIDDLE OF THE POLTERGEIST

AN OLD MYSTERY THAT IS ALWAYS RECURRING – NEW METHODS REQUIRED FOR ITS SOLUTION

Every few years attention is called to some house in which residence becomes so undesirable that the inhabitants have to go away for a holiday or even to move elsewhere.

The occurrences are always of the same nature.

Lumps of coal are said to come whizzing through the windows from nobody knows where. Tables are upset and chairs flung about.

Such happenings are trivial, ridiculous and annoying. Feats which may be amusing at the cinema cease to divert when it is your own coal that smashes your own window.

The publicity is, moreover, trying to the nerves of sensitive people. It is not pleasant to have to push your way out of your front-door in the morning through a crowd of gaping people waiting to see "the ghost". Your friends and relatives jump to the conclusion that you are trying to be funny.

Three chief theories have been advanced to account for the phenomena. According to one theory, spirits, poltergeists, light-hearted and light-headed entities of the Puck variety indulge from time to time in a kind of university "rag" lasting for three or four weeks. Another theory associates such happenings with some unknown force akin to electricity and magnetism.

SEARCH FOR TRUTH

Science is tending to the belief that animal organisms emit a great number of radiations. The electric eel will give you a severe shock if you touch him. It may be that Uncle Sidney's emanations are so strong at times that the dining-room table is literally upset when he enters the house.

Others – the sturdy die-hards of scepticism – refuse to see anything mysterious in such disturbances. "Trickery," they say, and infer that there is no mystery to be cleared up.

Phenomena of this nature have been recorded in all parts of the world and at all periods of history. Last year, in Italy, I frequently passed a deserted country house which had fallen into ruins. It was called La Casa degli Spiriti, The House of the Spirits, and the peasants would not pass that way after dark if they could help it. Some years ago an Anglican Bishop in his African diocese was puzzled by the strange behaviour of a mud hut in a native village. The Bishop went in and saw lumps of wall and roof hurtling about. If there was trickery his lordship failed to detect it.

It is hard to believe in the poltergeist theory but it is equally hard to believe in the practical joker theory. Throwing lumps of coal and cement through a window is such an extremely elementary joke that it is difficult to see how anyone could find much amusement in it.

Is it not time that such occurrences were investigated more closely than they have been hitherto?

The present method of procedure when a house misbehaves itself in this way is to surround it by a cordon of police – either to prevent the crowd from getting at "the ghost", or to prevent "the ghost from running away and hiding amongst the crowd".

Another method, only in favour when the inmates do not too strenuously disbelieve in spirits, is to call in a medium, hold a seance, and try to persuade the spirit to reveal something of his history and, having unburdened himself, to depart in peace.

Neither of these methods is particularly effective in helping us to get nearer the truth. The police, though skilful enough in dealing with the ordinary criminal, have not been trained either in scientific research or legerdemain. And the medium enters the field with a ready-made theory. Convinced of the agency of spirits, it is difficult for him fairly to weigh the pros and the cons of evidence.

AN IMPARTIAL INVESTIGATION

Would it not be better, instead of treating every fresh case of a house "possessed" by a coal-throwing maniac (whether of this world or of some other) as a more or less harmless joke, to appoint a commission to investigate all such occurrences as independently and intelligently as possible?

But such a commission should not consist entirely of spiritualists or scientific sceptics. Intelligent people with open minds are usually the best investigators.

1st October 1928

Viscount Gormanston.

A CASTLE WITH A BANSHEE

The premier viscount of Ireland, young Viscount Gormanston, will be fourteen this month. I hear that he is growing very popular with the tenantry at Gormanston Castle, which, like most Irish houses, has its own banshee.

This is said to emerge in vapoury white draperies crying piteously over the house.

I always wonder what is a banshee's status in a family. Is it feared and respected, or looked upon as a somewhat troublesome child?

Another story you will hear at Gormanston is that a band of foxes appears whenever misfortune is about to befall the family.

POLTERGEIST GIRL'S NEW ROLE

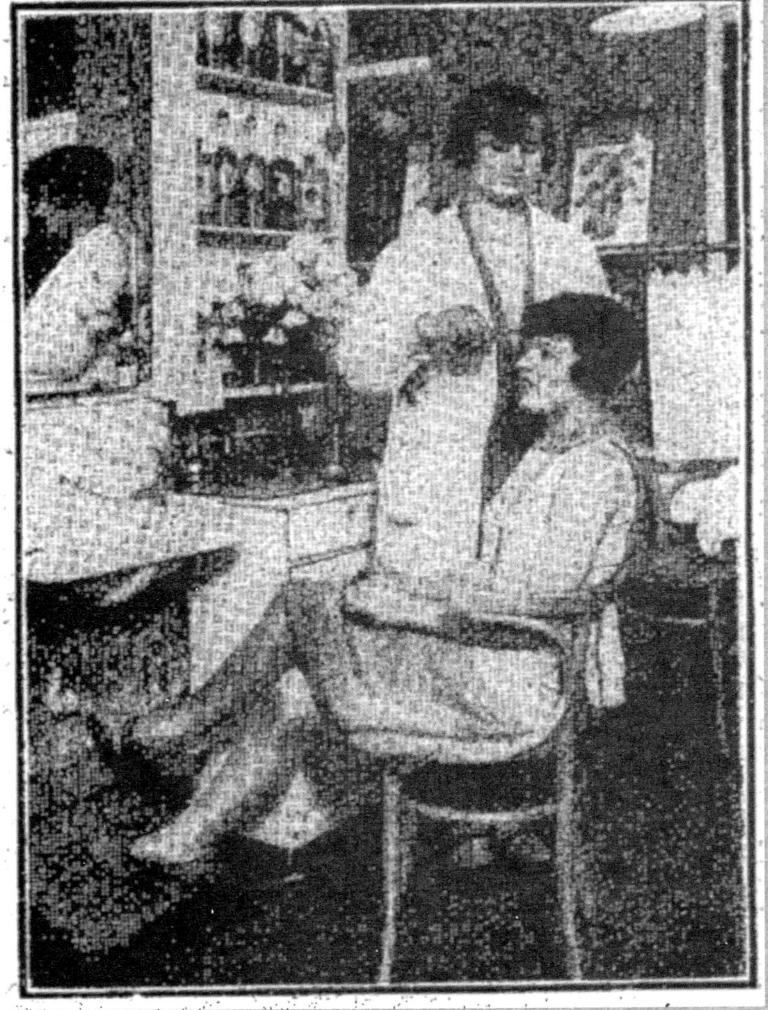

4th December 1928

POLTERGEIST GIRL'S NEW ROLE

Eleanora Zugun, the Rumanian peasant girl whose professed psychic powers created a sensation when they were tested in London two years ago, is now a hairdresser's assistant in Bukarest. After her visit to London she went to Munich (Germany), where it was alleged that the phenomena were produced by deceptive methods.

10th June 1929

PHANTOMS IN GARDEN

The summer house in the garden of Borley Rectory, near Long Melford, Suffolk, where phantoms of a nun, a headless groom and a carriage are said to be seen. These relate to an ancient tragedy.

14th June 1929

WEIRD NIGHT IN "HAUNTED" HOUSE

SHAPE THAT MOVED ON LAWN OF BORLEY RECTORY

STRANGE RAPPINGS

ARTICLES FLYING THROUGH AIR SEEN BY WATCHERS

There can be no longer any doubt that Borley Rectory, is the scene of some remarkable incidents.

Last night Mr. Harry Price, Director of the National Laboratory of Psychical Research, his secretary, Miss Lucy Kaye, the Rev. G. E. Smith, Rector of Borley, Mrs. Smith and myself were witnesses to a series of remarkable happenings.

All these things occurred without the assistance of any medium or any kind of apparatus, and Mr. Price, who is a research expert only and not a spiritualist, expressed himself puzzled and astonished at the results.

To give the phenomenon a thorough test, however, he is arranging for a seance to be held in the rectory with the aid of the

prominent London medium.

The first remarkable happening was the dark figure I saw in the garden.

We were standing in the summer-house at dusk watching the lawn, when I saw the "apparition" which so many claim to have seen but owing to the deep shadows it was impossible for one to discern any definite shape or attire.

FALLING GLASS

But something certainly moved along the path on the other side of the lawn, and although I immediately ran across to investigate, it had vanished when I reached the spot.

Then, as we strolled towards the rectory discussing the figure, there came a terrific crash, and a pane of glass from the roof of a porch hurtled to the ground.

We ran inside and upstairs to inspect the rooms immediately over the porch, but we found nobody.

A few seconds later we were descending the stairs, Miss Kaye leading and Mr. Price behind me, when something flew past my head, hit an iron stove in the hall, and shattered.

With our flashlamps we inspected the broken pieces and found them to be sections of the red vase which, with its companion, had been standing on the mantelpiece of what is known as the blue room and which we had just searched.

Mr. Price was the only person behind me and he could not have thrown the vase at such angle to pass my head and hit the stove below.

A maid at Borley Rectory, pointing out the bushes where she believes she saw the ghost of a nun.

RAPS ON MIRROR

We sat on the chairs in the darkness for a few minutes and just as I turned to Mr. Price to ask whether we had waited long enough something hit my head.

This turned out to be a common mothball, and had dropped from apparently the same place as the vase.

I laughed at the idea of a spirit throwing mothballs around, but Mr. Price said that such methods of attracting attention were not unfamiliar to investigators.

Finally came the most astonishing event of the night.

From one o'clock until nearly four this morning all of us, including the rector and his wife, actually questioned the spirit or whatever it was and received at times the most emphatic answers.

A cake of soap on the washstand was lifted and thrown heavily on to a china jug standing on the floor with such a force that the soap was deeply marked.

All of us were on the other side of the room when this happened.

Our questions which we asked out loud, were answered with raps apparently made on the back of a mirror in the room, and it must be remembered that no medium or spiritualist was present.

15th June 1929

SEANCE HELD IN HAUNTED HOUSE

MYSTERIOUS RAPPINGS IN THE RECTORY BORLEY

"FORMER RECTOR"

HOW QUESTIONS WERE ASKED AND ANSWERED

An informal seance at the "haunted" Borley rectory as a preliminary to an orthodox one with a medium produced astonishing results.

This took place in the presence of the rector and his wife, Mr. Harry Price, and Miss Lucy Kaye, director and secretary of the National Laboratory of Psychical Research, respectively, and myself.

Mysterious replies to our questions were given by means of one, two or three raps on the back of a mirror in the room.

Light in the room made no difference.

The replies came clearly and distinctly. At times we lit the lamp and sat around the mirror with everybody in the room in full sight, but there was no hesitation about the answers.

EMPHATIC "YES"

The only unsatisfactory feature was our inability to get a complete message by spelling out the alphabet; the "spirit" was either a bad scholar or was speaking in Hindustani.

Our first attempts were naturally to ascertain the identity of the rapper. We asked if it were the nun in the old legend or one of the grooms, and a single rap denoting "no" was the reply.

Then I suggested to Mr. Price that he should ask whether it were the Rev. H. Bull, the late rector. I had hardly finished the name when

three hurried taps came on the mirror, which meant an emphatic "yes".

The following dialogue then took place, sometimes with the lamp lit, sometimes in darkness: "Is it your footsteps one heard in this house?" – "Yes".

"Do you wish to worry or annoy anybody here?" – "No".

"Do you object to anybody now living in the house?" – "No".

SMOKING DURING SEANCE

"Do you merely wish to attract attention?" – "Yes".

"Are you worrying about something that you should have done when you were alive?" – "No".

"If we had a medium here, do you think you could tell us what is the matter?" – "Yes".

Here followed a series of questions dealing with the late Mr. Bull's private affairs, to which no answer at all was received.

The whole proceeding was entirely informal, and we even smoked and chatted as if we were in the rectory drawing-room instead of the room that is supposed to be haunted.

The worst part about these "manifestations", from the rector's point of view, is that Borley is fast becoming a show place for the whole of Suffolk and Essex.

Crowds of visitors arrive on foot and by motor-car to see the alleged haunted house.

17th June **1929**

SHY "GHOST" OF BORLEY RECTORY

DECLINES TO REVEAL ITSELF TO LONDON MEDIUMS

"ROWDY" VISITORS

READER AND FORMER RECTOR'S DECLARATION

Borley's ghost failed to rise to the occasion at a specially arranged seance in the now famous rectory.

While apparently willing to demonstrate at an informal sitting, it flatly declined to exhibit itself before the two mediums brought down specially from London.

For hour after hour we sat in the "haunted" room until dawn broke, but our weary vigil was unrewarded and we retired, yawning, to our beds.

Mr. C. Glover and Mr. Harry Collard, the mediums, waited anxiously for some phenomena to occur, and sat sometimes with the lamp lighted, but nothing happened.

"PEOPLED BY CHILDREN"

When on tour of inspection, however, Mr. Botham, on entering one room, declared that he "felt" this room was peopled by children. It transpired that it once had been a schoolroom.

The rectory continues to receive the unwelcome attentions of hundreds of curious people, and at night the headlights of their cars may be seen for miles around. The mediums expressed the view that these conditions were not conductive to manifestations.

With little or no respect for the Rector's wish for privacy, or the rights of trespass, these visitors last night invaded the gardens and lawn of the Rectory and the woods behind.

This morning the litter left behind, consisting of empty bottles, paper bags and remnants of food, had to be cleared away.

RECTOR'S APPEAL

One "enterprising" firm even ran a motor-coach to the Rectory, inviting the public to "come and see the Borley ghost", while cases of rowdyism were frequent, the noises at times being plainly heard inside the Rectory.

"I have no intention of forsaking the Rectory because of what has happened," the Rev. G. E. Smith told me to-day, "but may I appeal to people to be a little more considerate when they come here?"

The *Daily Mirror* has received scores of letters from readers pointing out "faces" in a photograph published of a clump of bushes in the rectory garden.

It may be pointed out that according to the answers received at the first informal "seance", the "spirit" was that of the Rev. H. Bull, the late rector of Borley, the following letter is interesting:–

"IGNORED" SPIRITS

"In 1922 I resided for some weeks at the rectory with the Rev. H. Bull," writes Mr. J. Harley, of Nottingham-place, W.1., "and I distinctly recall him assuring me that on many occasions he had had personal communications with spirits.

"In his opinion the only way for a spirit, if ignored, to get into touch with a living person, was by means of a manifestation causing some violent physical reaction, such as the breaking of glass or the shattering of other and similar material elements.

"The rector also declared that on his death if he were discontented, he would adopt this method of communicating with the inhabitants of the rectory."

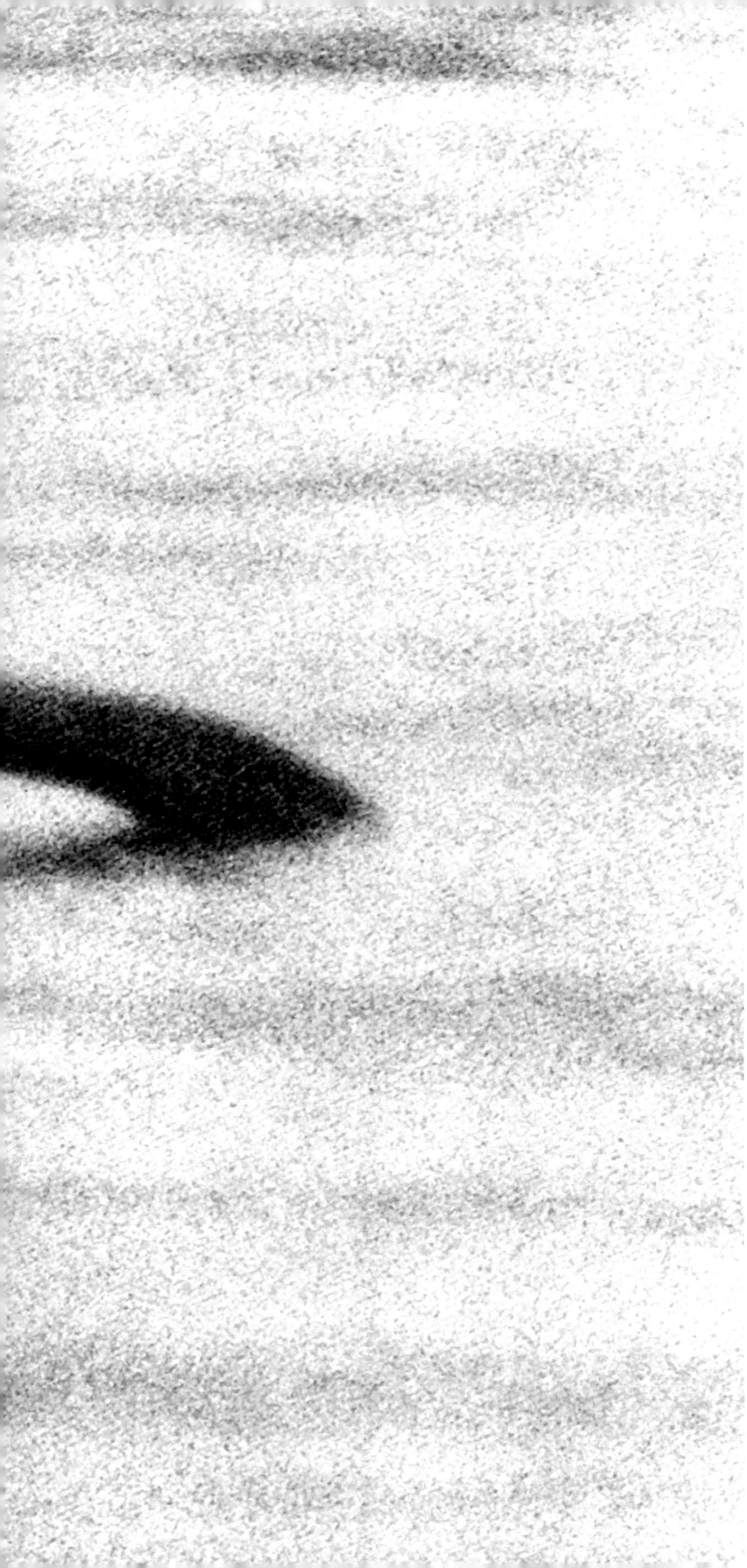

Loch Ness Monster – Stalking with Dinosaurs

One of Frank Searle's photographs of the Loch Ness Monster from 1972.

DAILY MIRROR, Friday, September 1, 1972 PAGE 3

Nessie's a little late this year

Nessie, 1972 . . . Frank Searle's new picture of the elusive Loch Ness Monster. "It was black and had two humps and a fin. I would say that it was twelve feet long."

Nessie makes a splash . . . an earlier picture of the monster by an amateur photographer.

FIRST PICTURE OF THE SEASON—BY A FULL-TIME MONSTER HUNTER

Some neck . . . the most famous picture of the Loch Ness monster.

Frank Searle. . . . Watching for the monster for three years.

MONSTER watchers who have been worried by the lack of news this season about the Loch Ness Monster can relax.

Nessie is alive and well and still living in Scotland.

By BILL MOWATT

He's just been a little late making his appearance this year.

Nessie was actually photographed a few weeks ago by Frank Searle, one of the most dedicated monster hunters in the business.

It was only yesterday that Frank got his roll of film back from the processers.

Frank, 46, has been living in a tent watching out for Nessie for the past three years.

Every day, summer and winter, he has kept a dawn-to-dusk vigil by the loch side.

Elusive

He has been rewarded by seventeen sightings of the monster. But this is by far his best photograph of the elusive beastie.

Yesterday it was hailed as a classic by the Loch Ness Phenomenon Investigation Bureau.

The bureau's young American secretary, Miss Holly Arnold, 25, said: "This is a really good picture—most exciting indeed.

"It's the first one in years to show any kind of detail."

Frank, who quit his greengrocer's business in London to become a full-time Nessie watcher, spoke yesterday of the exciting moments when the monster broke the surface of the loch just over a month ago.

He said: "The creature appeared eighty yards offshore for twelve seconds.

"There were two humps clear of the water and a fin. The humps were four and a half to five feet long each and including the tail fin I would say that it was twelve feet long.

"It was all black, but not shiny or anything. Through the viewfinder the tail seemed to have rough skin on it.

"There is no doubt in my mind that it was the monster."

TOP: Nessie, 1972 … Frank Searle's picture of the Loch Ness Monster. "It was black and had two humps and a fin. I would say that it was twelve feet long."
CENTRE RIGHT: Frank Searle.

It is most commonly held that the creature inhabiting Loch Ness is descended from a line of long-surviving dinosaurs, either a nothosaur, which were Triassic marine sauropterygian ("lizard flippers") reptiles, and first appeared about 245 million years ago, or one of its successors, a plesiosaur (plesios meaning "near to" and sauros meaning "lizard"), an order of Mesozoic marine reptiles, such as the Elasmosaurus, which appeared in the fossil record 199.6 million years ago. However, the scientific community considers the Loch Ness Monster to be a modern-day myth, and explains sightings as a mixture of hoaxes and wishful thinking. For example, the Great Glen was formed only 10,000 years ago, which makes it hard to explain how a long-extinct dinosaur might come to be trapped within. Despite this, Nessie remains one of the most popular and enduring examples of cryptozoology.

1st September **1972**

NESSIE'S A LITTLE LATE THIS YEAR

FIRST PICTURE OF THE SEASON – BY A FULL-TIME MONSTER HUNTER

Monster watchers who have been worried by the lack of news this season about the Loch Ness Monster can relax.

Nessie is alive and well and still living in Scotland.

He's just been a little late making his appearance this year.

Nessie was actually photographed a few weeks ago by Frank Searle, one of the most dedicated monster hunters in the business.

It was only yesterday that Frank got his roll of film back from the processers [*sic*].

Frank, 46, has been living in a tent watching out for Nessie for the past three years.

Every day, summer and winter, he has kept a dawn-to-dusk vigil by the loch side.

ELUSIVE

He has been rewarded by seventeen sightings of the monster. But this is by far his best photograph of the elusive beastie.

Yesterday it was hailed as a classic by the Loch Ness Phenomenon Investigation Bureau.

The bureau's young American secretary, Miss Holly Arnold, 25, said: "This is a really good picture – most exciting indeed.

"It's the first one in years to show any kind of detail."

Frank, who quit his greengrocer's business in London to become a full-time Nessie watcher, spoke yesterday of the exciting moments when the monster broke the surface of the loch just over a month ago.

He said: "The creature appeared eighty yards offshore for twelve seconds.

"There were two humps clear of the water and a fin. The humps were four and a half to five feet long each and including the tail fin I would say that it was twelve feet long.

"It was all black, but not shiny or anything. Through the viewfinder the tail seemed to have rough skin on it.

"There is no doubt in my mind that it was the monster."

1st November **1972**

THE MOST AMAZING PICTURES YET ...

(IS THIS THE FAMOUS LOCH NESS MONSTER?)

You should be able to tell straightaway what that thing is in the water, Frank Searle has been taking pictures of the monster fairly regularly since quitting his shop manager's job three years ago to watch the loch full-time.

As recently as September, he produced a portrait of Nessie hailed as a classic by the Loch Ness Phenomenon Investigation Bureau.

But now he has excelled himself with what he modestly admits are "by far and away the best and most exciting pictures yet".

Being a perfectionist, of course, he is not entirely satisfied with the new photographs.

At his lonely camp on the banks of Loch Ness last night, he said: "I have no doubts there will still be sceptics.

"No, I won't be happy until I have virtually rammed a camera lens down its throat."

SPLASH

Alas, he wasn't quite close enough to try that when he took the latest pictures ten days ago.

He was out in his boat, about 300 yards off-shore when, he said, "there was a tremendous splash and the monster appeared". Frank, 46, banged off four shots at a range of 250 yards before Nessie dived.

Two minutes later it emerged again on the other side of the boat. Unfortunately it was still 250 yards away.

Frank carefully recorded all the details of his eighteenth sighting, quietly rather pleased with himself.

DAILY MIRROR, *Wednesday, November 1, 1972* PAGE 3

NESSIE

The most amazing pictures yet..

(IS THIS THE FAMOUS LOCH NESS MONSTER?)

First it appeared on one side of the boat . .

. . . and then it turned up on the other side.

YOU should be able to tell straight away what that thing is in the water.

Frank Searle swears it is the dear old Loch Ness Monster. And he should know. He took the pictures himself.

He has been taking pictures of the monster fairly regularly since quitting his shop manager's job three years ago to watch the loch full-time.

As recently as September, he produced a portrait of Nessie hailed as a classic by the Loch Ness Phenomenon Investigation Bureau.

But now he has excelled himself with what he modestly admits are "by far and away the best and most exciting pictures yet."

Being a perfectionist, of course, he is not entirely satisfied with the new photographs.

At his lonely camp on the banks of Loch Ness last night, he said: "I have no doubts there will still be sceptics.

"No, I won't be happy until I have virtually rammed a camera lens down its throat."

Splash

Alas, he wasn't quite close enough to try that when he took these pictures ten days ago.

He was out in his boat, about 300 yards off-shore when, he said, "there was a tremendous splash and the monster appeared."

Frank, 46, banged off four shots at a range of 250 yards before Nessie dived.

Two minutes later it emerged again on the other side of the boat. Unfortunately it was still 250 yards away.

Frank carefully recorded all the details of his eighteenth sighting, quietly rather pleased with himself.

But he was right about the sceptics. A zoology professor at Glasgow University studied the pictures last night and actually doubted whether the "monster" was even alive.

He said: "My first impression is that this is the carcass of an animal which has been in the water for some time. Or perhaps a tree."

Frank is not terribly upset by such criticisms. He said: "I love this life.

"And I'm determined to get really close-up shots one day. . . ."

But he was right about the sceptics. A zoology professor at Glasgow University studied the pictures last night and actually doubted whether the "monster" was even alive. He said: "My first impression is that this is the carcass of an animal which has been in the water for some time. Or perhaps a tree."

Frank is not terribly upset by such criticisms. He said: "I love this life.

"And I'm determined to get really close-up shots one day …"

26th April 1973

THE DRAGON AND THE DISC A-GO-GO

The 1973 season for solving the mystery of the Loch Ness Monster is officially open. First on the scene is an old hand at the game, Ted Holland.

In 1968 he wrote a book proving that the monster does indeed exist. Today he publishes another book proving that it doesn't.

Poor old Nessie, says Holland, is a ghost.

In *The Dragon and the Disc*, Holland says the monster is an emanation which may possess an unimaginable

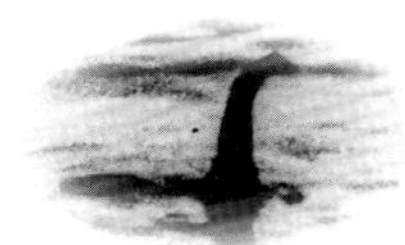

spiritual force. He reckons that flying saucers are only ghosts, too.

Holland bases his idea on his research into ancient symbols and reckons that Nessie might point the way to a new source of energy.

"It is shocking that so little is being done to investigate these phenomena," he says. "We need massive government or industrial backing."

Holland adds: "The potential is enormous." Yes, and so is Nessie, by all accounts.

27th March 1974

IN THE SWIM AGAIN

Pictures of the Loch Ness monster seem to indicate it really exists. And why not?

As Peter Costello points out in his book, *In Search of Lake Monsters*, sightings of sea serpents similar to Nessie have been reported from all over the world across the years.

Certainly Scotland would not be the same without its pet water dragon which, considering the tourists it attracts, is one of the country's growth industries. According to Costello, the creature is probably gentle and harmless. As one American woman observed: "Well, he certainly looks no worse than my husband in the morning."

22nd June 1974

A SUPPER SIZZLER

Britain basked in sizzling sunshine as temperatures scored into the eighties yesterday.

And for sun-seeking families planning weekend trips to the seaside and country, weathermen forecast another scorching couple of days at least.

Temperatures will probably stay "in the high seventies" through the weekend, say the London Weather Centre.

OLD NESSIE . . SPLENDID GOTHIC.

IN THE SWIM AGAIN

THESE two pictures of the Loch Ness monster, one a 19th Century imaginary (and splendidly Gothic) conception of the beastie, the other a 1930s photograph, seem to indicate it really exists. And why not?

As Peter Costello points out in his book, In Search of Lake Monsters, which Garnstone Press publish tomorrow, sightings of sea serpents similar to Nessie have been reported from all over the world across the years.

Certainly Scotland would not be the same without its pet water dragon which, considering the tourists it attracts, is one of the country's growth industries. According to Costello, the creature is probably gentle and harmless. As one American woman observed when she looked at the 19th Century picture: "Well, he certainly looks no worse than my husband in the morning."

NEW NESSIE . . . SPLENDID IMAGE.

The hottest spots in the country yesterday – the longest day of the year – were Blackpool, North Wales and the Lake District. There the temperature soared to a sweltering 81 deg. F.

UNLUCKY

The heatwave could last well into next week, the weathermen said.

Night-time temperatures in most areas are expected to rise as high as 59 deg. F. – six degrees above the normal for this time of year.

But some parts may not be so lucky.

The Weather Centre said some places around the east coast could have fog, with temperatures down into the fifties.

The hot weather brought into the open one elusive sunbather – Nessie, the legendary Loch Ness monster.

Furniture salesman Douglas Stewart, 22, and his mate George Thomson, 31, said they saw Nessie, a 60ft. long eellike creature, going for a swim.

18th June 1975

LOVE MESSAGE TO NESSIE

COME UP AND SEE ME SOMETIME!

Most tricks have been tried on the Loch Ness Monster.

Except romance.

Now these firemen hope that Nessie will rise to their bait: a 14ft.-high monster built on shapely lines from oil drums and papier mache.

The firemen from Hemel Hempstead, Herts, will take their sexy siren Nellie on a fundraising tour before launching her on to Loch Ness.

Sub-officer Maurice Langston said yesterday: "We have a recording of a bull walrus – the nearest thing we could think of for Nellie blowing a kiss."

11th October 1975

HAVE A HORROR HOLIDAY!

Imagine you are holidaying on a boat with the family on a placid lake when a hideous, primeval head rears out of the water. It's the sort of thing that would put most people off fish cakes for life. But an ideal start to a monster-hunting Highland holiday.

The people who helped change the flat, fenny wastelands of the Norfolk Broads into a watery wonderland are turning their expertise to Loch Ness.

Jim Hogan, who runs cruisers on the loch, plans to double his fleet to sixteen craft next spring.

He reckons to charge about £180 a week for a four/five berth boat in peak season.

Jim supplies a rubber dinghy – ideal bait for monster fishing.

There is no speed limit on the lochs and Jim's boats will do about fourteen knots.

But that won't help if the monster comes after you. It can do 25 knots.

How do I know? I met a keen monster hunter up there last week. Tim Dinsdale, former aeronautical engineer from Reading, has written three books about the monster.

RESPECT

He talks about it with respect and never stoops to familiarity by calling it "Nessie".

"I've seen it twice," he told me. "I was very frightened. My first sighting in 1970 was 10ft. of neck sticking up out of the water. At a range of half a mile, it was as thick as a telegraph post.

"I saw it next in 1971. I saw a 4ft.-high neck, very clearly, at about 250 yards.

"There's no doubt in mind the monster exists.

"We hope soon to have indisputable photographic evidence.

"I think there is a group of about fifteen of them. They have probably bred here since just after the last Ice Age.

"Lots of visitors see them. Their reports can be whittled-down to about thirty acceptable sightings a year.

"I'm not too happy about all these holidaymakers that are going to come cruising on the loch," Tim said. "I think they might frighten the monster."

On the other hand, Jimmy Hoseason, a marketing tycoon who plans to bring thousands of tourists to the monster's lair, has no time for Nessie.

"It's fantasy," he says.

24th November 1975

A MONSTER CLASH ON NESSIE

Experts were locked in battle last night over the answer to their fishiest question.

Does new film taken by American scientists prove there really IS a Loch Monster?

Yes say naturalist Sir Peter Scott and Nessie experts Nicholas Witchell and David James.

No say five experts at the Natural History Museum in London.

The film, taken by Dr. Robert Rines, will be shown to a world-wide gathering of scientists in Edinburgh next month.

But a dozen experts in Britain have already studied the pictures – with divided opinions.

The museum experts say that colour slides – showing what appears to be a long-necked creature like the extinct plesiosaur – do not prove that Nessie exists.

HOAX

Sir Frank Claringbull, director of the Museum said: "They have

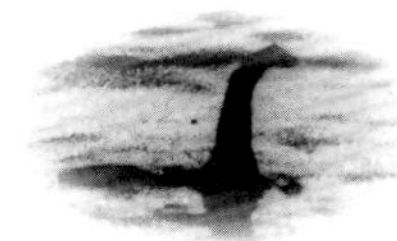

By ROGER TODD

A monster clash on Nessie

EXPERTS were locked in battle last night over the answer to their fishiest problem.

Does new film taken by American scientists prove there really IS a Loch Ness Monster?

YES say naturalist Sir Peter Scott and Nessie experts Nicholas Witchell and David James.

NO say five experts at the Natural History Museum in London.

The film, taken by a team led by Dr. Robert Rines, will be shown to a world-wide gathering of scientists in Edinburgh next month.

But a dozen experts in Britain have already studied the pictures—with divided opinions.

The museum experts say that the colour slides—showing what appears to be a long-necked creature like the extinct plesiosaur—do not prove that Nessie exists.

Hoax

Sir Frank Claringbull, director of the Museum, said: "They have been unable from the evidence to relate it to any particular animal.

"You can't eliminate the element of hoax from this."

But Sir Peter said: "The photos are not fakes.

"I'm absolutely satisfied it's not a hoax."

He believes the pictures are of one of a group of between twenty and fifty monsters which grow up to 40ft. in length.

Another firm believer is law student Nicholas Witchell, who has written a book on the hunt for the monster.

"It was hideous, angular, bony and revolting," he said.

Convinced

And Tory MP Mr. James, the founder of the Loch Ness Investigation Bureau, is also convinced of the picture's authenticity.

Mr. James, MP for Dorset North, said: "I have talked to dozens of witnesses and seen it at ranges of feet and yards myself."

THIS creature in London's Natural History Museum might have a mate soon—Nessie, the Loch Ness monster.

It is a prehistoric Plesiosaur. And Nessie hunters with underwater cameras are said to have produced shots bearing an amazing resemblance to it.

This photo was taken yesterday by Mirror photographer Alisdair Macdonald, who said: "The method used to take the new underwater pictures in Loch Ness appears to be workable."

He added: "One of the creatures was said to have been photographed from forty feet away. Usually that would be useless in any British waters because of the murky water we have.

"However, thanks to the vast improvements that the computer can make, it might now be possible."

been unable from the evidence to relate it to any particular animal.

"You can't eliminate the element of hoax from this."

But Sir Peter said: "The photos are not fakes.

"I am absolutely satisfied it's not a hoax."

He believes the pictures are of one of a group of between twenty and fifty monsters which grow up to 40ft. in length.

Another firm believer is law student Nicholas Witchell, who has written a book on the hunt for the monster.

"It was hideous, angular, bony and revolting." – he said.

CONVINCED

And Tory MP Mr. James, the founder of the Loch Ness Investigation Bureau, is also convinced of the picture's authenticity.

Mr. James, MP for Dorset North, said: "I have talked to dozens of witnesses and seen it at ranges of feet and yards myself."

This creature in London's Natural History Museum might have a mate soon – Nessie, the Loch Ness monster.

It is a prehistoric Plesiosaur. And Nessie hunters with underwater cameras are said to have produced shots bearing an amazing resemblance to it.

Mirror photographer Alisdair Macdonald said: "The method used to take the new underwater pictures in Loch Ness appears to be workable."

He added: "One of the creatures was said to have been photographed from forty feet away. Usually that would be useless in any British waters because of the murky waters we have.

"However, thanks to vast improvements that the computer can make, it might now be possible."

◀ A plesiosaur skeleton in London's Natural History Museum.

26th November **1975**

MIRROR CLOSE-UP ON THE LOCH NESS MYSTERY

NESSIE:
FACT OR MONSTROUS FICTION?

LEGEND OF THE LOCH

Fifteen hundred years ago – that's when the legend of Nessie began. And it was all started by a travelling saint.

St. Columba, the Abbot of Iona, spotted some men burying a body near Loch Ness and asked how the man had died.

When they said he had been bitten by a sea monster while swimming, St. Columba commanded one of them to plunge into the water as bait.

Nessie (or rather, a distant ancestor) obliged by rearing up out of the water, whereupon St. Columba made the sign of the cross and shouted: "Think not to go further nor touch that man. Quick, go back!"

There were further reported sightings in the 16th and 18th centuries, but it wasn't until the early Thirties of this century that they began to flood in.

In 1934, the most startling evidence of Nessie's presence was produced – the famous photograph taken by an unnamed surgeon.

It showed that unmistakable long neck and tiny serpent-like head rearing in front of a dappled wake.

This photograph has never been successfully explained. Could it be a fake?

NO say one lot of experts since photographic equipment wasn't sophisticated enough then.

YES, say other experts, for few people really questioned the photograph at the time and too long a period has elapsed since then for the material to be carefully scrutinized.

The picture remains as one of the few unchallenged pieces of evidence.

THE CASE "FOR"

The evidence for the presence of a large creature in the

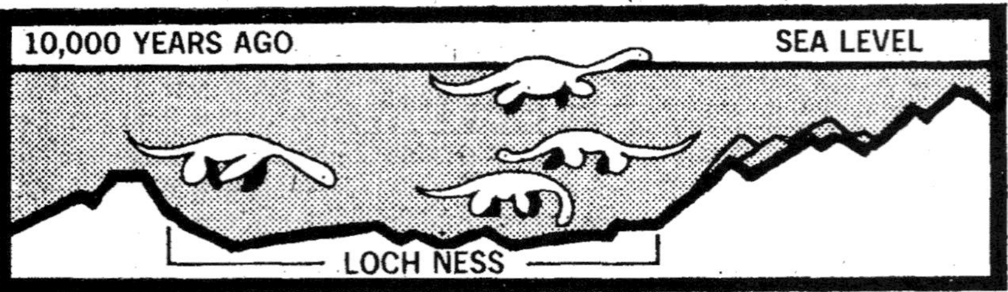

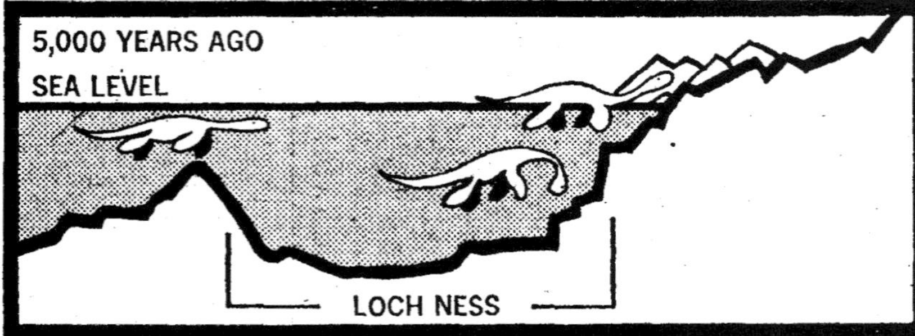

How they got there

AFTER the Ice Age 10,000 years ago the oceans flooded the land, enabling sea creatures to swim in and out of the submerged loch. About 3,000 years ago the water stopped rising. Eventually rising land reduced access to the sea and the animals which had swum into the loch in search of food or to escape from other sea beasts become trapped.

GRAPHICS by TERRY DICKIE

loch rests almost entirely on thousands of sightings – some remarkably detailed.

Witnesses include clergymen, doctors, lawyers, housewives, schoolboys, fishermen and holidaymakers.

The main supporter of the theory that a monster does exist is Tory MP David James, who is appealing for the monster to be made a protected animal.

Mr. James says: "We have established the probability of there being a large unidentified species in the loch and raised the whole subject to one of serious world-wide interest."

Naturalist Sir Peter Scott is another believer. He says: "I would say there must be between 30 and 50 of these animals."

Tim Dinsdale, author of several books on the monster, claims to have seen one swimming at great speed in the loch.

He says: "It was a black snake-like object, rearing out of the water, only 200 yards from me."

Is it possible that the loch contains such a creature?

Yes. The waters are tremendously deep in places – up to 754ft. A depth greater than the seas surrounding Britain.

As for food, the loch is rich in animal life. Fishermen estimate there are millions of eels and vast quantities of other fish.

Belief in the existence of a creature rests on the fact that thousands of people claim to have seen one. Researchers say that clearly each of them deeply believe that what they saw was an unusually large moving animal.

◀ How they got there.

THE CASE "AGAINST"

Scientists have forcefully discounted the idea of a super animal or monster existing in the loch since the first sightings this century.

The possibility of such an animal as the extinct plesiosaur being alive still after millions of years is too unlikely they say. If there is a monster – or monsters – why have no footprints been found, no evidence of droppings and why have no corpses floated to the surface over the years?

The main argument against a monster is that no really satisfactory picture has been taken in more than forty years of observation.

WHAT IS NESSIE?

Some of the scientific theories that have been put forward explaining Nessie are: A long-necked newt; a gigantic eel; a Pinniped (a sort of seal with a long neck); and a Plesiosaur the most popular opinion. Other explanations include: birds, otters, porpoises, turtles, ribbonfish, giant squid, sunfish, rays and sharks.

HOW THEY GOT THERE

After the Ice Age 10,000 years ago the oceans flooded the land, enabling sea creatures to swim in and out of the submerged loch. About 3,000 years ago the water stopped rising. Eventually rising land reduced access to the sea and the animals which had swum into the loch in search of food or to escape from other sea beasts become trapped.

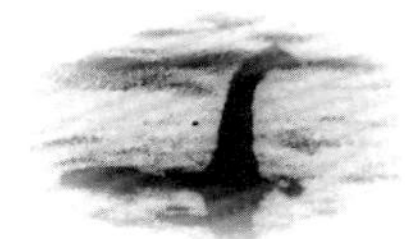

27th November 1975

Horned head, long neck, scaly humps, flippers and all.

JOIN THE FUN … AND WIN YOUR BEASTIE THIS CHRISTMAS

MAC'S MONSTER

This looks like being one of the great years for the Loch Ness monster. And as the sighting season goes well into extra time, *Mirror* cameraman Alisdair Macdonald explained how he succeeded where so many have failed, capturing his astonishing full-length study. He said: "Simple. I just took one pound of green Plasticine and a wire coat-hanger and made a model.

"Then I lined a bath with black paper and filled it up, adding a cup of office coffee and the contents of an ashtray for the murky look."

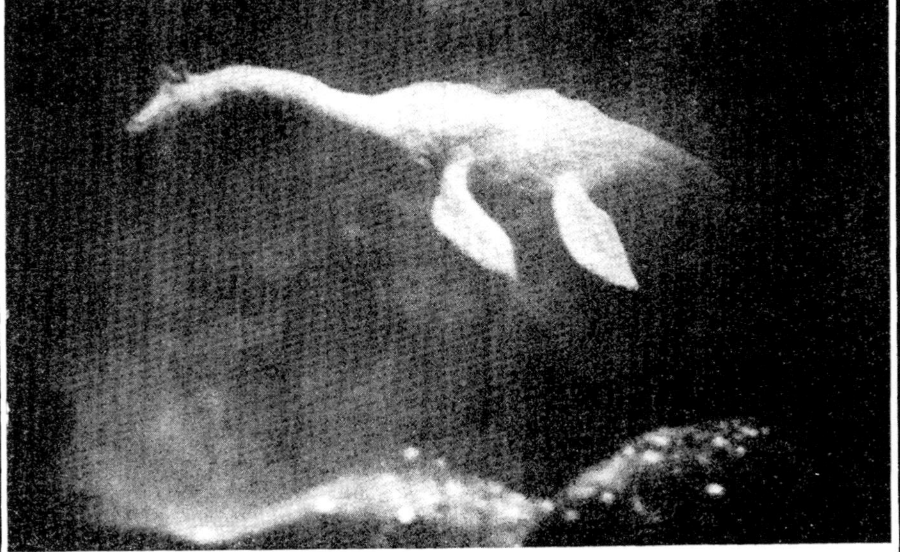

Join the fun . . and win your own Beastie for Christmas

MAC'S MONSTER

THIS looks like being one of the great years for the Loch Ness monster. And as the sighting season goes well into extra time, here is the most dramatic and revealing picture yet in the long line of dramatic and revealing portraits of Nessie.

Picture by ALISDAIR MACDONALD

Mirror cameraman Alisdair MacDonald explained how he succeeded where so many have failed, capturing this astonishing full-length study.

He said: "Simple. I just took one pound of green Plasticine and a wire coat-hanger and made the model.

"Then I lined a bath with black paper and filled it up, adding a cup of office coffee and the contents of an ashtray for the murky look."

Now send us a drawing of what you think Nessie looks like—with twenty-five words on what you think of Nessie—and you could win a monster prize.

The 100 best entries will each receive a Shakermaker Hairy Bunch monster kit in time for Christmas. Entries, giving your name, address and age, to Nessie, Daily Mirror, PO Box 221, London NW99 4XA.

CLOSE-UP: The full-length study of Mac's monster, with horned head, long neck, scaly humps, flippers and all.

28th November 1975

I DON'T SAY THEY DIDN'T FIND NESSIE, BUT …

My views on the Loch Ness Monster are much the same as my views on flying saucers. I do not deny they exist. I simply prefer to reserve my final decision until I have actually had a ride on one.

My feelings about the American scientists who claim to have photographed Nessie are slightly less impartial.

I do not doubt that they are honest men and that they have come close to something that they believe is a monster.

But I do think that a team of experts which has invested so much time, money and equipment in an investigation is not going to return home empty-handed.

If Dr. Robert Rhines [*sic*] and his monster-spotters had set up a hide in Piccadilly Circus to photograph the Abominable Snowman I think they would have returned home with some pictures that would certainly have created just as much controversy as is now raging about Nessie.

Incidentally I greatly admire Sir Peter Scott's sinisterly realistic painting of those bloated monsters. It could knock the bottom out of the flying duck business.

3rd December 1975

MR NESSIE HITS BACK

American Dr. Robert Rines yesterday blamed publicity by British scientists for the wrecking of his plan to prove that the Loch Ness monster exists.

"They have queered the atmosphere," he said. "All the publicity leaks have come from Britain."

Dr. Rines was commenting on Monday's cancellation of next week's conference at Edinburgh at which he aimed to show photos.

The conference was scrapped by its Scottish university sponsors because "too much publicity had made impartial discussion impossible".

5th December 1975

THIS PROVES IT IS NESSIE – SO THERE!

American Robert Rines has opened his photo album in a

DAILY MIRROR, *Thursday, December 11, 1975* PAGE 17

Today the Daily Mirror publishes the controversial pictures from Loch Ness

Nessie, is this REALLY you?

An artist's impression of how the monster, left, looks.

By ARTHUR SMITH, Science Correspondent

SO this is what all that fuss was about . . . the much-heralded proof that Nessie lives.

These are the pictures taken by a team of American scientists last summer, using an electronic flash 45ft. below the surface of Loch Ness.

The pictures weren't even this clear at first. They have been sharpened by a system known as computer-enhancement.

That full-body study on the left may look to you like a bursting haggis thrown over the side of a loch steamer.

But it's good enough to convince Sir Peter Scott, the painter and wildfowl expert, and Dr. Robert Rines, the Boston attorney who led the American team.

In Britain's leading scientific journal Nature, where the monster picture was first published yesterday, they even put forward a name for Nessie.

They called it Nessiteras Rhombopteryx — which means the Ness Monster with a diamond-shaped fin—and explained that if it wasn't named it couldn't become a protected species under British law.

Sir Peter and the doctor calculate that their monster is anything up to 65ft. long, living on fish and plant debris. And they reckon Nessies have been breeding in the loch ever since it ceased to be an arm of the sea 12,000 years ago.

The pair defended their evidence before a slightly sceptical Press conference in London last night, Dr. Rines calling his monster "the tenth wonder of the world."

THE SYSTEM: How computer enhancement works. The picture, left, of Mars satellite Phobus was taken by a Mariner spacecraft in 1971. It was fed into a computer which created the new, clearer close-up, right. The same process was used on the Nessie pictures.

BODY The speckled shape of Nessie, photographed before dawn 45ft. below the surface of Loch Ness—indicating, its supporters claim, a monster 65ft. long with a 12ft. neck

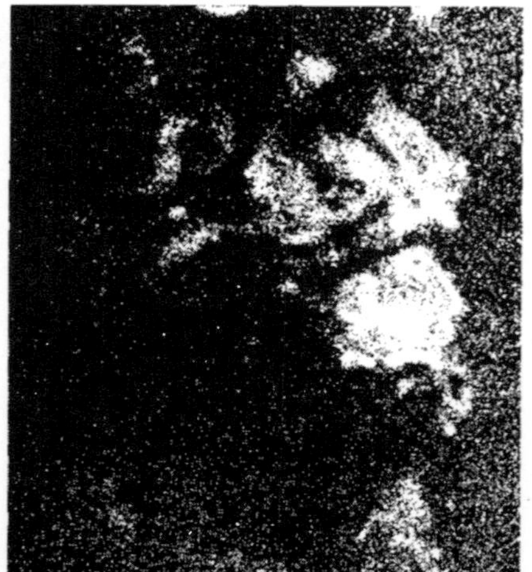

HEAD The splodge that believers call the head, with horns which may be schnorkel tubes—clearly shown in the artist's version—for breathing without causing a ripple on the loch.

Graphics by TERRY DICKIE.

new bid to prove that the Loch Ness monster really is alive and well.

He showed a picture of what he claims is Nessie to fifty students at the law school in Concord, New Hampshire, where he is dean.

Dr. Rines identified parts of the rust-coloured object as a body 12ft. wide and neck 8ft. long.

He said he showed the picture, taken deep down in the loch earlier this year, to counter claims by sceptical British scientists that no monster was recognisable on his team's film.

6th December 1975

NESSIE MAN FLIES IN WITH THOSE PICTURES

The man who claims he has discovered the Loch Ness monster flew to London yesterday in a last-ditch attempt to prove Nessie exists.

And last night the monster-hunter, Dr. Robert Rines, was locked in battle with experts from the British Museum.

Dr. Rines brought with him photographs which, he claims, show Nessie.

He met some of the experts on prehistoric monsters and fish who last week dismissed his photos as showing only a piece of tree.

A museum official said: "We sent Dr. Rines a three-page letter setting out our doubts and explaining why we didn't believe his pictures show a monster.

"He is now trying to convince our experts that they are wrong and that he is right.

"He is trying to back up his earlier evidence with more detailed discussion."

Body: The speckled shape of Nessie, 65ft long with a 12ft neck, photographed 45ft below the surface of Loch Ness, and an artist's impression. Head: Nessie's head and an artist's interpretation.

11th December **1975**

TODAY THE *DAILY MIRROR* PUBLISHES THE CONTROVERSIAL PICTURES FROM LOCH NESS

Pictures taken by a team of American scientists last summer, using an electronic flash 45ft below the surface of Loch Ness, and sharpened by a system known as computer-enhancement, are good enough to convince Sir Peter Scott, the painter and wildfowl expert, and Dr. Robert Rines, the Boston attorney who led the American team.

In Britain's leading scientific journal *Nature*, where the monster picture was first published yesterday, they even put forward a name for Nessie.

They called it *Nessiteras Rhombopteryx* – which means the Ness Monster with a diamond-shaped fin – and explained that if it wasn't named it couldn't become protected species under British law.

Sir Peter and the doctor calculate that their monster is anything up to 65ft. long, living on fish and plant debris. And they reckon Nessies have been breeding in the loch ever since it ceased to be an arm of the sea 12,000 years ago.

The pair defended their evidence before a slightly sceptical Press conference in London last night, Dr. Rines calling his monster "the tenth wonder of the world".

12th December **1975**

LIVE LETTERS CONDUCTED BY THE OLD CODGERS

WHAT WILLIAM, THE BUTLER, DID NOT SEE …

William Elliott, Puttocks Drive, North Mymms, Herts., writes:

Can you tell me when it was that Sir Edward Mountain was engaged on an investigation of the Loch Ness Monster, and its outcome?

I was Sir Edward's butler for some time, but left his service thirty-five years ago. I did go to Scotland with him, but the Loch Ness investigation was before my time up there.

It was in July, 1934, that Sir Edward, chairman of Eagle Star Insurance and keen angler, had a go at "catching" Nessie.

Staying at Beaufort Castle, he employed twenty men, armed with cameras and binoculars and stationed them at lochside vantage points.

In a fortnight these men took twenty-one photographs of a creature. After that, watch was continued by a Captain Fraser and an assistant with a cine-camera and they filmed a large creature swimming.

This was later shown to the Press and scientists in London, but Sir Edward, who died in 1948, apparently took the matter no further.

28th January **1976**

DO THE MONSTER MASH …

Scientists are trying to get Nessie rockin' around the loch … with swinging pop records. And they hope the monster will be so turned on by the music that she will fall into their trap.

An electronics firm has splashed out £45,000 on underwater broadcasting gear to find out what's top of the pops in Loch Ness. So far they've discovered that Beethoven's Fifth is a hit with the fish – while Elvis sends them diving for the bottom. The research team leader, Mr. Brian King, said yesterday: "Up to now we have found nothing, except that there are a lot of fish in Loch Ness. But we are going to find out once and for all if there really is a monster."

If Nessie responds to the music, the scientists will try to lure her in to the Caledonian Canal – then drain off the water.

3rd February **1976**

NESSIE

I hope, for its own safety, monster Nessie doesn't allow scientists to lure her into the Caledonian Canal to be prodded and probed.

Fortunately, Nessie seems to have more brains than the so-called scientists who've hunted her over the years.

D. Pickett, Southsea, Hants.

27th May **1976**

IT'S HUNT FOR NESSIE!

Social calendar note: June 1 marks the start of the biggest game season of the lot.

That's when the Americans jet in for a summer's sport trying to shoot the Loch Ness monster – on film.

Leading the team yet again will be Dr. Robert Rines, the Boston lawyer who unleashed "Nessie" pictures on a startled world last year.

With him will be Charles Wyckoff, head of Applied Photo Sciences, a firm specialising in advanced camera techniques.

They will be lugging along enough equipment to set up a TV studio on the bed of Loch Ness.

Observed Wyckoff: "We aim to get those critturs this time."

(Yes he actually did say critturs.)

7th August **1976**

NESSIE BAIT

A new hunt for the Loch Ness monster is to be made next week by two balloonists. They hope to attract it by skimming over the water trailing a huge bacon joint.

9th June **1977**

Nessie photographed from 100 yards away.

UP FOR THE JUBILEE NESSIE!

NESSIE HAS SURFACED AGAIN – BY APPOINTMENT

She could have told them all along, of course.

They wouldn't need their fancy gadgets to lure her from the deep. Not this year.

All they needed was … the Jubilee.

And the Beastie from Loch Ness popped up, right on cue, for a peek at the celebrations.

Nessie's Command Performance was captured by monster watcher "Doctor" Tony Shiels from Falmouth, Cornwall. The "Doc" – he bought a doctorate in the States for five dollars – reckons Nessie was 100 yards away when he took a picture. And he brought Nessie to the surface, he claims, by using telepathy.

Nessie might argue with that. She's as likely to have risen for a Jubilee knees-up.

24th June **1978**

NESSIE CATCHES AN ANGLER'S EYE

The Loch Ness monster reared its head again yesterday to start the summer season.

The first sighting of 1978 was reported by Bill Wright, a 52-year-old angler.

Bill, who was fishing from the loch shore at dawn, said: "I got the fright of my life. My eyes nearly popped out when it rose out of the water just thirty yards away."

According to Bill, Nessie had a black body shaped rather like an upturned rowing boat. Its brown neck was at least 12ft. long, he reckoned, and its round brown head about the size of a football.

Bill, an aluminium plant worker from Falkirk, stressed: "I really did see the monster.

"I was trying to get to a better vantage point when I slipped on some pebbles and the creature just slid under the water and disappeared."

Bill is now compiling a written report of what he saw in case it might be of help to marine biologists, or monster hunters. Or even Scottish tourism officials.

BRITAIN'S BIGGEST DAILY SALE 7p Thursday, June 9, 1977

Up for the Jubilee NESSIE!

NESSIE has surfaced again—By Appointment.

She could have told them all along, of course.

They wouldn't need their fancy gadgets to lure her from the deep. Not this year.

All they needed was . . . the Jubilee.

And the Beastie from Loch Ness popped up, right on cue, for a peek at the celebrations.

Nessie's Command Performance was captured in this believe-it-or-not photograph, right, by monster-watcher "Doctor" Tony Shiels from Falmouth, Cornwall. The "Doc" — he bought a doctorate in the States for five dollars — reckons Nessie was 100 yards away when he took the picture. And he brought Nessie to the surface, he claims, by using telepathy.

Nessie might argue with that. She's as likely to have risen for a Jubilee knees-up.

1964, let's see more.

ON time for '69.

STILL alive in '75. MORE tricks in '76.

IDI HERE? OR IDI THERE?

By NICHOLAS DAVIES, Foreign Editor

PRESIDENT Idi Amin is already in London, Uganda Radio sources claimed last night.

No details were given on the basis for the report—latest in the bizarre diplomatic drama.

Special Branch officers at Britain's ports of entry have orders to keep Amin out.

And Premier Jim Callaghan has his own idea of the illusive President's whereabouts. He thinks Amin is in Kampala, the Ugandan capital.

The Prime Minister made his guess while calling for everyone to "keep cool" over a threat to 240 Britons in Uganda.

The 240 have been ordered not to leave the country.

The order is part of a bid by President Amin to gatecrash the Commonwealth Conference which opened in London yesterday.

By holding the Britons "hostage," the Ugandans hope to blackmail the Prime Minister into allowing Amin into Britain.

But Mr. Callaghan told newsmen: "Why don't we all keep cool about this and not give President Amin the chance to think he is putting the wind up us?

"He may have put the wind up you, but he has not put the wind up me."

Foreign Secretary David Owen said that the Uganda Britons — mainly missionaries, teachers and businessmen—were committed to the future of the country.

He added: "They will know how to cope."

But Dr. Owen was still anxious about the safety of the Britons.

Yesterday's "hostage" order in the "Idi Coming, Idi Ain't" drama was made by the President's deputy, General Mustafa Adrisi.

The general warned in a statement on Uganda

Continued on Page Two

Anthony Shiels' 1977 photograph that came to be known as "The Loch Ness Muppet".

SKYSHIP

UFOs – Close Encounters

The world's first flying saucer, or Skyship as its designers prefer to call it, eased itself into the air in 1975, and science fiction became science fact. The 30ft saucer took off near Bedford to notch a first for British aviation.

Alien abductions started to be widely reported from the early 1960s. By the end of the millennium, it was estimated that as many as 1,700 people could have been captured against their will for examination and experimentation, or to take part in alien–human breeding programmes. Indeed, this has been the reason given to explain several phantom pregnancies. Otherwise, there seems to be no pattern in the choice of abductee, except that subsequent assessment has found these people to be quite ordinary and not delusional nor mentally ill; the aliens' motivations seem to vary from the curious to the malign.

30th November **1981**

A CASE FOR THE FLYING SQUAD

A Yorkshire policeman has, under hypnosis, described seeing a flying saucer manned – if that's the word – by "a tall humanoid and eight small robots".

Recognizing a humanoid when he sees one, especially at 5.15 a.m. in late November in Todmorden, proves again how wonderful our policemen are.

On the other hand, he could have seen a jet-powered pumpkin carrying Snow White and the Seven Dwarfs back from a night out in Barnsley with Arthur Scargill.

True, he says there were eight small creatures. But perhaps he counted Dopey twice. That would be understandable.

Alternatively, he may have stumbled upon a Tory Party meeting being addressed by Sir Geoffrey Howe. If "humanoid" means anything at all, it certainly describes Sir Geoffrey.

This theory would also account for the audience being mistaken for robots.

We can rule out that it was Count Dracula travelling with a miniaturized retinue. Contrary to legend, the count was a kindly man, not taken to frightening innocent coppers.

More boringly, the P.C. may just have been dreaming.

The world teems with solid, stolid, reliable, hardworking and trustworthy citizens who believe passionately in Atlantis, the Second Coming, the Bermuda Triangle, flying saucers and economic recovery under Mrs Thatcher.

Sad to say, they are all fantasies.

3rd February **1983**

MARCIA AND THE LITTLE GREEN MEN

Lady Falkender is about to reveal – to those of us that didn't have the foggiest idea – that she believes in flying saucers.

The ever-surprising Marcia has written a most enthusiastic foreword to a book on the matter in which she calls for a widening of interest in this "highly sensitive subject".

According to the authors, one of whom is Timothy Good, professional violinist and adviser to the House of Lords U.F.O. group, Lady Falkender actually knows that the Government knows that the Military know all about flying saucers.

And that there is, to use that dark and sinister phrase, a "cover-up".

My researchers were unable to discuss this amazing business with

Sunday Mirror

22p September 27, 1981

BINGO

Eyes down for Game No. 2

INSTANT BINGO

WIN £10,000 TODAY —See Page 3

First picture of the White Cliffs baby

AMAZING UFO DEATH RIDDLE

Experts baffled by burns on man

Victim — Mr. Adamski with his wife Lottie

Priscilla Presley's new life

CENTRE PAGES

MY LOVER AGED 22, BY OLIVIA NEWTON-JOHN —See Page 17

Crunch day for Labour

➧ Zigmund Adamski Unexplained Death. The *Sunday Mirror* newspaper headlines, 27th September 1981.

Marcia. One was told that "a friend has just popped in unexpectedly from Paris".

But in the foreword of the book *George Adamski – The Untold Story*, she writes: "This long overdue appraisal contains much that is exciting and new about the controversial claims of George Adamski.

"Something clearly of tremendous significance happened to this man and some of the information in the book is new, highly controversial and thought provoking."

The late Adamski's book was full of pictures of UFOs and even gave accounts of meetings with funny little men. He was regarded by many as an "outrageous hoaxer and a looney".

Still, Marcia evidently believes that – hoax or not – they are out there.

On the subject of that cover-up, Mr. Good says: "She says she knows an awful lot more than she has told me."

We put all this chilling stuff to Lord Clancarty, one of Britain's' leading flying saucer experts. He said: "The Russians and the West have discovered the secret of UFOs and have learned how to tap energy from them.

"If the public knew that both sides had these high powered things it might cause panic."

Quite. That is just why Steven Spielberg, who is in the pay of the Planetary Propaganda Unit on Uranus, gave us the lovable E.T.

To lure us into a false sense of security.

6th January **1988**

COPS SPOT A FLYING SAUCER ... AND THE UFO MYSTERY GROWS

'ELLO UFO!' COPS SPY A JELLY IN THE SKY

Eight policemen stood gaping as the grey-green, pink-blobbed UFO hovered before them. Laugh if you like … but they were convinced by the close encounter over Kensington, West London, as reported in the *Mirror* yesterday.

At Heathrow, officials could find no explanation and logged it as an official UFO – one more to add to the thousands reported in the last 40 years.

But are they fact or fiction? Here are some of the people who have had close encounters … and come away convinced.

It happened at midnight in August, 1967. Edwin Kembery had just found his lost collie in the fields close to his bungalow.

He was returning with the pet, and a fierce Alsatian watchdog, when he saw the shape of a huge cannon shell looming in the eerie gloom at Saddlescombe, Sussex.

"Two strange men appeared at my side," he says, "Each was about five feet tall.

"They twittered like birds. Gently, without touching, they led me and the dogs back to the bungalow.

"Inside, I could see them properly. They were identical with deep-set eyes, flat noses, thin lips and three fingers on each hand. They had no eyebrows, thin mouths and tiny teeth. Their skin was dry, creamy like parchment.

"They wore dull grey, tight garments of which the head-piece was like a balaclava. There were grids at the ear but no bulge to show they actually had ears at all."

Edwin, a retired audiologist, gave them cheese and biscuits, which they took away. He offered them whisky, which they spat out.

In return they gave him some "diamonds" and some seeds. A jeweller certified the stones were, in fact, rock crystal.

Edwin claims two of the seeds grew in his greenhouse, sprouting "caramel tasting" berries from thin brown stems.

He took one to Stricklands, a Hastings plant specialist, but they could not identify it. Edwin says the plants were killed by frost soon after.

The "men" returned some six more times during the next two months.

RIDICULE

Edwin gave them ornaments. He showed them TV, which amused them. He noted their bouncing walk, their physical weakness, yet their complete gentleness and lack of fear.

He reported their "visitations" to the police. "And I got a lot of ridicule for it," says Edwin. "Some people suggested I should enter the local asylum.

"But I know what I saw. It was marvellous."

He has stuck by his story for the past 20 years.

SPACE ODDITY CALLED ABNEMOS

It happened in July, 1942. Nine-year-old Ron Evans, a wartime evacuee, was staying with a village family in Frome, Somerset.

It was a hot day and he went off to collect firewood in the forest.

"I saw this green haze, like the sun streaming through the leaves," said Ron, now 54 and living in Southall.

"As I approached I saw a strange craft, big as a house, in the clearing. Then a man's voice said: 'Don't be afraid' and a hand stopped me.

"I was absolutely terrified but he calmed me.

"He had large eyes, a small nose. But his whole face looked as though a G-force was dragging it back. He was tall, with long hair and wore a matt grey skinsuit.

"Slowly he stepped into the green haze and immediately his body transformed like in an X-ray. He said that I would never come out if I walked into that haze.

"He told me his name was Abnemos. In the centre of his chest was a control panel. He touched some buttons and three silver balls emerged from the panel. Two hovered over my shoulders, one over my head.

"Then he walked back to his craft. As the bottom opened I could see about 20 more beings there, some like small children.

"Slowly the four claw legs buckled beneath the round craft and it rose turning bright white with a flashing red rim. It spun, then vanished."

Ron told nobody. Even then, he was used to confiding only in himself. His mother died giving birth to him. His grieving father died five months later.

GOOD

"It was years before I told a friend, but he said I was a loony. So I decided to keep it my own secret.

"I believe we were all like that man once. Maybe we became bad and lost those powers. I don't know who he was, but I know he was good.

"Call me a crank or a nutcase. But what I saw was beautiful – the most marvellous thing that ever happened to me."

VISIONS THAT ROCKED STAR

It happened on January 13, 1982. Dave Davies of The Kinks was relaxing with his wife Nancy in his tour hotel room in Hampton, Virginia, "when suddenly the sensation hit me. It was like being grasped round the neck," Dave, now 40, remembers, "except it was my mind that was gripped.

"I called to Nancy and tried to explain what was happening." He has tried to explain it ever since.

Dave leans forward, on the edge of his armchair, in his luxurious home in St John's Wood, London. His voice is barely audible. "Oh yeah, I know some people will say… 'Just another rich, druggie pop star freaking out.'

"But I was taken over by beings from another world."

Ask for descriptions, and Dave can't give them. He can only "visualise" the "beings" sitting round an imaginary table taking turns to speak to him.

"They showed me the world in a new light.

"They manipulated my arms. They changed the feelings in my body. Everything below my solar plexus went numb."

Throbbing visions bombarded his mind for the next six days. Yet he was able to play the gigs, feeling strangely relaxed throughout.

"The visions ended in Indianapolis," Nancy recalls. "Dave woke up and they were gone."

15th July 1992

SHAMEN SPARK OFF UFO ALARM

Police rushed to the shoot of a Shamen video when locals thought they were being invaded by aliens.

The London rave band were filming a mind-boggling £30,000 futuristic video in the Lake District when neighbours mistook the special effects for a flying saucer.

The police arrived after they received reports that a UFO full of aliens had landed on a lake.

The band's front man Colin Angus, whose record 'LSI' has entered the charts at No. 9, says: "We chose the Lake District because it has a magical and mystical feel, but what happened to us was even weirder than we expected.

SIGHTINGS

"Our singer Jhelisa was floating on a flowered float in the middle of a lake, Mr C and me were wearing strange space-type suits and there were strobes flashing everywhere.

"There were a lot of UFO sightings and the police had to check them.

"Then they realized we weren't menacing aliens about to take over the world, but boring old human beings."

5th June 1993

SPACED OUT JONATHAN

Heavens above! Chat show host Jonathan Ross has seen a flying saucer.

The normally down-to-earth telly star has kept the experience quiet for years. Until now.

He confided his schoolboy sighting to guests he was interviewing for his new ITV series, *Fantastic Facts*.

One of his guests on the show, Phillip Mantle, of the British UFO Research Organization, said: "He was really great with us. We

are used to people taking the mickey about UFOs but Jonathan took the subject very seriously.

"I was stunned when he admitted that he had seen something strange in the sky some years ago."

Elsie Oakensen, another guest in the show dedicated to UFO sightings, said: "Jonathan was wonderful. He told me that as a young man he had seen strange lights and objects in the sky.

"It was an experience he would never forget."

22nd December **1993**

SPIELBERG TO EXPOSE UFO COVER-UPS

Ace director Steven Spielberg is deserting science fiction – for science fact.

The genius behind movie blockbusters *ET*, *Close Encounters of the Third Kind* and *Jurassic Park* is secretly working on a £50 million movie that he claims will unmask a government cover-up of an alien spaceship crash in New Mexico in 1947.

Project X is based on the Roswell Air Force base incident which gave the world the term "flying saucer". Spielberg believes the US military took away alien bodies from the crashed UFO.

Hollywood insiders say the director has got hold of previously unseen film footage of the flying saucer crash scene taken by a military officer. "Everybody is talking about *Project X*," says a Tinseltown source.

"Spielberg has already got a team at Hamlin Productions working on the script.

"This is going to be a totally different film from the likes of *ET* which was just a fairy story.

"It's about the UFO crash and the political intrigue that followed."

The movie is due for release in 1997 – the 50th anniversary of the alleged alien landing.

20th June **1994**

CROP CIRCLE MAKER MOURNS END OF FIELDS OF DREAMS

It is midsummer. A time of long shadows and hazy days. Of busy bees and cuckoos.

Doug creating a corn circle with a plank and a wire sight on his cap.

But none so busy, nor so cuckoo, as those who frolic in the fields in search of extra-terrestrial doodlers.

Yes, it's crop circle time again. The season of corn fakes and cereal chillers. Of hills alive with the sound of experts and "cerealogists" voicing their theories and fantasies into the wide, blue yonder.

For one elderly gent, the call of the corn fields will go unheeded. Never again will he tread those familiar ways.

Doug Bower, self-confessed corn circle faker, has hung up his cap, put away his plan – and called it a day.

"Well, I'll do it once so you can take some pictures. But that's it. It got beyond a joke," he says. "Whatever I did, wherever I went, there was always someone, somewhere, ready to give an explanation for the circles I made.

"In the end I was even signing the patterns. But it made no difference. If people want to believe in alien beings rather than a 69-year-old man from Southampton, that's their look-out.

"I wasn't put on this earth to stop potty people acting daft."

There is a gleam in his eye but bitterness in his voice. His tale is one of innocent beginnings soured by experience.

"It all began over a couple of pints at the Percy Hobbs pub in Alresford, Hampshire, one Friday evening in 1978," he says. "Little did I know then what seeds I planted."

HUDDLED

There was Doug and his mate Dave, huddled over their beer, chatting idly about landscape painting.

"Then it came to me," says Doug. "I'd lived in Australia and remembered reading about a circle which appeared in a reed bed. There was all sorts of speculation that aliens may have caused it.

"I said: 'Dave, I have an idea!'"

So the pair took their cheese rolls and bottles of ale and set forth where no men had boldly gone before.

"It became an obsession," says Doug.

"For 13 years we trod the fields. First we did simple circles. Then I started designing more complicated patterns and the world went mad.

"As a child I marvelled at the possibility of beings from another planet. But I gradually realized there was no one out there.

"That's when I decided I would be the 'alien'. I would make the dream come true. And there was no shortage of experts to prove me right."

But fame was slow a-coming. "It was two years before the Press really got hold of the circles.

"The main problem was that the places where we made our early circles weren't visible enough. We were using four-foot planks at Westbury and Warminster in Wiltshire and all over Hampshire, but nobody was getting excited."

Then, in 1981, the Devil's Punchbowl at Cheesefoot Head near Winchester was planted with cereal crop for the first time. It was a natural canvas – one offering breathtaking views to passing motorists. Doug's big break had arrived.

By the end of the week every newspaper and TV station had carried stories about the weird corn circle. Circlemania was born. By 1985, Doug and Dave had branched out. From his small workshop Doug would devise patterns, including quintuplet circles, pictograms, ladders and swirls.

He devised an "eye-liner" – a piece of wire attached to his baseball cap – to align his wondrous shapes. But as fast as the pair trod the corn, the experts found an explanation. Chief among them was Dr Terence Meaden, an Oxford physicist and meteorologist.

He said that the circles were caused by "vortices" – mini-whirlwinds which could flatten the corn.

"It really annoyed me," says Doug.

WEIRD

"I didn't want anyone coming up with a natural explanation. I wanted people to believe these patterns were caused by aliens. That's when we started concentrating on our 'pictograms'."

The weird shapes, full of boxes and ladders, boosted the True Believers' faith.

Doug says: "We'd watch the experts measuring our designs and try to keep straight faces as people lay down in our circles to 'absorb the cosmic energy'."

Doug pauses. "It was seven years before I told my wife what I was up to. She got suspicious about the miles I was doing in my car at the weekend.

"So I went to my workshop and returned with a pile of Press cuttings. She still didn't believe me, so I took her out and showed her how it was all done.

"But eventually it got beyond a joke. People took to sleeping in the fields waiting for the aliens to arrive. The farmers and police were getting fed up.

"By 1991 we decided to go public."

Their story produced a furore. Here were Doug and Dave, two sprightly pensioners, announcing the A-cropalypse. Corn-spiracy theories were developed, accusing the duo of being agents in a Government cover-up.

"People needed something to believe in and we gave it to them," says Doug,

"When we told them the truth, it was like attacking a religion."

He sighs: "I only wish there were aliens from another planet – rather than some of the cereologists who just act like they are from another planet."

4th February 1995

FLYING SAUCIES

Apparently, more and more divorcing couples in America are naming an alien from outer space as the third party.

One woman said her husband lost his sex-drive after affairs with a flying-saucer crew.

He struck lucky. The chances of getting picked up by an entire flying saucer are pretty slim.

The chances then of the whole crew being up for a quick one must be millions to one.

The only things that ever land in our garden are starlings and you can't have sex with them.

They just fly off.

27th March 1995

SECRET FILM OF ALIENS TO HIT SCREENS

A top secret film said to show dead aliens is to be screened for the first time – in Britain.

It will be revealed at a UFO conference in Sheffield, Yorks, in August and feature in a BBC TV documentary.

It is said to show US military scientists examining a creature after a flying saucer crashed in New Mexico in 1947.

One cameraman, now 82, secretly kept a copy and gave it to a British TV film maker to expose the cover-up. Conference organiser Phillip Mantle said: "I've seen one reel and it's very intriguing."

22nd August 1996

PHOTOS NASA HID FOR 20 YEARS

DO ASTRONAUTS' PICTURES PROVE WE ARE NOT ALONE?

It's the controversial subject that has divided scientists – are there aliens out there?

Sightings of UFOs have been reported time and time again – and they have never been refuted with total authority. It is even claimed that when Apollo 11 landed on the Moon, the spaceship was watched by aliens.

NASA has dismissed the [resulting] pictures as photos of meteors, clouds of debris or even huge ice crystals.

But a growing number of top scientists and space experts are amassing a convincing body of evidence to counter NASA's denials.

They even believe America's Area 51, a closed-off region of the Nevada desert which does not appear on any map and features in *Independence Day* contains the remains of a crashed alien craft.

Former Apollo astronaut Dr Brian O'Leary claimed: "There's plenty of scientific evidence of contacts with aliens but NASA has suppressed it."

He added: "There have been a lot of unearths and misinformation. Anybody with access to the truth has been sworn to secrecy.

"I am convinced crashed alien craft has been discovered. The evidence is out here."

He also claims ancient alien constructions have been photographed on the Moon. And he claims a NASA source at the Johnson Space Centre in Houston admitted "airbrushing" UFOs from photos released to the media.

Maurice Chatelain, who designed and ran communications systems on the Apollo missions and died recently, said: "All the flights were followed.

"Astronauts saw things during their missions that could not be discussed with anyone outside of NASA."

He adds: "Every time it occurred, they notified mission control who ordered complete silence.

"Walter Schirra aboard Mercury 8 in the early Sixties used the codename 'Santa Claus' for ETs. Chatelain wrote in a book: "James Lovell on board Apollo 8 came out from behind the Moon and reported back: 'We've been informed Santa Claus exists'."

He also claimed that Gemini 4 pilot James McDivitt was the first to take a photograph of a UFO.

Frank Borman and James Lovell, on board Gemini 7, also snapped UFOs following them at distances of just a few hundred yards, it is believed.

"The UFOs looked like huge mushrooms with propulsion systems, and clearly showed a glow on their underside," said Chatelain.

"When Apollo 11 landed on the Moon in 1969, and just before Neil Armstrong set foot on it, two UFOs hovered overhead. Edwin 'Buzz' Aldrin took several pictures of them."

Dr Jack Kashner, professor of physics at Nebraska University, has

Photos NASA hid for 20 years

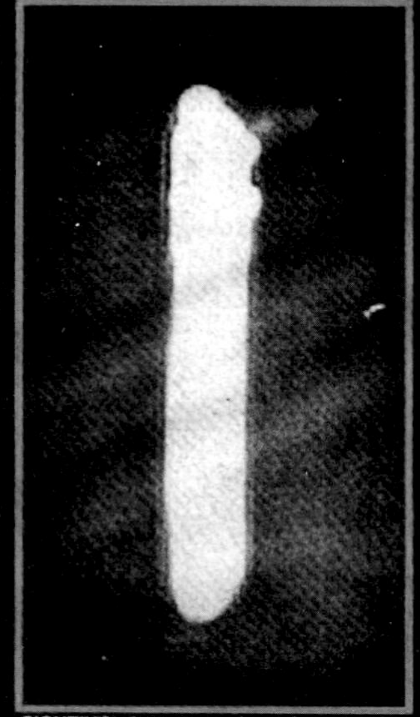

SIGHTING: A mystery cigar-shaped craft

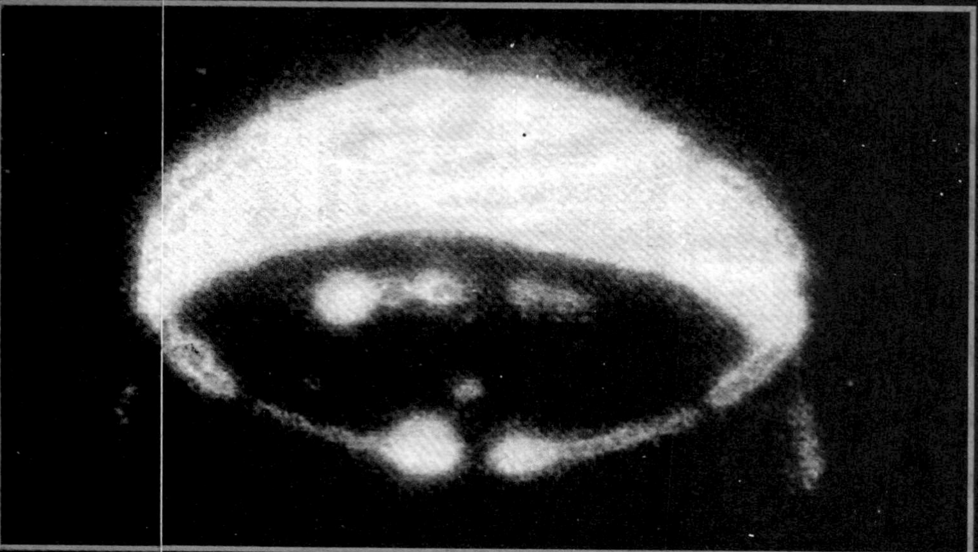

SIGHTING: An enormo, dazzling object which appeared to flying above the Moon, stunned astronauts on the Apollo 12 mission in 1969

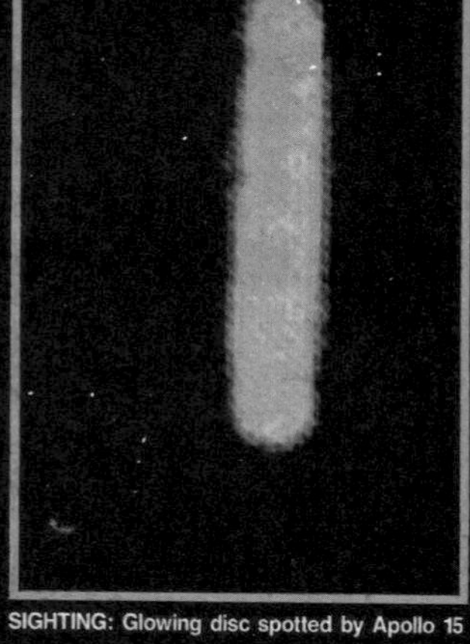

SIGHTING: Glowing disc spotted by Apollo 15

DO ASTRONAUTS PICTURES PROVE WE ARE NOT ALONE?

By JUSTIN DUNN

DAILY Mirror EXCLUSIVE

THESE pictures could come from the alien invasion movie *Independence Day*. But they don't.

They are believed to be real and some respected professors and astronauts claim they are part of a sensational cover-up by America's space centre, NASA.

It's the controversial subject that has divided scientists — are there aliens out there?

Sightings of UFOs have been reported time and time again — and they have never been refuted with total authority. It is even claimed that when Apollo 11 landed on the Moon, the spaceship was watched by aliens.

NASA has dismissed the pictures on this page as photos of meteors, clouds of debris or even huge ice crystals.

But now a growing number of top scientists and space experts are amassing a convincing body of evidence to counter NASA's denials.

They even believe America's Area 51, a closed-off region of the Nevada desert which does not appear on any map and feres in *Independence Day*, contains thmains of a crashed alien craft.

mer Apollo astronaut Dr Brian O'ary claimed: "There's plenty of sctific evidence of contacts with als but NASA has suppressed it."

added: "There have been a lot of untths and misinformation. Anybowith access to the truth has been swi to secrecy.

m convinced crashed alien craft habeen discovered. The evidence is ouhere."

also claims ancient alien contstions have been photographed on the Moon. And he claims a NASA source at the Johnson Space Centre in Houston admitted "airbrushing" UFOs from photos released to the media.

Maurice Chatelain, who designed and ran communications systems on the Apollo missions and died recently, said: "All the flights were followed.

"Astronauts saw things during their missions that could not be discussed with anyone outside of NASA."

HE ADDS: "Every time it occurred, they notified mission control who ordered complete silence.

"Walter Schirra aboard Mercury 8 in the early Sixties used the codename 'Santa Claus' for ETs." Chatelain wrote in a book: "James Lovell on board Apollo 8 came out from behind the Moon and reported back: 'We've been informed Santa Claus exists'."

He also claimed that Gemini 4 pilot James McDivott was the first to take a photograph of a UFO.

Frank Borman and James Lovell, on board Gemini 7, also snapped UFOs following them at distances of just a few hundred yards, it is believed.

"The UFOs looked like huge mushrooms with propulsion systems, and clearly showed a glow on their underside," said Chatelain.

"When Apollo 11 landed on the Moon in 1969, and just before Neil Armstrong set foot on it, two UFOs hovered overhead. Edwin 'Buzz' Aldrin took several pictures of them."

Dr Jack Kashner, professor of physics at Nebraska University, has studied video footage of objects taken by the 1991 space shuttle flight STS 48.

"NASA claimed they were ice crystals," he said. "We proved that was physically impossible.

KASHNER added: "Ice crystals couldn't change direction the way these objects could.

"We managed to eliminate meteors, satellites and space junk.

"There were six to eight UFOs. We calculated that if they were ten miles from the shuttle, the biggest went from zero to 2,500 mph in one second."

Former NASA consultant Richard Hoagland, head of a four-year study of the photographic evidence, said: "NASA has been involved in a cover-up using misinformation and confusion.

"They've destroyed photographs and edited films — we proved they even issued 13 versions of what was supposed to-be the same photo.

"NASA has been funded with billions of US taxpayers' dollars and this information should be in the public domain," he added.

"It's time for President Clinton to bite the bullet, open NASA's files on all of this, and come clean."

●TOMORROW: An alien story that tests your imagination.

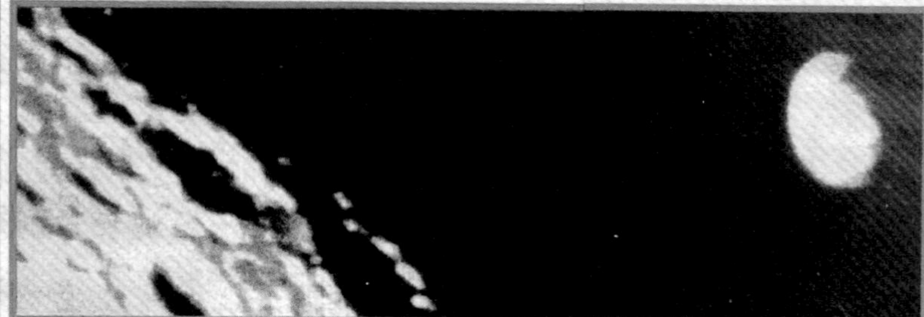

SIGHTING: The vast craft-like object, shown as a close-up in the main pictureove, nears Apollo 12 on its orbit of the Moon

SIGHTING: Three enormous objects hover above the moon, photographed from a long distance by astronauts on the Apollo 13 mission

studied video footage of objects taken by the 1991 space shuttle flight STS 48.

"NASA claimed they were ice crystals," he said. "We proved that was physically impossible."

Kashner added: "Ice crystal couldn't change direction the way these objects could.

"We managed to eliminate meteors, satellites and space junk.

"There were six to eight UFOs. We calculated that if they were ten miles from the shuttle, the biggest went from zero to 2,500 mph in one second."

Former NASA consultant Richard Hoagland, head of a four-year study of the photographic evidence, said: "NASA has been involved in a cover-up using misinformation and confusion.

"They've destroyed photographs and edited films – we proved they even issued 13 versions of what was supposed to be the same photo.

"NASA has been funded with billions of US taxpayers' dollars and this information should be in the public domain," he added.

"It's time for President Clinton to bite the bullet, open NASA's files on all of this, and come clean."

TOP LEFT: A mystery cigar-shaped craft.
TOP CENTRE: An enormous dazzling object, which appeared to fly above the Moon, stunned astronauts on the Apollo 12 mission in 1969.
TOP RIGHT: A glowing disc spotted by Apollo 12.
BOTTOM LEFT: A vast craft-like object nears Apollo 12 on its orbit of the Moon.
BOTTOM RIGHT: Three enormous objects hover above the Moon, photographed from Apollo 13.

23rd August **1996**

DAY 2 OF A SPECIAL INQUIRY

A RESPECTED AMBULANCE CHIEF AND HIS FRIEND REVEAL UNDER HYPNOSIS THEY WERE ABDUCTED BY A SPACESHIP ON A LONELY ROAD

Case 1: The ambulance chief

Dateline: 17th August 1992

Location: A70, nr Edinburgh

It takes only a dark road with a dip in it, or a blind corner, and Gary Wood is gripped by fear.

Nightmares shatter the four hours' sleep he has now learned to live with.

Every day the words echo in his head: "We are already here – and we are still coming."

Yet this is a man who holds down the vital job of keeping Scotland's ambulances on 100 per cent call-out readiness.

In a country pub, his drink untouched, making his story as detailed as possible, 32-year-old Gary shoots embarrassed glances at his listeners.

He shakes his head. "I'm sorry. I know it sounds nuts, but I can only tell it how it happened … I don't want this. I would rather have my life back the way it was."

Gary tells a story of alien abduction on a Scottish road. Of beings who probed his body and mind and left him terrified that one day they will return – for him.

Of all the encounters claimed around the world, Gary's is considered one of the most authentic. For he was not alone on the night of August 17, 1992, when he was plucked from his car.

Friend Colin Wright was with him. Separately, under hypnosis, they have told the same story.

Colin has coped with it better, refusing to talk publicly. Gary talked and suffered ridicule and hostility. It took much persuasion to arrange this rare interview.

Nervous, and watching for the first hint of derision, he begins: "I was just a normal guy. All I wanted was my job, plenty of money, a nice house, a family…"

Today he shrugs as if these things are lost forever.

At about 10pm that August night, Gary set off with Colin on a 40-minute journey to another friend's house outside Edinburgh.

Driving at a safe 45mph, the pair had just passed Harper's Ridge reservoir on the A70 when they approached a blind dip in the road.

Before them, floating about 20ft above the ground, was a black, domed object measuring 30–35ft across. It was a classic flying saucer shape.

A curtain of light bathed the width of the road.

"Suddenly, it was like I was in a black void," says Gary. "There I am, standing up and thinking: 'Where's my car? Where's Colin?' I wondered if I was dead.

"Another 15 seconds went by and I was back in my car on the wrong side of the road, shunting diagonally into the banking."

At their friend's home, the terrified pair told what had happened.

Independently, in separate parts of the house, they drew what they had seen. The drawings were identical.

They also discovered that somehow, they had lost an hour and a half en route.

For Gary, the ordeal was just beginning. He began to suffer severe headaches and flashbacks which left him screaming in bed.

The fear was so crippling he couldn't go out alone, except to work.

Nine months after his encounter, Gary was prepared for hypnosis. Colin also agreed to undergo testing.

The regression was video-taped. Horror is stamped over Gary's face as he relives the meeting.

"I saw three creatures coming towards my car. I felt intense pain, like an electric shock. Then I was in some room.

"I saw these things like wee men moving about, doing something to me. I could only see up. Then this six-foot creature approached.

"It was white-grey in colour with a large head and dark eyes with a long, slender neck, very slim shoulders and waist.

"There were either ribs or folds of skin on its body. The arms were like ours but there were four very long fingers.

"The little ones were about three feet tall and seemed to do all the work while the big ones did the communication.

"I felt that some of them felt sorry for me. One of them looked into my life and I looked into it – it couldn't stop me. It was hiding something.

"One of the big creatures put his face close to mine and I was so frightened I could hardly breathe.

"It never spoke to me, but something came to my head.

"I heard a voice saying: 'I have a life like you but different things happen to us – but it's got to be done.'

"I was crying like a baby – I wanted to get away. I must have asked what it wanted. It said: 'Sanctuary – we are here already and we are coming here.'

"Just to the left of me I saw a girl. She was on the ground, her hands clasping her knees to her chest. She was naked and crying.

"She looked at me, but I couldn't do anything. Tears were coming down her face. She was in her early twenties, with shoulder-length blonde hair. I would recognise her face if I saw it again but it was nobody I'd met before."

In separate sessions, Colin remembered being in a different room. He was naked and sitting in a chair.

If he tried to move, one of the creatures would stop him.

In his head he heard: "Gary's all right, you don't have to get off the chair."

Hanging from the ceiling were cylinder-shaped objects which made him think of containers for people.

After the regression, Gary became obsessed with research and tracking down other people who have had similar experiences.

He now has his own page on the Internet. Along with Edinburgh author John Jenkins, he has recorded the stories of them – debunking many of them.

Every spare hour is devoted to seeking an answer to what

Case 3: The forester
Dateline: Nov, 1979
Location: Scotland

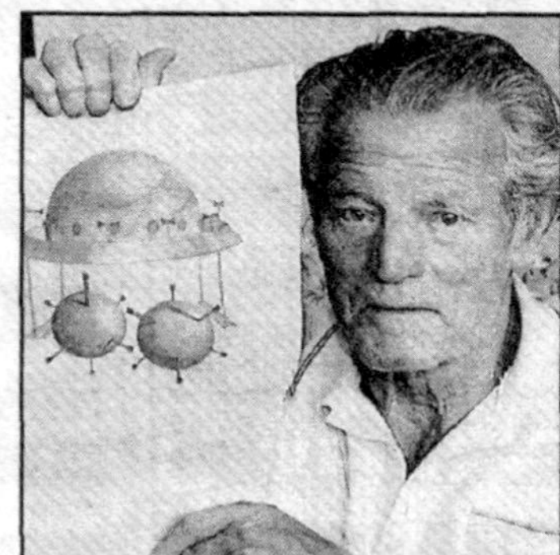

ATTACK: Bob's picture of his assailant

SPIKES WENT FOR MY LEGS

RETIRED forester Bob Taylor will never forget that day in November 1979 when he was attacked by a UFO in a Scottish wood.

Bob, 78, who now lives in Tayside, says: "I was walking through Dechmont woods with my red setter Lara and as I turned this corner there was this 250ft spinning top thing in front of me.

"These sea-mine-type things with spikes on them came out of the back and grabbed my trousers ripping right through to my skin."

Bob passed out.

"When I came to, I heard a sound of something moving very fast away in the distance. I eventually got on my knees and crawled to my truck but it was dead."

Dad-of-five Bob crawled the mile to his home and told his wife he'd been attacked by a UFO.

The police were called to the scene and their report states: "The marks indicated an object of several tons had stood there but no information has been gained to explain them."

But widower Bob says: "I know there is something out there.

TERROR DRIVE: Rose and Val and an impression of the UFO

OUR LOST 30 MINUTES

Case 3: The girlfriends
Dateline: July, 1981
Location: A5, Shropshire

IT WAS 2am and the road was deserted. Suddenly, bright lights appeared to hover in front of Vivien Hayward's car.

She, Rosemary Hawkins and Valerie Walters noted that the huge object ahead was silent.

Foster carer Rosemary, 40, recalls that night 15 years ago: "Our engine lost power. Then the object's lights dimmed and it disappeared. We arrived at a police station at 2.50 – we'd lost half an hour."

Under hypnosis, Rosemary remembered being scanned in a machine. Valerie recalled: "Something grabbed my shoulders and a voice told me not to be afraid.

"I was in a room with no doors and a tall, long-haired man and woman appeared. The female tried on my shoes and fell. I asked what they wanted and was told: 'There will be a time when you'll understand'."

TOP RIGHT: A picture of a spiky assailant.
CENTRE RIGHT: Bright lights appeared to hover in front of the car.

happened to him.

"I know that something is going to happen. I believe they are here and they are coming.

"I want to be ready."

MANY CASES INVOLVE SANE, HONEST PEOPLE

Phillip Mantle, of the British UFO Research Association (BUFORA), has interviewed many of the 80 Britons claiming alien encounters. He says: "There are too many cases involving sane, sober, decent people for it to be discounted.

"The fact that alleged abductees risk ridicule when they talk publicly must deter the cranks."

An MoD spokesman dismissed the threat of aliens arriving here as "negligible". He said: "We don't perceive any threat from extra-terrestrials.

"Around 99.9 per cent of cases are explained by natural phenomena like lighting, weather balloons or aircraft."

Nick Pope spent three years at MoD, investigating and researching the UFO mystery. He says: "I have absolutely no doubt that some of these accounts do happen and that some sort of alien intelligence may be involved.

"Of the MoD UFO sightings, five to ten per cent are unexplained.

"On a number of occasions RAF jets have been scrambled to try and intercept UFOs."

SPIKES WENT FOR MY LEGS

Case 2: The forester

Dateline: November 1979

Location: Scotland

Retired forester Bob Taylor will never forget that day in November 1979 when he was attacked by a UFO in a Scottish wood.

Bob 78, who now lives in Tayside, says: "I was walking through Dechmont woods with my red setter Lara and as I turned this corner there was this 250ft spinning top thing in front of me.

"These sea-mine-type things with spikes on them came out of the back and grabbed my trousers ripping right through to my skin."

Bob passed out.

"When I came to, I heard a sound of something moving very fast away in the distance. I eventually got on my knees and crawled to my truck but it was dead."

Dad-of-five Bob crawled the mile to his home and told his wife he'd been attacked by a UFO.

The police were called to the scene and their report states: "The marks indicated an object of several tons had stood there but no information has been gained to explain them."

But widower Bob says: "I know there is something out there."

OUR LOST 30 MINUTES

Case 3: The girlfriends

Dateline: July 1981

Location: A5, Shropshire

It was 2 am and the road was deserted. Suddenly, bright lights appeared to hover in front of Vivien Hayward's car.

She, Rosemary Hawkins and Valerie Walters noted that the huge object ahead was silent.

Foster carer Rosemary, 40, recalls that night 15 years ago: "Our engine lost power. Then the object's lights dammed and it disappeared. We arrived at a police station at 2.50 – we'd lost half an hour."

Under hypnosis, Rosemary remembered being scanned in a machine. Valerie recalled: "Something grabbed my shoulders and a voice told me not to be afraid. I was in a room with no doors and a tall, long-haired man and woman appeared. The female tried on my shoes and fell. I asked what they wanted and was told: 'There will be a time when you'll understand.'"

Case 4: Phillip Spencer

Dateline: 1st December 1987

Location: Ilkley Moor, Yorkshire

Former policeman Phillip Spencer was walking across Yorkshire's Ilkley Moor just after dawn when he encountered something incredible.

Phillip (not his real name) was carrying a camera to take some snaps of the town when it got lighter.

Hearing a humming sound, he looked up to see a figure he is convinced wasn't human.

He took a photo and followed it to what appeared to be two giant silver saucers stuck together.

The craft shot upwards and into the clouds.

When he got back into town, Phillip realized it was 10 am – he'd "lost" two hours. He had the photos developed – to find the creature had been captured on film. During later hypnotic regression Phillip described entering the craft and being put on a table by creatures with pointed ears.

He said they showed him two films, the first containing scenes of destruction and starvation. He said he was not allowed to discuss the second.

UFO Hunters June 1967. An International Sky Scout or UFOLOGISTS as they prefer – pictured in Enfield London as they try to spot Unidentified Flying Objects in the night sky.

Ghosts – Peeves and Woooooster

The Enfield Poltergeist threw furniture and toys at the Hodgson household in Green Street, Enfield, September 1977.

"Harry witnessed Professor McGonagall walking right past Peeves who was determinedly loosening a crystal chandelier and could have sworn he heard her tell the poltergeist out of the corner of her mouth 'It unscrews the other way.'"
– J K Rowling, *Harry Potter and the Order of the Phoenix*

If you only know the Harry Potter stories from the movies, then you'd be excused for not knowing Peeves, the Hogwarts poltergeist: the part, played by Rik Mayall, was cut. But, in the books, he is very much the typical blithe spirit (Noël Coward's play of the same name features another literary poltergeist). Full of high jinks, their mischief is enough to make you lose your marbles.

2nd November **1931**

"OLD WIVES" FABLES

"The less we have to do with spiritualism the better," said Dean Inge yesterday.

Preaching at All Hallows, Tottenham, he said he was almost ashamed to mention the spiritualistic superstitions now so rife.

"Old wives' fables about ghostly apparitions have been popular always and everywhere, but that is not the kind of immortality that Christianity teaches us, nor that which any sensible person would desire for himself or his friends.

"Even when this superstition masquerades in scientific dress, avoid it."

26th September **1934**

VISION OF DEATH

There is a legend that the house of Beresford was "cursed" in penal days.

A woman, an aged mother, so the story goes, laid her curse upon the house of Beresford and prophesied that no head of the family would die in his bed.

A banshee is accredited to the family. There are many who believe that a white garbed fairy woman, who is the grim foreboder of death to the house, wails by the banks of the Clodiagh River when death threatens the house.

When Lord Charles Beresford, the famous Admiral, was a midshipman on a South American station he went one day into his cabin, and there saw the apparition of his father, the fourth Marquis of Waterford, lying in his coffin.

Lord Charles was out of reach of any communication with home, but carefully noted the time of this appearance.

Some weeks later news came to him of his father's death. At the time when he saw the vision of his father lying in his coffin his father was lying in state at Curraghmore.

Lord Charles never attempted to give any explanation or to propound any theory as to this incident.

"I cannot explain it," he said. "I cannot account for it except on the ground that the relations between my father and myself were those of extraordinary affection. I can only testify to what I have seen."

20th January **1937**

BELIEVES IN THE BANSHEE!

In Irish folklore there are many stories of weird visitations from the mysterious banshee or woman of the fairies.

Most people are inclined to scoff at these tales.

However, I have knowledge of two cases where the banshee actually warned people of the death of their dear ones.

Some years ago a rate collector was murdered on a lonely road. That night his wife heard pitiful lamentations outside her bedroom window.

She knew it was the banshee warning her that her husband was dead.

In the other case a doctor was very ill. At midnight I heard unearthly cries in the shrubbery which separated his house from ours.

Next day the doctor died.

The banshee only follows Irish families of ancient lineage.

– Jean, Co. Dublin

7th October **1947**

HIS PIANO TELLS TIME BUT IT WON'T SAY WHY

The upright piano that stands against the wall in the kitchen of Mr. John Turner, of Salford, Lancs, was bought in a junk shop three months ago for 35s. Ever since, according to Mr. Turner, it has been behaving as if it were a clock instead of a musical instrument.

"For," says Mr. Turner, "it never misses striking the hours and half-hours."

"Punctually on the hour it strikes the time on the G string," declares the mystified owner. "I just can't make it out.

"With the help of my brother, a piano repairer, I have stripped it six times. Still we don't get it.

"Even when double British Summer Time ended the piano didn't let us down. It went back an hour, too."

At the invitation of the *Daily Mirror*, three experts tried to solve the riddle of the striking piano yesterday.

DIDN'T ANSWER

They were Mr. G. T. Elkes, manager of Messrs Crane and Sons, piano manufacturers; Mr. H. V. Barker, ex-major, secretary of the Manchester Psychical Research Institute, and Mr. John Riding, Manchester business man, its president.

A careful check of the time was made on the telephone with Manchester's "Tim".

At three o'clock the three experts heard the piano ping three times. It was twenty seconds before "Tim" time.

In silence one ping was heard at 3.30 p.m.

Mr. Riding said quietly, "If you have a spirit entity, will you strike the note again, please?"

There was no response.

STILL MYSTIFIED

Mr. Elkes stripped the piano, examined the action, tested each individual wire, and looked for any hidden automatic or electrical mechanism.

Still mystified, he put the parts together again.

He said: "I can see no reason why the piano should strike.

"It is an old bi-chord – two wires against the modern three – yet only a single wire sounds. I cannot discover any cause."

Mr. Barker and Mr. Riding gave the view that the phenomenon was not due to any poltergeist activity.

"CONTACT WITH EARTH"

Mr. Barker said: "It is probably a direct spirit manifestation of a being who has 'gone over' with a strong attachment to the piano and not likely to be connected with the Turner family.

"He is using the instrument to make contact with the earth.

"In the house there may be one member of the family with a tendency towards psychical medium.

"Now a scientific medium is to make a test."

30th March **1953**

THE POT-SHOT GHOST

A curious and frequently noted phenomenon in connection with poltergeist [noisy ghost] cases is that of stone-throwing.

Showers of pebbles, dirt, rock and even large-sized stones have been known to fall, both inside and outside the house – and this despite the most constant watch, maintained by a number of observers.

Such odd occurrences have been reported from China, Iceland, Java, South Africa, England, France, Germany, and in fact from every part of the habitable globe …

Still another peculiarity consists in the fact that the objects thrown appear unduly warm, and even hot, to the touch. This has even been noted in extremely cold climates (such as Iceland and Siberia).

THROWN BACK

In many instances stones have been marked and then thrown out of the house on to some open space, or even into a river, in which they were seen to sink.

Within a few minutes, however, these marked stones were again thrown into the house, where they were identified.

13th March **1956**

MYSTERY FIRE AFTER A 'GHOST' TAPS WARNING

A mystery fire at a house said to be haunted was investigated by detectives yesterday.

They talked to fifteen-year-old Shirley Hitchings who said she was warned beforehand about the fire by a poltergeist – a "mischievous spirit" which tapped messages to her on the wall.

Shirley's father, Mr. Walter Hitchings, 47, was burned on both hands when he beat out flames on an eiderdown in a downstairs bedroom at their home in Wycliffe-road, Battersea, London, yesterday morning.

Shirley – who was upstairs at the time – said later: "I smelt burning and from the stair landing I saw a green flash and flames shoot from the bedroom.

"Daddy was in the kitchen. He ran in and put out the flames.

"The poltergeist was tapping out messages all last night and this morning until the fire started."

17th March **1956**

SHIRLEY GOES – SO DOES THAT 'GHOST'

Fifteen-year-old Shirley Hitchings, the girl who has been pursued

by a tapping poltergeist – a mischievous spirit – for two months has left home. And so has the poltergeist.

Her father, Mr. Alfred Hitchings, of Wycliffe-road, Battersea, said last night: "I have sent Shirley away. She is in need of rest. I am keeping secret where she has gone. We are not being troubled with the poltergeist now."

Mabel Chinnery, 48, a housewife from Ipswich, Suffolk, took this photograph of her husband Mr Chinnery, seated in the driver's seat of their motorcar, when they went to visit her late mother's grave on 22nd March 1959. When Mrs Chinnery developed her negatives, she was shocked to find her mother, Mrs Ellen Nammell, sitting in the back seat … in the place she normally sat when the family went out for a drive. The *Sunday Pictorial* has examined the negative of Mrs Chinnery's photograph and is certain it has not been inadvertently tampered with. Photographic expert Bill Turner of Ipswich reports, "I stake my reputation on the fact the picture is genuine."

6th May **1964**

JUST IN CASE YOU'VE NEVER MET A BANSHEE

Sure, if you're after being one who doesn't believe in leprechauns and banshees and such, you won't be needin' *A Short Guide To The Little People*, which is out today.

But if you are going for a holiday in Ireland and would like to look for the Little People, the guide tells you where and how to spot them.

SHOES

Best known of the Little People is the leprechaun – a solitary sort of bloke, according to the guide.

Watch out for a little old man, about 24in. high, brightly clad.

He is generally engaged in making shoes for the Good People – another type of Little People – and apparently makes a good thing out of it.

"Hardly one of them is without a little hidden hoard of golden coins of ancient minting," the guide says.

Jacky-The-Lantern alias Will-o'-the-Wisp, is more spooky – "the shade of a misguided human who sold his soul to the Devil … and was condemned to wander through bogs and marshes for ever holding a burning wisp".

Not very friendly, either, is the Banshee – "a white-clad woman, pale of face, with long flowing hair". She floats gently along above the ground and wails plaintively.

Other Little People whom the tourist is advised to treat with extreme reserve are the Gruagach – "Meanly clad and excessively hairy creatures" found in wells.

Puca – A large black horse, which offers rides to unwary travellers, and then hurls them into bogholes.

Mermen and Mermaids in the coastal waters, and . . .

If by now you are thinking of cancelling your trip to Ireland, it must be said that no tourist has ever been proved to have seen one of the Little People.

The guide book is issued by the Irish tourist office … just in case.

26th May **1964**

BISHOP SEES GHOST HOUSE

A Bishop has been called in to help three families who say a poltergeist is bombarding them with lumps of coal.

The families, who live in flats at Clifton Place, Plymouth, say that the poltergeist has moved furniture, scattered ornaments and hit a two-year-old girl in the eye with a piece of coal.

INCIDENTS

Mr. and Mrs. Brian Goldstone who have three children, Deborah, four, Julie, two, and Barry, 12 months, have been so upset by the poltergeist that they now stay with relations in Plymouth.

Mrs. Joyce Goldstone, who lives in the ground-floor flat, said: "After several incidents we locked the bedroom door.

"During the night we were awakened by a lump of coal hitting the head of the bed. It's uncanny. Nobody could have thrown it."

It was the last straw when Julie was hit in the eye while playing in an empty passage.

They were so upset they called in the Rev. J. G. Byrnell, the Rural Dean of Plymouth.

He called in the Bishop of Plymouth, Dr. W. G. Sanderson.

Said Mrs. Goldstone: "We've been told that the Bishop of Plymouth is asking the Bishop of Exeter to conduct a service of exorcism. We shan't rest until something is done."

Two other families who live in the house are worried.

30th October **1964**

MRS W'S COUNCIL FLAT IS HAUNTED BY A CHEEKY GHOST

Priests have tried twice to exorcise a poltergeist from Mrs. Patricia

Wright's council flat – and failed.

Mrs. Wright, 32, spoke yesterday of the mischievous spirit, which she says arrived a year ago and nearly scared her into moving house.

"The furniture seemed to come to life. Books, the coffee table and ornaments rose in the air and hovered in space.

"At first I thought I was seeing things. But neighbours who dropped in saw it happening, too. So did my husband.

MARBLES

"Now almost daily jars of face cream float across the room, my son's marbles fly through the air like bullets, and plastic flowers rise out of their vases and collapse.

"Milk bottles left in the passage soar into the living room and smash against the walls."

Mrs. Wright, of Westcroft Way, Cricklewood, London, said the spirit used to frighten her, but now she has become quite used to him.

"He seems to be mischievous rather than harmful," she said.

A spokesman at St. Agnes's Catholic Church Cricklewood said:

"Prayers were said and holy water was sprinkled in Mrs. Wright's flat to exorcise the spirit on two separate occasions early last year.

"We advised her and neighbours to pray that peace would be restored to the house."

Now Mrs. Wright has decided to ask a spiritualist circle for help. "Maybe they can contact the spirit and find out what it wants from me," she said.

27th March 1971

BOY 'HAUNTED BY EVIL SPIRIT' TAKEN AWAY FROM HOME

A boy who was said to have started a £70,000 school blaze while he was possessed by an evil spirit was taken from his home by a court yesterday.

The boy, who has gone through an exorcism ceremony to try to get rid of the spirit, was put in the care of the local authority.

He had pleaded not guilty to starting the fire which destroyed a science block at a secondary school in Braintree, Essex, because, he said, he was "possessed" at the time.

At an earlier hearing Mr. Peter Perrins, for the boy, told Braintree juvenile court that to be guilty of the offence he needed to have exercised free will.

The Rev. Christopher Neil-Smith, the vicar of St. Saviour's, Hampstead, who had been called in to perform an exorcism service on the boy, said he gave off evil vibrations after the ceremony.

HURLED

He said the boy had improved after the service.

The court was also told of poltergeist activities at the 13-year-old boy's home, in which heavy furniture was hurled about.

At the resumed hearing yesterday, magistrates studied reports from psychiatrists before deciding to remove the boy from his home.

Two other boys aged 11 and 13, who were said to have helped to start the blaze, were put on probation for three years.

18th December 1971

SCARED OUT OF HER NIGHTDRESS

Ghosts are still haunting houses in Britain, but the wail of the banshee is seldom heard in Ireland nowadays.

Banshees haunt families, not places. Only the oldest families have one. Most really ancient families (and their banshees) have become extinct, according to *Elliott O'Donnell's Ghost Hunters*.

This fascinating new collection is compiled from recently discovered papers of O'Donnell, who died, aged ninety-three, six years ago.

As an Irishman, O'Donnell was particularly interested in banshees, which, apparently, were seen or heard (sometimes both) to warn their families of imminent deaths.

CURSES

Most banshees wailed, groaned, clapped, or screamed blood-curdlingly. O'Donnell once encountered one which chuckled.

But some banshees appeared as lovely girls with long, flowing, red, golden, or black hair. Others looked like hags as they called out curses on those about to die.

O'Donnell claimed to be on familiar terms with his own family's banshee but was disappointingly reticent about it – no doubt to avoid its wrath – preferring to write about other people's banshees.

For instance, he told this story about:

The O'Brien Banshee: The night Anne Lady Fanshawe saw it she shook with fright so much her nightdress fell off.

SIGHS

She was sitting up in a four-poster gazing through parted bed-hangings, at an apparition of a moon-lit red-haired woman peering through her bedroom window.

From time to time it sighed woefully. It vanished with a final heartrending lamentation.

Anne was not an O'Brien, but she and her husband, who slept through it all, were visiting Lady Honora O'Brien, daughter of the 17th-century fifth Earl of Thomond, in the castle of Lemaneagh, thirty miles from Limerick.

Next day, Honora told Anne a cousin had died in the castle during the night. The banshee had cut it fine, arriving only an hour or so before her death.

Sometimes Banshees travelled abroad, if the last scion of an old family emigrated, said Mr. O'Donnell, introducing:

The O'Neill Banshee: A widowed Italian count was staying, sad and alone, in a hotel in North Italy.

Three nights in succession an English visitor called Mrs. Dempsey saw standing beside him on the veranda a tall, slim girl with red-gold hair, bare feet and a filmy green dress.

She had one hand caressingly on his shoulder. Her face was "filled with infinite sorrow and affection".

Mrs. Dempsey tackled the astonished count about his unconventional companion. He said no one had been with him.

However, he remembered his descent from the southern O'Neills and the family tradition of the banshee. But he laughed it off.

Next day, on his way to the railway station, he fell dead.

3rd April **1972**

HAUNTING SECRET OF A HOUSE FULL OF GHOSTS

Thousands of tourists flocked to a village's "haunted house" when it was announced that ghosts actually talked to each other in the building.

Each day 5,000 visitors paid 15p each to go into the house to see strange apparitions stare up from the kitchen floor.

Professional ghost-hunters were baffled … until yesterday, when the haunting was revealed as a gigantic hoax.

The aim: To attract tourists to the picturesque Spanish village of Belmez de la Moraleda.

Parish priest Father Antonio Molina accused the mayor of being implicated in the plot, together with the local police chief.

The priest said that trick projectors produced the "ghosts" faces, and their voices were really tape recordings.

4th February **1978**

FLYING TONIGHT … AT THE CHINESE QUAKEAWAY!

It was enough to make a bamboo shoot. Or send a Chinaman off his noodle. For it wasn't just the prawns that went crackers the night a ghost turned sour in a Chinese takeaway.

Before you could say beansprout, bowls of rice whizzed across the room. Chop suey sailed through the air. And frightened customers dived for cover.

The normally inscrutable staff had to duck as platefuls of food flew around the kitchens.

Finally a police patrol car was called to the Lotus House in Lea Road, Wolverhampton.

UNSOLVED

But last night the great Chinese Who Flung Food mystery was still unsolved.

Takeaway owner K. Lee said simply: "It all very funny business. I not want to talk about it." A police spokesman said: "When we arrived there were several rather frightened people outside and Mr. Lee has told us that there is some sort of poltergeist haunting his premises.

"Our men were told of food and even a torch apparently just floating in the air.

"But I'm afraid investigating poltergeists isn't quite our beat and we've just put it down as an unsolved mystery."

30th March **1978**

GHOST STORY

Scientists from all over the world are now attending a conference on psychic phenomena at Cambridge University – and one subject on the agenda was a haunted council house in North London. The incredible story of one of the most fascinating ghost hunts of modern times is told here, just as it happened. But we have disguised the name of the family involved to save them further stress.

THE STRANGE CASE OF THE DANCING TEAPOT

One hot August evening a chest of drawers took off across the floor of Peggy H's sitting room.

This started an eerie chain of events that have terrified the family,

PAGE 20 DAILY MIRROR, Thursday, March 30, 1978

GHOST STORY

BRYAN RIMMER investigates a mystery that has scientists guessing

SCIENTISTS from all over the world are now attending a conference on psychic phenomena at Cambridge University — and one subject on the agenda was a haunted council house in North London. The incredible story of one of the most fascinating ghost hunts of modern times is told here, just as it happened. But we have disguised the name of the family involved to save them further stress.

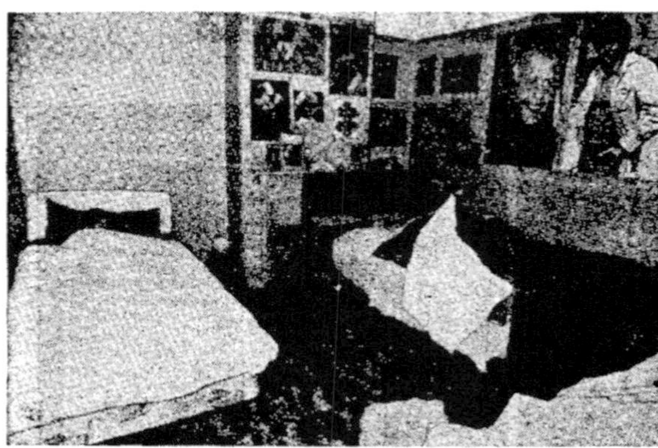

PILLOW FLIGHT THIS pic shows one girl's pillow apparently flying of its own accord while her sister looks on.

PILLOW FLIGHT THE pillow is folding about 1ft off the floor. The girl reacts by raising a hand in alarm.

amazed police and journalists and baffled scientists, doctors and researchers.

For the mystery of the moving chest has been followed by other amazing goings-on in the North London council house – flying objects that seem to be propelled by a supernatural force, a dancing teapot and a spine-chilling voice, apparently from the grave.

Perhaps the voice was the most frightening of all the sinister happenings that have surrounded the family of five.

It started in mid-December … and it was no ghostly shriek heard only by members of the family. It was a rich, deep male voice.

Since then, I have spent hours chatting with it – and so have the baffled boffins.

Usually the voice speaks through Mrs. H's daughters, aged 12 and 13, though often their lips do not move.

It chats to them as they lie in bed at night, wishes each of the family "Good morning" and often asks for dance music to be played.

It also gives itself a variety of names: Andrew Garner, Stewart Certain and Dirty Dick.

The *Daily Mirror* has spent weeks investigating this amazing story and talked to many people who claim to have seen mysterious happenings in the house.

SPENT

Psychic investigator Maurice Grosse has spent more than 1,000 hours watching the story unfold.

Grosse, a level-headed middle-aged businessman has made a signed, typewritten statement to the *Mirror*.

These are the astonishing events he claims to have witnessed:

Marbles and plastic blocks flying across a room – after apparently materialising from walls and windows.

A teapot dancing on a kitchen cabinet top.

The shade on a bed-lamp tilting 45 degrees, then straightening up.

The lavatory door opening and closing when there was no one near it.

A cardboard box full of cushions thrown at him while he was trying to communicate with the entity by knocking.

A slipper thrown at him across a bedroom.

A settee thrown up in the air and overturned when he was standing no more than a foot from it.

Hearing footsteps walking across the ceiling when there was no one upstairs.

Says Grosse: "I have studied psychic phenomena for 40 years and this is the most exciting case I have come across or even read about. And I believe it will be the best documented poltergeist case in history.

"Much of what is going on here is unique and the tests carried out are the most exhaustive in the history of psychic research.

"The family are going through a period of tremendous stress because of what happened."

Grosse remains convinced, despite the fact that in a harrowing scene in the family kitchen one of the girls tearfully confessed to TV ventriloquist Ray Allen that the whole voice episode was a hoax.

Ray, better known as the sidekick of dummy Lord Charles was called in by the *Mirror* to use his special knowledge to find out if the voice was a spoof.

The younger girl admitted to him, in my presence, that she and her sister had invented the voices to keep attention centred on them.

The next day the girl retracted her admission.

But even if her retraction were not valid, it still does not account for the other odd events in the house.

Photographs capture poltergeist activity as a pillow flies through, and hovers in, the air.

SAD

The sisters knew nothing about the moving furniture and flying objects, but Dirty Dick and Andrew Garner were products of their imagination.

Ray Alan said later: "It's very sad, but these little girls obviously loved all the attention they got when objects were mysteriously moved around the house and they decided to keep the whole thing going by inventing the voices.

"But it got too big for them and they didn't know how to stop what they had started."

Many people, however, as well as Grosse, feel certain that the manifestations are genuine.

AND BUMPS THAT BAFFLE BOFFINS

Maurice Grosse was not the first person to witness things going bump in the North London night.

Before he was called in by the Society for Psychical Research, other independent witnesses had been amazed by what they saw. They were:

The policewoman: WPC Carolyn Beeps, one of the first outsiders called to the house, could scarcely believe her eyes as an armchair moved across the living room, apparently of its own accord.

The author: Guy Lyon Playfair has spent countless days and nights observing the case. He has written two books on supernatural activity and spent four years observing ghostly goings on in Brazil.

He says: "This is my fifth poltergeist case and by far the most interesting. I, personally, have witnessed five incidents for which no reasonable normal explanation has yet been suggested. Each was recorded on tape."

On one occasion, as the younger girl got out of a heavy armchair, Playfair saw it slide forward and then overturn backwards. Next, while he was watching the girl, a table overturned in the kitchen.

"One morning I saw a red slipper go over the top of the door of the bedroom opposite mine. I went into the room at once. There was only one place the slipper could be and it wasn't there. Only the elder girl was in the room.

"When we went downstairs, there was the slipper on the doormat. Either it went round a corner on its own, or it went through the wall."

Other incidents included a flying book that turned corners, a short conversation with "the voice" by means of rapping, and recording tapes and cables that mysteriously snapped.

The hypnotist: Ian Fletcher is a surgeon, a hypnotist and a member of the Magic Circle and it was in this role that he made two visits to the "haunted" house.

VISITED

He says: "Happenings in that house are very strongly suggestive of paranormal phenomena.

"I hypnotized the younger girl, and from what she told me and from what other observers have said, I feel there is a poltergeist presence in the house."

The engineer: David Annette, product manager of Pye's business communications closed circuit television, and four other Pye technical experts visited the house with highly sophisticated camera equipment.

They set it up in the main bedroom where the girls were sleeping. But the camera jammed and they found the film had come out of the cassette and got entangled with the drive mechanism – so tightly that it would have taken the force of a sledgehammer to get it there.

David says "There's definitely something odd which I can't explain."

The researcher: David Robertson is assistant to Professor John Hastead, head of physics at London University's Birkbeck College, who is supervising a series of tests on the girls.

He has heard knockings from empty rooms – one that he locked himself.

He says: "Once I saw a sideboard lift up at an angle and fall face down on the floor. Many strange things are unexplained."

The physicist: Dr. Bernard Carr, Fellow of Trinity College, Cambridge, said that many odd things happened while he was there, but he did not see anything that was obviously paranormal.

The girls were being thrown out of bed and there were terrified cries from them – but always after he had left the room.

The magician: Milbourne Christopher is one of the world's most skilled magicians. He is also chairman of the Occult Investigation Committee of the Society of American Magicians.

He believes the only spirits responsible for the events are high spirits of the girls.

Loch Ness Monster – How to Catch a Star

The vast waters of Loch Ness could easily conceal a sizeable monster.

The most promising method for detecting the Loch Ness Monster has proved to be sonar (SOund Navigation And Ranging): emitting pulses of sound and listening for their echoes as they bounce off objects, or simply listening for the sounds made by other targets. Many commercial fishing vessels now employ sonar to find their catches, and several of the Loch Ness tour boats are also fitted with the equipment. Attempts to find Nessie using the technology have been going on since the 1950s, with several positive sightings. The most ambitious expedition was called Operation DeepScan, which was mounted in 1987 by Adrian Shine, leader of the Loch Ness and Morar Project. It involved sweeping the entire length of the loch with a flotilla of boats. Three distinct contacts of large moving objects were recorded at 78, 171 and 178 metres.

Model of the Loch Ness Monster in the American film *The Loch Ness Horror*.

14th December **1981**

MONSTROUS!

OCH, HOLLYWOOD'S TURNING OUR NICE NESSIE INTO A KILLER

Something monstrous has happened to Nessie, the lovable Loch Ness monster.

Movie chiefs in Hollywood have made her the star of a horror film.

They see Nessie as a smoke-snorting killer, who climbs out of Loch Ness to attack people.

Of course, things are not quite what they seem.

Beneath her foam skin, thirty-foot Nessie is a complicated machine made up of stainless steel tubes and the sort of hydraulics used to move the wing flaps and undercarriage in aeroplanes.

Nessie stars, naturally, in *The Loch Ness Horror*, a film made by producer Larry Buchanan, one of the masters of Hollywood blood and gore.

LOVE

Larry, who was responsible for classics such as *Goodbye Norma Jean*, *Pretty Boy Floyd* and *It's Alive*, researched around the shores of Loch Ness for six months before writing the script.

He said: "We loved it there. People were doing crazy things. We interviewed one character who plays Beethoven on the loch shores because he reckons Nessie will fall in love with the music.

"Another guy goes out every day with his fishing line trying to hook the monster. He throws any fish he catches back."

Hollywood special effects artists Pete Chesney and Tom Valentine created Larry's monster.

They are proud of their toy's movement and expressions. The head has eleven movements. She wrinkles her nose, rolls her eyes and sprays smoke from her nostrils.

Tom said: "We had only one problem. When we put her together she had a terrible squint, a sort of monstrous Marty Feldman.

"We had to cut open the back of her head and do a quick job with a welding torch to realign her eyes."

Filming *The Loch Ness Horror* was done secretly at Lake Tahoe, a holiday resort in the mountains on the California–Nevada border.

SECRET

Larry said: "We kept it secret because we didn't want people watching and finding out the ending."

In the film, Nessie gets mixed up with a young scientist, a sunken World War Two German bomber the British Government wants to keep hidden, and a group of American campers.

Larry said: "They think Nessie is a big joke until the heads start to roll."

Then, of course, she's a riot.

▲ Filming *The Loch Ness Horror*.

27th April **1983**

CRUMBS! NESSIE BAIT

Ten tons of breadcrumbs may be scattered on Loch Ness in the hope of tempting the monster to the surface. The crumbs, worth about £3,000, are being offered free by a German industrialist. Nessie hunters want sixty volunteers to help to sprinkle the bait this summer.

▲ The Loch Ness Project boat in 1983.

9th August **1983**

NESSIE! SEXY MONSTERS ARE BACK FROM HOLIDAYS

Loch Ness is the breeding ground for the world's sea monsters, says an American researcher.

Wildlife photographer Erik Beckjord, who claims he has photographed Nessie twice in the last week, says monsters are returning to the lock after a "holiday" in the world's ocean.

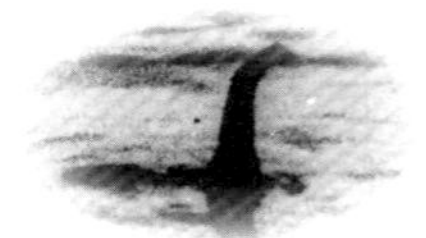

But to get there they have to swim five miles along the River Ness through the centre of Inverness and pass close to ships berthed in the town's harbour.

Local swimmers have now been persuaded to make the journey to prove his migration theory.

Mr Beckjord says he thinks a video tape recording shows Nessie swimming in the loch on Thursday evening and Saturday lunchtime. "I cannot say it is definitely the monster but it is very interesting."

28th June 1986

➧ Early morning sighting of Nessie turns out to be a Greenpeace publicity stunt.

NESSIE'S BACK AGAIN – OR IS SHE?

OCH AYE, PULL THE OTHER ONE!

Here she is again, folks. Or so a Scotsman would have you believe.

The old girl popped up from her dark still waters to have a canny look-around. By chance canny Alan Greig, 33, popped out of his tent at the same time – 4.15 in the morning – camera ready and film loaded.

And his snap looks convincing … blurred, out of focus with a ghostly mist skimming the water's edge. Alan, who is on a camping holiday, said yesterday: "I got up to see the sun rise. Suddenly Nessie appeared about 150 yards offshore. I couldn't believe it – I was shaking like a leaf."

But wait a minute. Nessie doesn't exist, does she? "Oh, yes she does," says Alan. "I took three shots before she simply slid under the surface. They may be a bit blurred because I was so excited."

But it wasn't Nessie, Alan. It was a phoney. Environment group Greenpeace came clean last night and admitted that they had put a Nessie model in Loch Ness as a publicity stunt to warn of acid rain.

NESSIE'S BACK AGAIN—OR IS SHE?

Och aye, pull the other one!

★ *HERE* she is again, folks. Or so a Scotsman would have you believe. The black silhouette in the middle of this fuzzy snapshot is no less than the ever-elusive Nessie.

★ The old girl popped up from her dark still waters to have a canny look-around. By chance canny Alan Greig, 33, popped out of his tent at the same time — 4.15 in the morning — camera ready and film loaded.

★ And his snap looks convincing … blurred, out of focus with a ghostly mist skimming the water's edge. Alan, who is on a camping holiday, said yesterday: "I got up to see the sun rise. Suddenly Nessie appeared about 150 yards off-shore. I couldn't believe it — I was shaking like a leaf."

★ But wait a minute. Nessie doesn't exist, does she? "Oh, yes she does," says Alan. "I took three shots before she simply slid under the surface. They may be a bit blurred because I was so excited."

★ But it *wasn't* Nessie, Alan. It was a phoney. Environment group Greenpeace came clean last night and admitted that they had put a Nessie model in Loch Ness as a publicity stunt to warn of acid rain.

24th August 1987

FISHING CHIPS HUNT FOR NESSIE

The chips are down for Nessie – a fleet of floating computers is on her tail.

They are aboard an armada of boats which will go "fishing" for Nessie in October.

The 20 motor cruisers, loaded with computers and sonar equipment, will sail side by side along the 23-mile Loch Ness, recording every fish and beastie that moves and everything else that doesn't.

CURTAIN

A back-up flotilla will scan the 700ft depths with cameras.

Adrian Shine, leader of the three-day Anglo-American operation, said: "It will be the largest scientific expedition ever undertaken on the loch."

One of the team said: "This is a curtain through which nothing can escape."

DAILY MIRROR, *Monday, March 14, 1994* PAGE 7

Loch Ness Fraudster

KEY TO THE LOCH: The surgeon's famous photo is an elaborate hoax

The world's best loved monster is just a toy sub and plasticine

THAT strangely curved neck, rearing above a grainy pattern of ripples on a cold Scottish loch, was the image that launched a legend and a thousand souvenir shops.

It sent the rich and famous scurrying North in search of the elusive monster said to dwell there.

It has taken 60 years to reveal what experts and computer enhancement signally failed to do — that the Loch Ness Monster in one of the most famous pictures of the 20th Century was a fake.

The "creature" was really a toy submarine bought for a few pence in a London shop, topped off with a serpent-like head made out of Plastic Wood and weighted with a lump of lead.

That is the rather disappointing truth about the "Surgeon's Photograph" taken by respected gynaecologist Colonel Robert Wilson on April 19 1934.

It seems the Colonel was just a frontman for an actor and adventurer — Marmaduke "Duke" Arundel Wetherell — who decided the public should "have their monster".

Footprints

Wetherell didn't waste any time when he was hired to track down the beast in 1933. Within 48 hours after arriving on a lochside beach by motor boat, he claimed to have found huge footprints in the mud — but experts at the Natural History Museum in London poured scorn on his "discovery".

Furious, Wetherell returned home to Twickenham and plotted to get his own back. He succeeded beyond his wildest imaginings, and made Loch Ness a magnet for monster-hunters for six decades.

His son Ian, then 21, was sent out to buy a model submarine and Plastic Wood. Stepson Christopher Spurling sat down and spent eight days making the model. After trials in a pond, they took their creation North and the famous picture was taken.

The stunt quickly got out of hand as news of the "find" spread. The photograph excited monster-fever all over the world, and wild theories spread as to the creature's identity. It was 60 years before the truth came out. Before his death last November at the age of 90, Wetherell's stepson Christopher revealed the secret to two researchers.

His confession will do little to dampen interest in the monster. In fact, it may intensify it. This spring, the hunt for Nessie will be on yet again — with boats and a privately-owned submarine searching the loch's murky depths for the famous "beastie".

The legend has been demolished — but still, it seems, people *want* to believe in Nessie.

SCORN CIRCLES: "Alien visitors" were local pranksters

'The stunt quickly got out of hand and the world went wild'

Patterns

Adrian Shine, director of the Loch Ness Project, said last night: "I don't think it will affect the tourist trade. People will still want to see if they can spot something."

The "Surgeon's Photograph" isn't the only hoax to have fooled a world that seems desperate to believe.

● CORN circle fever spread in the mid-1980s after mysterious patterns appeared in fields throughout the South of England. It was claimed they had been made by alien spacecraft. The circles were apparently a message to the Earth from beyond the stars. But then two men came forward to show how they created them, using a plank and pieces of string.

● "FROZEN Fritz" was thought to be a man more than 5,000 years old when his body was found under a glacier on the Italian-Austrian border three years ago.

As scientists around the world seethed with excitement, a TV company pointed out that the man was found with a bronze axe. Yet he was supposed to have died before the Bronze Age.

● A SPANISH history student was awarded £55,000 by delighted tourist officials after he discovered "Stone Age" cave paintings while potholing in 1992.

By the time experts discovered the paintings had been done only two years earlier, the hoaxer had vanished.

● IN the 1920s, Sir Arthur Conan Doyle, creator of Sherlock Holmes, failed to sleuth out the truth about "The Cottingley Fairies".

A photograph showing two little girls posing with pixies and fairies convinced him and a lot of other people that fairies really exist.

It wasn't until the Eighties that one of the women pictured, Frances Griffiths, confessed in her old age that the girls had faked the scene by cutting out pictures of fairies from storybooks.

Maybe it's true after all that the camera never lies but it sometimes gets a helping hand.

STEPHEN WHITE

Opt-out heads blast Patten

By RICHARD GARNER
Education Correspondent

HEADTEACHERS of the Tories' flagship opt-out schools have delivered an astonishing snub to the Government: You're not fit to run education.

The scope of their dismay at the way state schools are being manhandled emerged in private talks with Labour Education spokeswoman Ann Taylor.

"Their views show they are waking up to reality," says Mrs Taylor.

"If the Tories are returned to power in another election, it really will be central control of education with two capital C's." Heads of the country's 1,000 opt-out institutions admit in a paper to Mrs Taylor that they "clearly recognise the concerns" voiced by Labour over the running of state schools.

They feel that Education Secretary John Patten, has "too much power in his hands".

Other fears include the setting-up of a quango to run their schools which has ten Tory party sympathisers on its 12-strong committee.

The heads firmly reject the idea of a single organisation running all state schools "whether local education authority, school board or (most of all) Government department".

They also stress the "importance of all state schools being treated equally in cash handouts" – a reference to crude Tory attempts to "bribe" opt-out schools by giving them more cash for equipment while threatening the reverse for council-run counterparts who hold out.

Their views are a major embarrassment for Mr Patten who is considering compelling all secondary schools to opt out. His unease will be increased by the opt-out schools' expression of "warm approval" for Labour's education Green Paper.

The party wants to scrap many reforms set in motion by the Tories, including publishing national exam league tables of GCSE and 'A' level results.

● THE gravy train could be over for opt-out schools, reveal figures out today. They asked the Government for £448 million to repair crumbling buildings this year – but ended up with a measly £34 million.

8th October 1987

SMILE, NESSIE

A fleet of boats carrying sophisticated TV and sound equipment will set out tomorrow on the most intensive search yet for the Loch Ness monster. The three-day hunt will cost £1 million and expedition leaders are confident that the monster will be found at last. But canny Highland bookies are laying 100–1 that the camera won't catch Nessie within the next year.

23rd June 1992

NESSIE SEARCH

A new high-tech search is being launched for the Loch Ness Monster.

A Government-backed team of scientists using military equipment will sweep every cubic foot during next month's hunt.

28th December 1992

NESSIE JET-SET

Virgin Airways chief Branson plans flying-boat trips for Loch Ness monster hunters. An aide said: "We will have to do a fly-past to see if Nessie is in the way before we land."

5th March 1993

KEY TO LOCH

Actor Nicolas Cage wants to lead an expedition to prove the Loch Ness Monster exists. The Hollywood star is fascinated by the legendary Nessie.

And thanks to the success of his latest film *Honeymoon in Vegas* which grossed £200,000-plus during its first few days in the U.K and topped the U.S box office, he can afford to mount a dive to search the mysterious loch. Last time he was there he was a struggling actor armed only with binoculars.

14th March 1994

◆ The surgeon's famous photograph is an elaborate hoax.

LOCH NESS FRAUDSTER

THE WORLD'S BEST LOVED MONSTER IS JUST A TOY SUB AND PLASTICINE

That strangely curved neck, rearing above a grainy pattern of ripples on a cold Scottish loch, was the image that launched a legend and a thousand souvenir shops.

It sent the rich and famous scurrying North in search of the elusive monster said to dwell there.

It has taken 60 years to reveal what experts and computer enhancement signally failed to do – that the Loch Ness Monster in one of the most famous pictures of the 20th century was a fake.

The "creature" was really a toy submarine bought for a few pence in a London shop topped off with a serpentlike head made out of plastic wood and weighted with a lump of lead.

That is the rather disappointing truth about the "Surgeon's Photograph" taken by respected gynaecologist Colonel Robert Wilson on April 19 1934.

It seems the Colonel was just a frontman for an actor and adventurer – Marmaduke "Duke" Arundel Wetherell – who decided the public should "have their monster".

FOOTPRINTS

Wetherell didn't waste any time when he was hired to track down the beast in 1933. Within 48 hours after arriving on a lochside beach by motor boat, he claimed to have found huge footprints in the mud – but experts at the Natural History Museum in London poured scorn on his "discovery".

Furious Wetherell returned home to Twickenham and plotted to get his own back. He succeeded beyond his wildest imaginings, and made Loch Ness a magnet for monster-hunters for six decades.

His son Ian, then 21, was sent out to buy a model submarine and plastic wood. Stepson Christopher Spurling sat down and spent eight days making the model. After trials in a pond, they took their creation North and the famous picture was taken.

The stunt quickly got out of hand as news of the "find" spread. The photograph excited monster-fever all over the world, and wild theories spread as to the creature's identity. It was 60 years before the truth came out. Before his death last November at the age of 90, Wetherell's stepson Christopher revealed the secret to two researchers.

His confession will do little to dampen interest in the monster. In fact, it may intensify it. This spring, the hunt for Nessie will be on yet again – with boats and a privately owned submarine searching the loch's murky depths for the famous "beastie".

The legend has been demolished – but still, it seems, people want to believe in Nessie.

PATTERNS

Adrian Shine, director of the Loch Ness Project, said last night: "I don't think it will affect the tourist trade. People will still want to see if they can spot something."

The "Surgeon's Photograph" isn't the only hoax to have fooled a world that seems desperate to believe.

Corn circle fever spread in the mid-1980s after mysterious patterns appeared in fields throughout the South of England. It was claimed they had been made by alien spacecraft. The circles were apparently a message to the Earth from beyond the stars. But then two men came forward to show how they created them using a plank and pieces of string.

Frozen Fritz was thought to be a man more than 5,000 years old when his body was found under a glacier on the Italian–Austrian border three years ago.

As scientists around the world seethed with excitement, a TV company pointed out that the man was found with a bronze axe. Yet he was supposed to have died before the Bronze Age.

A Spanish history student was awarded £55,000 by delighted tourist officials after he discovered "Stone Age" cave paintings while potholing in 1992.

By the time experts discovered the paintings had been done only two years earlier, the hoaxer had vanished.

In the 1920s Sir Arthur Conan Doyle, creator of Sherlock Holmes, failed to sleuth out the truth about "The Cottingley Fairies".

A photograph showing two little girls posing with pixies and fairies convinced him and a lot of other people that fairies really exist.

It wasn't until the Eighties that one of the women pictured, Frances Griffiths, confessed in her old age that the girls had faked the scene by cutting out the pictures of fairies from storybooks.

Maybe it's true that the camera never lies but it sometimes gets a helping hand.

17th August 2005

MOCK NESS MONSTER

It certainly looks real … and a massive model of the Loch Ness monster had around 600 people thinking it was.

Nessie fans were stunned – and no doubt thrilled – when they spotted the 16ft dummy, which has a moving head and jaws, gliding through the water.

But the beast was part of a TV stunt by Five who were filming a show for Sunday called *Loch Ness Monster: The Ultimate Experiment* – to find out if people still believe it exists. Five said the response proved they do.

A source added: "People still want to believe in the myth."

DAILY MIRROR, Wednesday, August 17, 2005

Mock Ness Monster

By LOUISE HOSIE

IT certainly looks real...and this massive model of the Loch Ness monster had around 600 people thinking it was.

Nessie fans were stunned – and no doubt thrilled – when they spotted the 16ft dummy, which has a moving head and jaws, gliding through the water.

But the beast was part of a TV stunt by Five who were filming a show for Sunday called Loch Ness Monster: The Ultimate Experiment – to find out if people still believe it exists. Five said the response proved they do.

A source added: "People still want to believe in the myth." Anyone bumping into this convincing-looking creature is unlikely to hang around to find out if it's real or not.

SCARY: 'Monster' in water

HIT AND MYTH: Divers help model Nessie into the loch

Anyone bumping into this convincing-looking creature is unlikely to hang around to find out if it's real or not.

16th January 2006

THATCH: DOLPHINS COULD HUNT NESSIE

HI-TECH SEARCH PLAN UNCOVERED

A Nessie hunt using a team of dolphins was planned by the Tory government, according to declassified secret documents.

Within days of the 1979 election, officials in Margaret Thatcher's regime proposed importing the mammals from America and fitting them with hi-tech equipment to scour Loch Ness.

Despite opposition from animal rights groups, it was argued that finding the monster would benefit local tourism.

A letter from Environment Department civil servant David Waymouth to Stewart Walker at the Scottish Home and Health Department, showed the Government wanted a licence to initiate the plan.

It stated: "This department is presently considering the issue of a licence to import two bottle-nosed dolphins from America for the purpose of exploring Loch Ness.

"Inquiries have been made with the mammal experts on the Scientific Authority for Animals and their advice is that there are no conservation or welfare reasons for refusing a licence.

"Clearly, however, there are other factors, mainly political, that you might wish to consider before the licence is issued."

The National Archive of Scotland contains no record of a response to the letter, which was released under the Freedom of Information Act.

However, Adrian Shine, a naturalist who has been investigating the Loch Ness mystery for several decades, said he believed the dolphin plan was the brainchild of veteran monster hunter Dr Robert Rines.

Dr Rines was the founder of the American-based Academy of Applied Science who took a now-famous underwater photograph in 1972, which appeared to show a large flipper in the loch.

The Academy of Applied Science in New Hampshire confirmed that dolphins were being trained with mini cameras and strobe lights that could have been activated if they encountered any large objects.

Last week, it was revealed that civil servants made plans to give Nessie legal protection from poachers and bounty hunters in the early 80s.

The plan was instigated when the Swedish government asked for help to preserve their equivalent, the Storsjo monster.

UK officials then realized there was nothing to stop a trophy hunter from tracking down the beast and killing her.

It was eventually decided that Nessie should be protected as part of the Wildlife and Countryside Act 1981, rather than specific legislation.

Under the provisions of the Act it is illegal to snare, shoot or blow up the monster.

20th January 2006

I SPY WITH MY LITTLE EYE A TWO-FACED MP

Always thought she was round the twist, and news that Maggie Thatcher wanted to get dolphins to track down the Loch Ness monster confirms my suspicions.

Didn't any of her ministers have the guts to tell her Nessie is a Highland invention?

I suppose not. Which reminds me of the time she took her cabinet out to a restaurant for dinner. "And what will madam have?" asked the waiter. "A steak, with blood dripping from it," she snarled. "And the vegetables?" he grovelled. "Oh, they'll all have steak as well."

29th November 2006

BIG HIT: MONSTER NESSIE VOTED AS TOP SCOT

The Loch Ness Monster is the most famous Scot, a survey said yesterday.

Nessie won almost a third of votes to beat poet Robert Burns and Sean Connery into second and third places.

Robert the Bruce, victor at Bannockburn, and Sir William Wallace, who trounced the army of Edward I at Stirling, came fourth and fifth. Robbie Coltrane was sixth, Billy Connolly seventh, Lorraine Kelly eighth, Ewan McGregor ninth and Lulu tenth.

More than 2,000 adults across the UK were questioned in a survey for Crabbies Green Ginger Wine. Caroline Glenn, of the Robert Burns National Heritage Park in Alloway, Ayrshire, said: "Burns will always be No 1 in our eyes."

21st April 2012

GREEN MONSTER

Sonar image of 70ft 'serpent' that may be Nessie lurking in depths of loch …

An image of a giant "serpent-like creature" is being hailed as the best possible sighting of the Loch Ness Monster for decades.

The sonar picture appears to show a beast up to 70ft long prowling the murky depths.

It was taken by Loch Ness tour boat skipper Marcus Atkinson, whose sonar fish-finder recorded the shape 23 metres down.

Marcus, 43, said: "I was in shock. It looked like a big serpent. It's the clearest picture I've seen in 21 years here."

Excited Nessie experts say it is too big to be a fish, seal or debris and it has won the Best Nessie Sighting of The Year Award from bookies William Hill.

Others say it may just be algae in the Scottish Highlands loch.

Open for business, the official Loch Ness Monster Exhibition Centre, 24th January 1996.

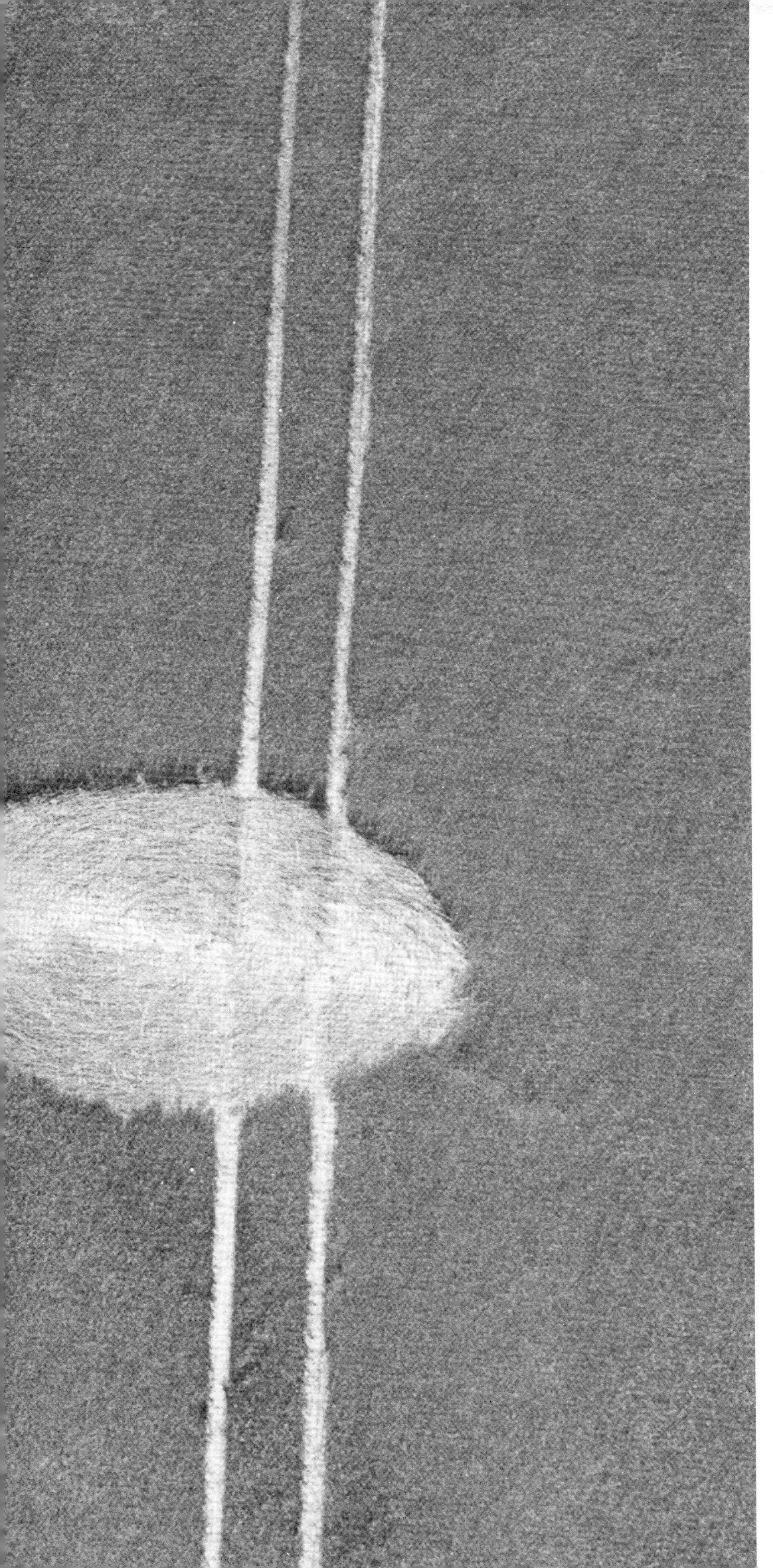

UFOs – The Circle of Life

Serial visitors, or corny joke?

Even if life is not obviously teeming throughout our universe, it has been suggested that microorganisms could have arrived here on Earth from outer space. Complex life then developed from these simple precursors into the diversity of nature that exists today. Consequently, the Astronomer Royal suggests, "life has abundant time to spread through the galaxy and beyond. Even if intelligent life is now unique to Earth, it could nonetheless become a significant feature of the cosmos … I believe we are part of some marvellous evolutionary process which still has a long way to go beyond the human stage, here on earth and far beyond … Extra-terrestrial life will use genetic engineering to quickly modify themselves into new post-human species better adapted to an alien habitat."

4th November **2000**

IN DOCK OVER CROP CIRCLES

A man became the first person in Britain yesterday to be charged in connection with creating crop circles.

Matthew Williams, 29, was arrested after a crop pattern appeared in farmer's cornfield at West Overton, Wilts, in July.

He was charged with one count of criminal damage and will appear before magistrates on Monday.

Crop circles have been blamed on freak weather, hoaxers and even aliens.

7th November **2000**

CROP CIRCLE FINE

A man who created a "crop circle" was fined £100 yesterday in the first such prosecution.

Matthew Williams, 29, made the seven-pointed star in a field at West Overton, Wilts, after an expert said it was impossible for a human to do it.

Then he emailed pictures to Professor Michael Glickman, who called the police. Williams said after the case: "Most crop circles are man-made."

13th September **2001**

THE FACE FROM SPACE?

A face is causing a sensation around the world. It appears to have been transmitted from outer space, but who is it meant to be? Elvis? Jesus? Your average ET? And is it male or female? Black or white? Good or evil? Everyone I ask gives a different answer.

The only certainty about the face is that it appeared overnight on August 19 in a Hampshire wheat field. Not just any field, but right beside the Chilbolton radio telescope. That is where they look deep into space for evidence of alien life. While they looked, alien life came up behind them and left its mark on their back yard. So there is a sense of humour beyond Earth.

With the Face came a message, also imprinted on the wheat field. It was a reply to the data about ourselves and our planet which we sent into space in 1974. It gives the corresponding data about another part of the universe. Astronomers are now trying to decode it.

This is the most exciting thing that has happened in my lifetime. Earlier this year I promised to keep readers in touch with crop-circle events. No one expected much because of foot and mouth closing access to the countryside. But it turned out to be a spectacular summer. A huge crop formation, 1,000 feet wide and made up of 409 separate circles, appeared in Wiltshire, and there were other beautiful designs. Then came the Face and the Message.

Perhaps it really is communication from space, but I am suspicious. It is all too neat, too carefully set up. There is humour in it, all right. But it is the sort of humour I know well, because it is human. I think there is human intelligence behind crop circles. Some are made by hoaxers, stamping out patterns. The masterpieces are generated on a computer screen and then beamed on to a field.

That is impossible, I know it is, but perhaps some genius has discovered how to do it, and is treating us to a show of miracles.

THE CROP-CIRCLE SAGA

Crop circles have been in the news for about 20 years. At first they were simple circles of laid-down crops. Then more complicated designs appeared. In 1991 a pair of elderly tricksters, "Doug and Dave", claimed they had been making the circles. The media lost interest in the subject, but the phenomenon went on. It has continued each year to produce ever more wonderful patterns. Who, or what, is behind it all? You can believe what you like, because no one really knows.

28th December **2002**

"We made all life on earth, you mistook us for gods, we were at the origin of your religions. Now that you are mature enough, we'd like to set up an embassy" – what 'alien' told cult leader Rael.

The Raelian Movement is a religious sect set up by Rael – French former racing driver and journalist Claude Vorilhon – who believes mankind was created by aliens.

He claims he was contacted by an extraterrestrial called Elohim in 1973. A flying saucer appeared from the crater of a volcano and took him to another planet where he was told he was a clone of the supreme extraterrestrial being and prophets including Jesus and Mohammed. Elohim was about 4ft. tall, with long black hair, almond shaped eyes, olive skin and he exuded harmony and humour.

He told Vorilhon, whom he renamed Rael, that the aliens "were the ones who made all life on Earth, you mistook us for gods, we were at the origin of your main religions.

"Now you are mature enough to understand this, we would like to enter official contact through an embassy." Back on earth Rael – The Messenger – started teaching and founded the Raelian Movement, now the most widespread UFO cult in the world.

Rael, who is in his 50s, lives in Quebec, Canada, but the group's HQ is in Geneva, Switzerland.

His followers, who once built an alien theme park in Quebec, believe all humans have the right to reproduce any way they can so that man can survive.

They believe in free love and allow children to divorce their parents and choose new guardians if they are abusive. But their beliefs have led to allegations of paedophilia and incest in the sect.

Rael believes that the aliens will return to Earth in 2025 and he has been instructed to set up an embassy to welcome them.

They will give humans the chance to live on other unknown planets and mate with extraterrestrials.

Raelians are initiated into the cult in a public baptism called "transmitting the cellular plan".

Each year members, who are asked to give 10 per cent of their income, hold a rally at a nudist camp in the south of France.

The group, which is said to have 55,000 members in 84 countries, and is especially strong in Japan, set up Clonaid five years ago and believes cloning will ensure eternal life.

15th July 2003

Are all crop circles hoaxes?

CROP CIRCLES WERE ALL THE RAGE A FEW YEARS AGO

Then it turned out that some had been made by a pair of pranksters.

Yet just because it is possible to fake a crop circle, must we assume that all crop circles are hoaxes?

One appeared last week in the West Country.

It could have been made by a team of meticulous artists working long hours in the darkness but I, frankly, find that harder to believe than the idea that it was caused by a UFO!

What do you think?

DAILY MIRROR, Tuesday, July 15, 2003 PAGE 37

Visit Jonathan at: www.cainer.com

Jonathan CAINER

CROP circles were all the rage a few years ago.

Then it turned out that some had been made by a pair of pranksters.

Yet just because it is *possible* to fake a crop circle, must we assume that *all* crop circles are hoaxes?

These pictures were taken last week in the West Country.

It *could* have been made by a team of meticulous artists working long hours in the darkness but I, frankly, find that harder to believe than the idea that it was caused by a UFO!

What do you think?

14th August 2003

LIKE SPACESHIPS PASSING IN THE NIGHT

TODAY'S LETTER, I THINK, SPEAKS FOR ITSELF …

Dear John,

I have hardly talked about this before (people tend to look at you as if they see water burning), but I have seen something UFO-like twice in my life.

The first time, it didn't seem to notice or frighten me or my friend. We simply concluded, "Oh look, a UFO", as if that is something you see flying around every day. Yet it felt very special.

The second time was more peculiar. We were bringing my boat home and had suffered some serious technical problems. It was the middle of the night and we were in the middle of nowhere, tired and very anxious to reach a safe harbour.

I started to think, "If the engine fails now, or the boat sinks we will be lost. If there is something out there please help us, I can't keep on like this."

I was keeping my mouth shut because the tension was quite enough without expressing my fears when whatever it was suddenly came floating from behind some dark treetops ashore on our right.

A bright light dimmed every time I looked at it, only to brighten again when I turned my gaze away.

It kept changing speed and hiding behind trees but it never changed its altitude. At first I thought it was my fatigue playing tricks on me, but after a while I informed my friend.

I thought he would see nothing, proving that the whole thing was just my imagination. But he saw exactly what I saw. He froze and felt goose-bumps, too.

The light stayed close to us until we finally reached a harbour.

In the morning, we woke up to find ourselves next to a big cargo boat which was willing to tow us home.

Without that tow, we might never have reached home safely.

Best regards,

Hanneke van Dongen

21st August 2003

OUT OF THIS WORLD

Last week's letter, about a reader's UFO experiences, brought a big response. I am not surprised. The UFO phenomenon is perhaps the most important happening of our times.

Millions of people have seen these mystery objects. But no one knows what they are or where they are from.

The one thing I know for sure is that UFOs have an effect on minds. Some people have been inspired and gained benefit from a UFO experience.

Others have been confused. It may be that Carl Jung was right. He said in 1959 that the purpose of UFOs is to change our old ways of thinking, to make us more attuned to the spirit of the Aquarian Age. That is a good way of seeing things, but does it fit the phenomenon? Here are two personal accounts from readers:

Kathie Marshall, from Wiltshire, writes:

"It was around September 20, 1982, about 9 pm on a clear, starlit night at Wilcot Road, Pewsey, Wilts, where we lived. Me, my then husband and our five-year-old daughter were walking home from the annual fair.

"Suddenly in front of us, skimming rooftops, was a flying saucer. It was very large, rotating and silent. It was the standard saucer shape, but around its perimeter were beautiful lights in shimmering, rainbow colours. Truly beautiful and amazing.

"We must have watched this UFO for about a minute until it disappeared over the roof of our house. I phoned the RAF at Upavon and asked if there was anything at that time that could fly without sound. They said no."

Maria, in Huddersfield, has seen two UFOs. The first was like Kathie's, very big with coloured lights around it. Maria writes:

"I saw my second flying saucer when I was picking my daughter up from babysitting. It was after midnight. We were just approaching our house when we saw something in the sky.

"The clouds looked to be parting to allow its entry. This time its shape was more cigar-looking, and again it was very large. I stopped the car to get a better look. My daughter, who was 16, was near hysterical, telling me to drive home.

"But I was transfixed. We remained looking at it for a while longer, but then I felt that for my daughter's sake I should take her home. I haven't seen anything since that time but I feel sure that one day I will."

23rd August 2003

UFAKEO

HOW THE WORLD WAS FOOLED INTO AN ALIEN ALERT BY A BALLOON

A "UFO" got the world asking if aliens were about to land

in Britain.

But it was hardly little green men many had feared were on board.

They were hoaxers who ran the stunt in a bizarre TV experiment.

The 25ft "flying saucer" stunned villagers on Saturday as it spun across the sky 200ft above their heads.

The outlandish sighting made the headlines as far away as Australia.

But the down-to-earth truth behind the "space craft" emerged yesterday.

TV firm Chrysalis had it built for a Channel 4 documentary with the working title *How To Build a Spaceship*.

Danny Cohen, of Channel 4, said: "We were trying to see whether we could build a convincing looking spaceship and in that regard undoubtedly we succeeded.

"Dozens of people saw it and couldn't quite understand what they had seen. So I think it did work.

"It stayed quite high in the sky and looked harmless, so it frightened nobody. I think people were more bewildered by what they were seeing.

"People were left rubbing their heads, wondering what was going on." It took eight months to research, design and build the £50,000 aircraft.

Model flight specialists Cutting Edge Effects – veterans of four Bond films – built it using a carbon fibre hoop as the skeleton.

This was set in a reflective-plastic balloon filled with helium.

After a US military engine was ditched as too heavy, electric fan engines from Germany proved the key to making the "saucer" fly at just the right speed – 20mph.

It was tested in an aircraft hangar at a secret location.

The out-of-this-world con included using seven pilots to fly the aircraft by remote control for three miles.

Suspicion for the hoax first fell on UFO buffs holding their annual Skywatch in the village, Avebury, Wilts.

But producer Mark Raphael said they weren't fooled – despite the eerie setting of a stone circle.

He said they spent the rest of the night "looking at nothing, and yet when the craft flew over they hardly got out of their seats".

20th February **2004**

UFO captured in the early evening above the St Budeaux area of Plymouth.

THE TRUTH IS OUT THERE

DAILY MIRROR, *Friday, February 20, 2004* PAGE 31

THE TRUTH IS OUT THERE

SIGHTING: The UFO is captured in early evening above the St Budeaux area of Plymouth

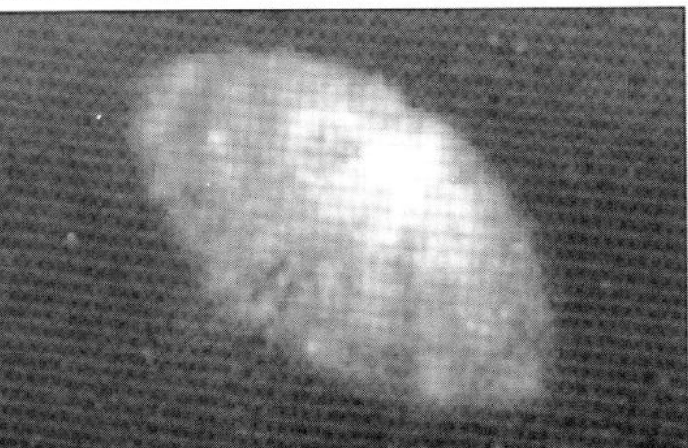

PERFECT: Snap of the UFO that has caused such excitement

Navy to probe 'one of best five UFO pictures ever seen'

By GEOFFREY LAKEMAN

AN extraordinary image of a shimmering disc-shaped object above the English coast has been hailed as one the best pictures of a UFO ever taken.

With a pinkish outer rim, golden middle and a light at its centre, there is no explanation for the "flying saucer".

Photographic experts say the pictures are not faked and a Royal Navy team has launched an investigation.

An un-named dockyard worker captured the image with his new digital camera in Plymouth. And Bob Boyd, chairman of the city's UFO research group, said: "It's one of the five best I've seen. There is no doubt it is the real thing."

There were no other sightings on the night of January 28, but he added: "If 100 people see a UFO, only one will report it."

lakers@cix.co.uk

NAVY TO PROBE 'ONE OF BEST FIVE UFO PICTURES EVER SEEN'

An extraordinary image of a shimmering disc-shaped object above the English coast has been hailed as one of the best pictures of a UFO ever taken.

With a pinkish outer rim, golden middle and a light at its centre, there is no explanation for the "flying saucer".

Photographic experts say the pictures are not faked and a Royal Navy team has launched an investigation.

An un-named dockyard worker captured the image with his new digital camera in Plymouth. And Bob Boyd, chairman of the city's UFO research group, said: "It's one of the five best I've seen. There is no doubt it is the real thing."

There were no other sightings on the night of January 28, but he added: "If 100 people see a UFO, only one will report it."

13th March 2004

➧ The existence of extraterrestrials is an alien concept.

BELIEVING THE IMP-OSSIBLE

Some people get angry when I say I do not believe in extraterrestrials or intelligent life in space. They point out that the universe contains billions of stars and planets.

Some of these must surely be, like earth, able to support life. And what about those thousands of "UFO sightings" over the years?

The problem is that beyond our solar system the distances are far too great to allow space travel. These vast distances are measured in light years.

Light travels at 186,000 miles a second. It takes 1.5 seconds just to reach us from the Moon, eight minutes to travel from the Sun, and four years to reach us from the next nearest star. So that star is four light years away.

Beyond that the distances become so enormous that, even if we could travel at the speed of light, it would take millions of years to explore other galaxies. No physical body can approach the speed of light, and if there are extra-terrestrial beings, the same goes for them.

Even so, we are not exactly alone. I have seen UFOs several times but I have never met "aliens". But I have interviewed several "contactees".

They had all been changed from their meetings with other-worldly beings. Some had become psychics, others were mentally disturbed. Their experiences were genuine. But who are these beings and where are they from?

The psychologist Carl Jung concluded that they are signs of coming changes. He said, these changes take place when one sign of the zodiac gives way to another. Such periods are always marked by "signs and wonders" – strange things in the sky.

I agree with Jung. The creatures reported by UFO contactees were quite familiar to our ancestors. They knew them as "elves, imps, or mischievous spirits". We may no longer believe in these things, but we never got rid of them, and now we call them extraterrestrials.

DAILY MIRROR, Saturday, March 13, 2004 PAGE 59

Believing the imp-ossible

CLASSIC MYSTERIES with JOHN MICHELLE: The world's most respected observer of the Unexplained

SOME people get angry when I say I do not believe in extra-terrestrials or intelligent life in space. They point out that the universe contains billions of stars and planets.

Some of these must surely be, like earth, able to support life. And what about those thousands of "UFO sightings" over the years?

The problem is that beyond our solar system the distances are far too great to allow space travel. These vast distances are measured in light years.

Light travels at 186,000 miles a second. It takes 1.5 seconds just to reach us from the Moon, eight minutes to travel from the Sun, and *four years* to reach us from the next nearest star. So that star is four light years away.

Beyond that the distances become so enormous that, even if we could travel at the speed of light, it would take millions of years to explore other galaxies. No physical body can approach the speed of light, and if there are extra-terrestrial beings, the same goes for them.

Even so, we are not exactly alone. I have seen UFOs several times but I have never met "aliens". But back in 1966, while writing my first book, The Flying Saucer Vision, I interviewed several "contactees".

They had all been changed from their meetings with other-worldly beings. Some had become psychics, others were mentally disturbed. Their experiences were genuine. But who are these beings and where are they from?

The psychologist Carl Jung concluded that they are signs of coming changes. He said, these changes take place when one sign of the zodiac gives way to another. Such periods are always marked by 'signs and wonders' – strange things in the sky.

I agree with Jung. The creatures reported by UFO contactees were quite familiar to our ancestors. They knew them as "elves, imps, or mischievous spirits". We may no longer believe in these things, but we never got rid of them, and now we call them extra-terrestrials.

2nd September 2005

I WAS ABDUCTED BY ALIENS …

UFO spotter Russ Kellett reckons he is a real-life X-Files agent – and says he's got the scars to prove it. He believes he saw his first alien spaceship when he was 10.

"I'll never forget it," he says. "It was a huge disc covered with red and white flashing lights. It hovered for a few seconds above the street before shooting off at high speed."

Since then the alien expert has had two more close encounters. The 41-year-old says: "I was driving my motorbike back home from work one night.

"When I came to the level crossing the barrier was down so I

stopped. Suddenly I was bathed in a hot, bright light. I turned around, expecting to see a car or truck but there was nothing there.

"Then just as quickly as the light appeared, it was gone."

The next morning he left for work – without looking in the mirror. As soon as he walked into the factory, where he worked as a forklift truck driver, one of his colleagues started to snigger and point in his direction.

"It was one of the girls in admin and she laughed and said 'You've overdone it on the sun bed'," recalls Russ, from Filey, North Yorks.

"I looked in the mirror and couldn't believe it: my face and neck were red raw. It was midwinter so there was no logical explanation for it."

He went to the doctor when his skin started to peel and blister – but nothing helped.

"I felt like a leper," he remembers. "Big patches of my skin started to fall off. And then overnight it cleared up. But I've still got a tiny scar as a reminder. I know it was caused by my close encounter at the crossing."

But if he thought that his skin condition was weird, a year later he was abducted by aliens. Russ continues: "I was out on my motorbike when I noticed a bright ball of light in the sky."

"Suddenly a black tunnel appeared in front of me. I tried to brake but they didn't work. I began to panic and was sweating with fear as I was pulled into blackness. My next memory is of arriving home. I've no recollection of how I got there."

But looking at his watch Russ realized he was missing two hours. Convinced he was imagining things he went to bed, but the next day the flashbacks began. "I remembered being inside a circular room standing between two silver poles with a hand on each and I couldn't move," he says.

"I was surrounded by 9ft figures wearing what looked like black wet suits. I remember not wanting to look into their eyes. They were trying to read my mind."

From reading books on the subject, Russ was horrified to realise he had the classic checklist for alien abduction.

"I had missing time, seen odd lights in the sky, had burns and flashbacks of encounters with strange beings.

"It was too much to take in but I knew I'd not imagined it," he says. "Before I'd always dismissed such claims as madness but I know what happened to me and I'm utterly convinced that I was abducted."

Still it took Russ two years to go public. But when he did he went one step further and set up a support group for others who felt they had been abducted too.

"For every encounter, like Mulder in the *X-Files* I fill in a detailed report. There is definitely something out there, we just don't know what.

"One thing is for certain – they're not human."

15th June 2006

MATT'S POLLEN OUT

Crop circle king Matt Williams has been forced to quit – because he has hay fever.

Matt, 35, is giving up his controversial hobby after being laid low by high pollen levels.

He sniffed yesterday: "I'll not be out this year – the hay fever is getting too bad. After a night in the fields, it takes me at least a day to recover." Matt, of Devizes, Wilts, is the only person ever convicted of crop circle-making.

He was fined £100 in 2000 for damaging crops after setting out to debunk claims that the complex circles could only be made by aliens.

20th July 2007

I'M AN ALIEN ABDUCTION AGONY AUNT

Hilary Porter claims she has been seeing aliens all her life. Now she helps others to cope with their own close encounters.

Every month agony aunt Hilary Porter receives hundreds of calls from confused and frightened clients. But they are not people with relationship problems – every plea for help is from someone who believes they were taken away by extra-terrestrial beings.

"The first reaction abductees have is relief that someone understands what they are going through. I'm the only alien abduction agony aunt in the UK," explains Hilary.

"Usually they won't have spoken to anyone about being taken away in a spaceship by aliens.

"They are worried about coming across as fruitcakes."

During the four years she's been offering her free service, Hilary has heard many strange stories.

She recalls: "One very successful businessman contacted me because of a recurring nightmare about being abducted.

"He thought it was his imagination then one morning he woke up with a strange 2 cm triangular scar on his hand.

"Over breakfast he noticed his six-year-old daughter had the same mark and she said, 'Daddy, I don't like the little men who come into my bedroom.' His blood ran cold when he heard this and finally he realized it really was happening – and to his daughter too."

Hilary's own extra-terrestrial contact began when she was five. She was playing on farmland when she saw a strange craft land close by.

"I crawled on my hands and knees to get a better look. The next thing I remember is this dark being in a suit dragging me into the spacecraft.

"I woke up with grass on my clothes and my knees were bleeding. My mum was furious with me for being late and ruining my clothes, I didn't tell her what had happened because I didn't know how to express it." Hilary forgot about this strange memory until one night 20 years ago she woke up with seven small grey beings in her bedroom poking her.

"I was sleeping alone. I'm divorced, and I was terrified. I don't remember what happened after that and don't want to either."

Since then, she's regularly seen strange craft in the skies in her local area and experienced episodes of lost time. "About five years ago I set out for the bus, looked at my watch, then came round on the other side of the road and it was two hours later. It was weird, and I know I'm not crazy so what was happening?"

Determined to find out, the 61-year-old from Farnborough, Hants, contacted UFO research organization Quest International. She says: "I was told I lived in a UFO hotspot. They also have a checklist to determine if you are being abducted and it was confirmed, my experiences are genuine and not my imagination.

"I set out on a mission and found everything I could about abductions. This is how I ended up an agony aunt. Now helping others is a major part of my life. I tell people, 'if I can live through this so can you'."

Nick Pope, who used to run the government's UFO project at the Ministry of Defence, says: "People think alien abduction only happens in science fiction movies, but it happens here in the UK too. I've come across around 100 British people who claim to have had these sorts of experiences.

"Research suggests these people aren't lying and they aren't mad. Something's going on, but we don't know what. I received several alien abduction reports alongside the hundreds of UFO reports at the MoD, but there was no official policy on this. I just had to counsel the people to the best of my ability."

08 M Daily Mirror THURSDAY 15.05.2008

BRITAIN OPENS ITS X FILES

EXCLUSIVE
BY MATT ROPER
matt.roper@mirror.co.uk

A FLYING saucer hovering over Central London, an alien craft as big as a football pitch in the skies above Yorkshire and a strange meeting with little green men on the Basingstoke canal...

These are just some of the unexplained encounters of the extra-terrestrial kind contained in Britain's X-files, released for the first time yesterday by the government.

The documents, which for years were hidden away in classified MoD files, include accounts of strange lights in the sky and unexplained objects being spotted by the public, serving soldiers and police officers.

They also include drawings of aliens, sketched by the people who saw them, including one of a flying saucer witnessed by two London policemen.

> MoD does not deny strange things in the skies

A government memo from 1983, also released yesterday, says: "The Ministry of Defence does not deny that there are strange things to see in the sky." But it adds, somewhat disappointingly, that the MoD "has no evidence that alien spacecraft have landed on this planet."

Another briefing paper, prepared in 1979 by the MoD for Lord Strabolgi, then government chief whip, states: "Her Majesty's government has never been approached by people from outer space."

Those who claim to have seen them, however, think otherwise...

IN May 1965 a woman from Ilfracombe, Devon, was in her garden when she saw a large, cylindrical object with a light at each end in the sky above her. "The object stopped some distance from my cottage, turned on its axis, and vanished," she wrote.

A FARMER'S wife from **Pencader, Dyfed,** *reported seeing a UFO on two consecutive nights in February 1985. In a report to the MoD, she said: "It appeared about six times larger than the brightest constellation that night and seemed to hover as if dangling from a string."*

THE child of an air traffic controller reported a red flying saucer with a dome on top and a shiny underside over **Jesmond, Newcastle,** in June 1985. It hovered before disappearing into cloud.

ONE of the MoD's classified files recounts the experiences of a 78-year-old man who claimed he had met an alien beside Basingstoke Canal in Aldershot, Hampshire in 1983. He said: "They were about four feet high, dressed in pale green overalls from head to foot, and they had helmets of the same colour with a visor that was blacked out. One of them beckoned me with his right arm. I took it that he wished me to follow, which I did."

He said he went on board the craft, – later doing a detailed drawing of it – before being quizzed by the aliens. He was then told: "You can go. You are too old and too infirm for our purpose."

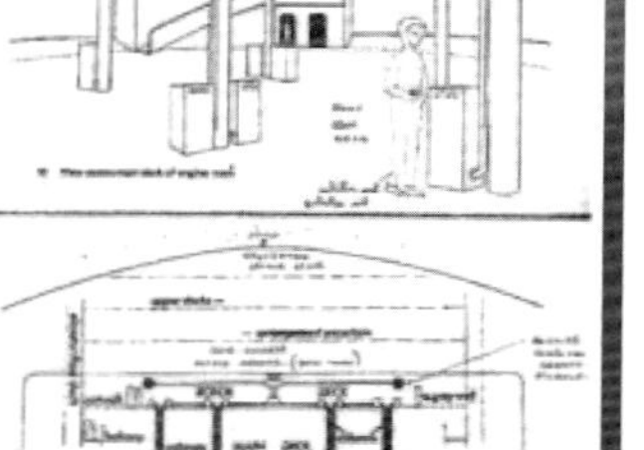

BEAM ME UP Drawings from inside an alien spacecraft

SAUCERS What the cops saw and, right, the airfield visitor

ON April 26, 1984 three Metropolitan police officers were called to a house in **Harrow, West London,** *and spent an hour observing an object in the sky which "moved erratically from side to side, up and down and to and fro, not venturing far from the original position." One of the officers described it as "circular in the middle with what appeared to be a dome on top and underneath".*

ONE man detailed his "physical and psychic contact" with green aliens since he was a child. The writer said that one of them, called Algar, was killed in 1981 by another race of beings as he was about to make contact with the UK government. The letter's author said he visited their bases in **Cheshire**. An airport worker independently reported six fast-moving golden spheres over **Kingsley, Cheshire** in December 1986.

> The little green men told me I was too old for them

AN air traffic controller at Dunsfold Aerodrome, Surrey, reported seeing a spherical object in the sky in July 1985, "approx 30-40 feet diameter, with appearance of highly polished silver metal, with a protruding lip a third of the way from the bottom. The object emitted a throbbing double-beat sound somewhat akin to a ship's propeller."

The report stated that the observer was "teetotal, excellent eyesight, not on any drugs".

AN ex-RAF officer wrote to the MoD's chief of air staff in 1987 retelling an incident he witnessed while stationed in the Far East. He wrote: "Suddenly and in full view of everyone at the base we were deliberately buzzed by a large flying disc which glowed red on the trailing edge as it made several passes over us and is glowed silver in the middle. It then shot straight up at a speed our radar chaps estimated to be about 600 knots. We were told not to write home about it, or to talk about it."

A REPORT from **RAF West Drayton** to the MOD in September 1987 described: "Orange/red flickering bright lights, oval in shape with dark band across the middle. Informant stated it was the size of a football pitch."

There's definitely something out there..

BY NICK POPE
FORMER MoD UFO INVESTIGATOR

IT is one of the most profound questions the human race can ask: are we alone?

Is it just us or do we share this universe with a multitude of other life-forms?

The quest for the answer to that question has been an obsession. First, we simply wondered. Then we built telescopes. Now we're sending up space probes. But even travelling at 100,000 miles an hour – the speed of the Galileo probe – it would take us 20,000 years to reach the nearest star.

Many scientists are convinced that in our infinite universe, life abounds. Accordingly, radio astronomers in the SETI (Search for Extraterrestrial Intelligence) programme listen expectantly for a signal. Other radio astronomers send transmissions to stars.

In a few years' time the most powerful radio telescope ever built will come on line. Many believe that if there's life out there, the Square Kilometre Array will detect it.

It's arrogant to assume that given the vastness of space, Earth would be the only planet where life has developed. What happened here must surely have happened somewhere else. So it's logical to assume that extra-terrestrial life exists.

The MoD files will cause many a discussion on the separate but related questions: "Do aliens exist?" and "Have we been visited?"

TELL US WHAT YOU THINK AT WWW.MIRROR.CO.UK/FORUMS

15th May 2008

Abductees' sketches of the inside and outside of alien spacecraft.

BRITAIN OPENS ITS X-FILES

A flying saucer hovering over Central London, an alien craft as big as a football pitch in the skies above Yorkshire and a strange meeting with little green men on the Basingstoke canal …

These are just some of the unexplained encounters of the extra-terrestrial kind contained in Britain's X-files, released for the first time yesterday by the government.

The documents, which for years were hidden away in classified MoD files, include accounts of strange lights in the sky and unexplained objects being spotted by the public, serving soldiers and police officers.

They also include drawings of aliens, sketched by the people who saw them, including one of a flying saucer witnessed by two London policemen.

A government memo from 1983, also released yesterday, says: "The Ministry of Defence does not deny that there are strange things to see in the sky." But it adds, somewhat disappointingly, that the MoD "has no evidence that alien spacecraft have landed on this planet".

Another briefing paper, prepared in 1979 by the MoD for Lord Strabolgi, then government chief whip, states: "Her Majesty's government has never been approached by people from outer space."

Those who claim to have seen them, however, think otherwise …

In May 1965 a woman from Ilfracombe, Devon, was in her garden when she saw a large, cylindrical object with a light at each end in the sky above her. "The object stopped some distance from my cottage, turned on its axis, and vanished," she wrote.

A farmer's wife from Pencader, Dyfed, reported seeing a UFO on two consecutive nights in February 1985. In a report to the MoD, she said: "It appeared about six times larger than the brightest constellation that night and seemed to hover as if dangling from a string."

The child of an air traffic controller reported a red flying saucer with a dome on top and a shiny underside over Jesmond, Newcastle, in June 1985. It hovered before disappearing into cloud.

One of the MoD's classified files recounts the experiences of a 78-year-old man who claimed he had met an alien beside Basingstoke Canal in Aldershot, Hampshire in 1983. He said: "They were about four feet high, dressed in pale green overalls from head to foot, and they had helmets of the same colour with a visor that was blacked out. One of them beckoned me with his right arm. I took it that he wished me to follow, which I did."

He said he went on board the craft, – later doing a detailed drawing of it – before being quizzed by the aliens. He was then told: "You can go. You are too old and too infirm for our purpose."

On April 26, 1984 three Metropolitan police officers were called to a house in Harrow, West London, and spent an hour observing an object in the sky which "moved erratically from side to side, up and down and to and fro, not venturing far from the original position". One of the officers described it as "circular in the middle with what appeared to be a dome on top and underneath".

One man detailed his "physical and psychic contact" with green aliens since he was a child. The writer said that one of them, called Algar, was killed in 1981 by another race of beings as he was about to make contact with the UK government. The letter's author said he visited their bases in Cheshire. An airport worker independently reported six fast-moving golden spheres over Kingsley, Cheshire in December 1986.

An air traffic controller at Dunsfold Aerodrome, Surrey, reported seeing a spherical object in the sky in July 1985, "approx 30–40 feet diameter, with appearance of highly polished silver metal, with a protruding lip a third of the way from the bottom. The object emitted a throbbing double-beat sound somewhat akin to a ship's propeller."

The report stated that the observer was "teetotal, excellent eyesight, not on any drugs".

An ex-RAF officer wrote to the MoD's chief of air staff in 1987 retelling an incident he witnessed while stationed in the Far East. He wrote: "Suddenly and in full view of everyone at the base we were deliberately buzzed by a large flying disc which glowed red on the trailing edge as it made several passes over us and it glowed silver in the middle. It then shot straight up at a speed our radar chaps estimated to be about 600 knots. We were told not to write home about it, or to talk about it."

A report from RAF West Drayton to the MOD in September 1987 described: "Orange/red flickering bright lights, oval in shape with dark band across the middle. Informant stated it was the size of a football pitch."

15th May 2008

THERE'S DEFINITELY SOMETHING OUT THERE …

It is one of the most profound questions the human race can ask:

are we alone?

Is it just us or do we share this universe with a multitude of other life-forms?

The quest for the answer to that question has been an obsession. First, we simply wondered. Then we built telescopes. Now we're sending up space probes. But even travelling at 100,000 miles an hour – the speed of the Galileo probe – it would take us 20,000 years to reach the nearest star.

Many scientists are convinced that in our infinite universe, life abounds. Accordingly, radio astronomers in the SETI (Search for Extraterrestrial Intelligence) programme listen expectantly for a signal. Other radio astronomers send transmissions to stars.

In a few years' time the most powerful radio telescope ever built will come on line. Many believe that if there's life out there, the Square Kilometre Array will detect it.

It's arrogant to assume that given the vastness of space, Earth would be the only planet where life has developed. What happened here must surely have happened somewhere else. So it's logical to assume that extra-terrestrial life exists.

The MoD files will cause many a discussion on the separate but related questions: "Do aliens exist?" and "Have we been visited?"

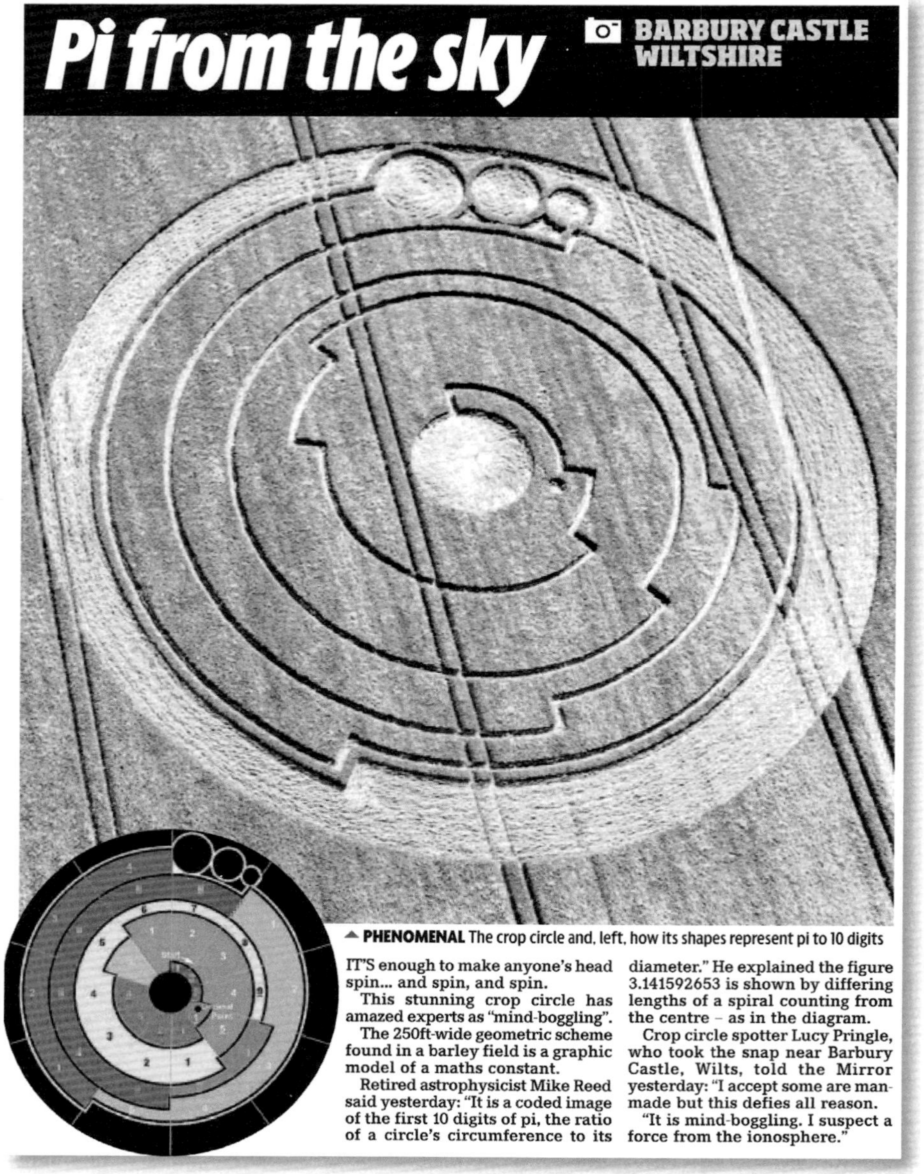

Pi from the sky

BARBURY CASTLE WILTSHIRE

▲ PHENOMENAL The crop circle and, left, how its shapes represent pi to 10 digits

IT'S enough to make anyone's head spin... and spin, and spin.

This stunning crop circle has amazed experts as "mind-boggling".

The 250ft-wide geometric scheme found in a barley field is a graphic model of a maths constant.

Retired astrophysicist Mike Reed said yesterday: "It is a coded image of the first 10 digits of pi, the ratio of a circle's circumference to its diameter." He explained the figure 3.141592653 is shown by differing lengths of a spiral counting from the centre – as in the diagram.

Crop circle spotter Lucy Pringle, who took the snap near Barbury Castle, Wilts, told the Mirror yesterday: "I accept some are man-made but this defies all reason.

"It is mind-boggling. I suspect a force from the ionosphere."

18th June 2008

◄ A crop circle and how its shapes represent pi to 10 digits.

PI FROM THE SKY

BARBURY CASTLE, WILTSHIRE

It's enough to make anyone's head spin … and spin, and spin.

This stunning crop circle has amazed experts as "mind-boggling".

The 250ft-wide geometric scheme found in a barley field is a graphic model of a maths constant.

Retired astrophysicist Mike Reed said yesterday: "It is a coded image of the first 10 digits of pi, the ratio of a circle's circumference to its diameter." He explained the figure 3.141592653 is shown by differing lengths of a spiral counting from the centre – as in the diagram.

Crop circle spotter Lucy Pringle, who took the snap near Barbury Castle, Wilts, told the *Mirror* yesterday: "I accept some are man-made but this defies all reason.

"It is mind-boggling. I suspect a force from the ionosphere."

3rd June 2009

SOME STING HAS LANDED

A huge jellyfish appears to have fallen to Earth in this bizarre crop circle.

Circle-watchers wobbled with joy when the 600ft jelly – two soccer pitches long and the first of its kind – appeared in Kingstone Coombes, Oxon.

Crop circle expert Karen Alexander said: "It's a complete monster."

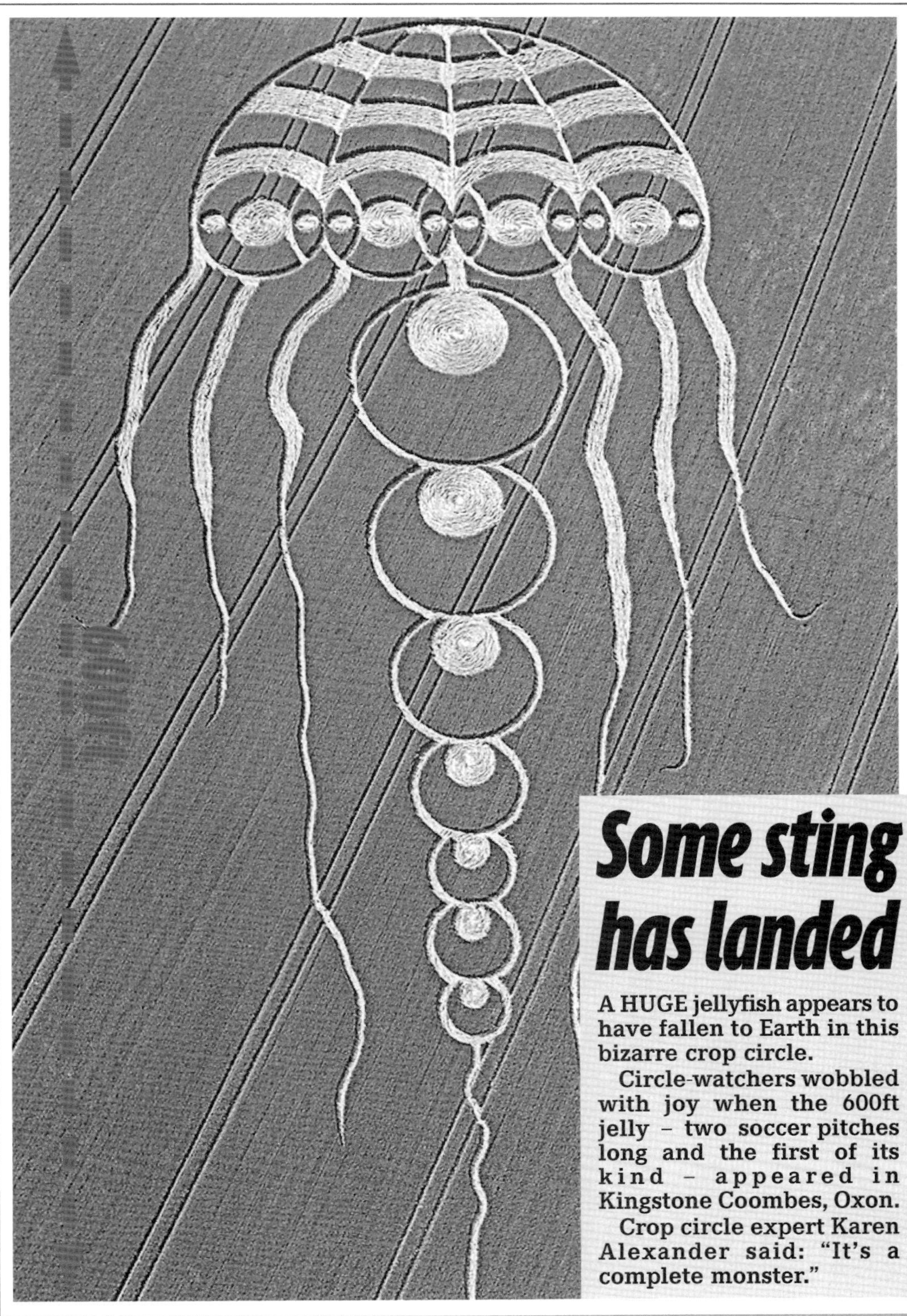

Some sting has landed

A HUGE jellyfish appears to have fallen to Earth in this bizarre crop circle.

Circle-watchers wobbled with joy when the 600ft jelly – two soccer pitches long and the first of its kind – appeared in Kingstone Coombes, Oxon.

Crop circle expert Karen Alexander said: "It's a complete monster."

A huge jellyfish crop circle.

21st October 2009

CLOSE ENCOUNTER COP

A police officer has contacted UFO experts after claiming to see three aliens examining a crop circle then zoom off at super-speed.

The unnamed off-duty sergeant saw the giant blond figures in white overalls in a Wiltshire field and stopped his car to investigate.

The officer heard "static" and watched as they ran off "faster than any man he had ever seen".

Crop circle expert Andrew Russell said yesterday: "I am quite convinced the officer had an experience that day." Wiltshire Police said: "It is a personal not a police matter."

23rd June 2010

U.F.OOOOOOH!

LIGHT FROM SUN TURNS CLOUD INTO 'SPACESHIP'

A couple had a close encounter of the cloud kind.

Brian Wilton and wife Isobel captured an optical illusion as the setting sun threw an eerie light into a dense almond-shaped cloud. The unusual "spaceship" cloud was spotted in the sky above Crieff, in Perthshire, at the weekend.

The dramatic clouds – altocumulus

For breaking news go to: **www.mirror.co.uk** RELATED LINKS

DMIST

Daily Mirror WEDNESDAY 23.06.2010 M 33

U.F.OOOOOOH!

Light from sun turns cloud into 'spaceship'

HERE'S the moment a couple had a close encounter of the cloud kind.

Brian Wilton and wife Isobel captured the optical illusion as the setting sun threw an eerie light into a dense almond-shaped cloud. The unusual "spaceship" cloud was spotted in the sky above Crieff, in Perthshire, at the weekend.

The dramatic clouds – altocumulus lenticularis – are usually found in mountainous regions due to very specific atmospheric conditions. Brian said: "We couldn't believe it. It was like the scene in the film Close Encounters of the Third Kind when the big spaceship comes down."

He said the clouds are usually slow-moving and evaporate quickly.

A cloud at sunset creates an optical illusion of a UFO above Crieff, in Perthshire.

lenticularis – are usually found in mountainous regions due to very specific atmospheric conditions. Brian said: "We couldn't believe it. It was like the scene in the film *Close Encounters of the Third Kind* when the big spaceship comes down."

He said the clouds are usually slow-moving and evaporate quickly.

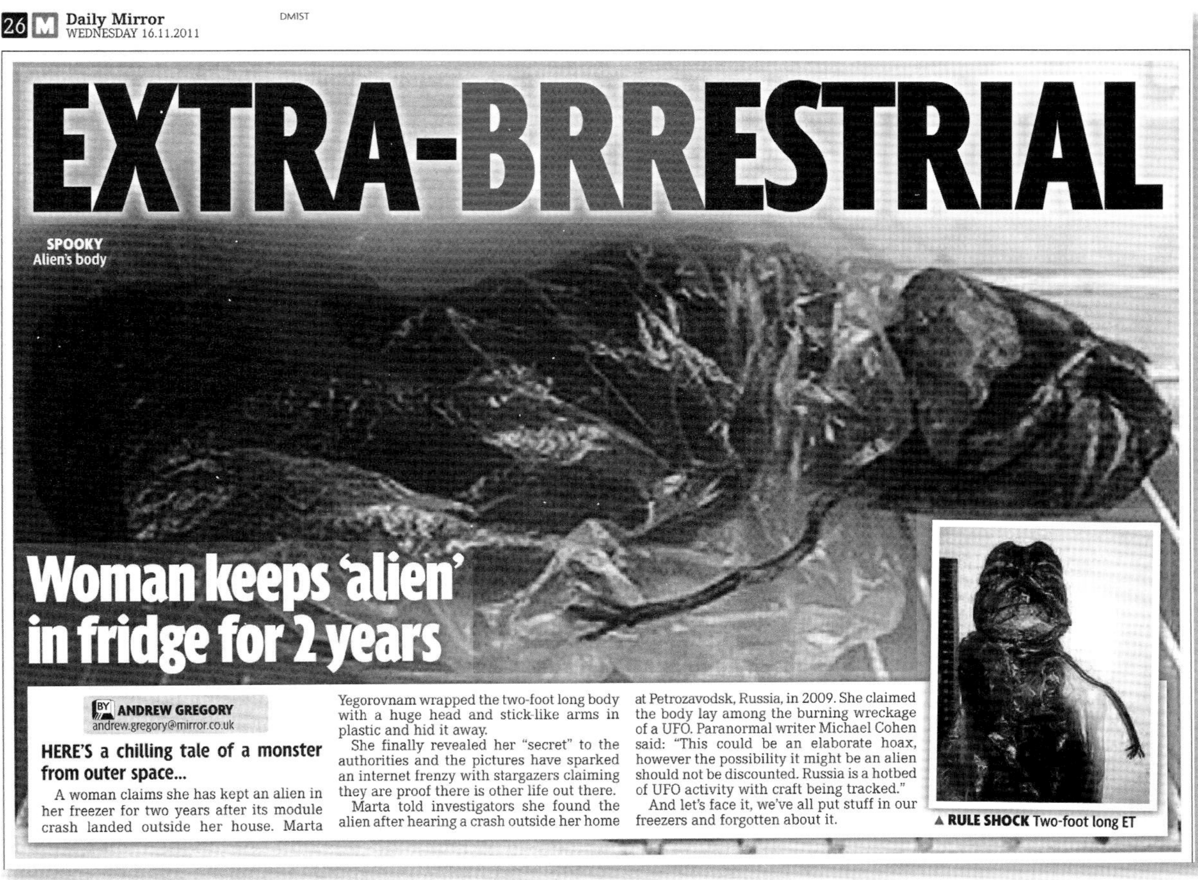

26 M Daily Mirror WEDNESDAY 16.11.2011

EXTRA-BRRESTRIAL

SPOOKY Alien's body

Woman keeps 'alien' in fridge for 2 years

BY ANDREW GREGORY andrew.gregory@mirror.co.uk

HERE'S a chilling tale of a monster from outer space...

A woman claims she has kept an alien in her freezer for two years after its module crash landed outside her house. Marta Yegorovnam wrapped the two-foot long body with a huge head and stick-like arms in plastic and hid it away.

She finally revealed her "secret" to the authorities and the pictures have sparked an internet frenzy with stargazers claiming they are proof there is other life out there.

Marta told investigators she found the alien after hearing a crash outside her home at Petrozavodsk, Russia, in 2009. She claimed the body lay among the burning wreckage of a UFO. Paranormal writer Michael Cohen said: "This could be an elaborate hoax, however the possibility it might be an alien should not be discounted. Russia is a hotbed of UFO activity with craft being tracked."

And let's face it, we've all put stuff in our freezers and forgotten about it.

▲ RULE SHOCK Two-foot long ET

7th March 2011

ALIEN LIFE IN SPACE ROCKS

A NASA scientist claims he has found alien life forms inside meteorites.

The microscopic worms were found inside three rocks that are four billion years old and fell from space.

Dr Richard Hoover denied they could be contaminated and said they prove life is widespread in the universe.

Writing in the *Journal of Cosmology*, he said: "Although many of the bacteria resemble species on Earth, there are others which are alien. I have no idea what they are."

NASA has not made any official comment.

16th November 2011

EXTRA-BRRESTRIAL

WOMAN KEEPS 'ALIEN' IN FRIDGE FOR 2 YEARS

Here's a chilling tale of a monster from outer space …

A woman claims she has kept an alien in her freezer for two years after its module crash landed outside her house. Marta Yegorovnam wrapped the two-foot long body with a huge head and stick-like arms in plastic and hid it away.

She finally revealed her "secret" to the authorities and the pictures have sparked an internet frenzy with stargazers claiming they are proof there is other life out there.

Marta told investigators she found the alien after hearing a crash outside her home at Petrozavodsk, Russia, in 2009. She claimed the body lay among the burning wreckage of a UFO. Paranormal writer Michael Cohen said: "This could be an elaborate hoax, however the possibility it might be an alien should not be discounted. Russia is a hotbed of UFO activity with craft being tracked."

And let's face it, we've all put stuff in our freezers and forgotten about it.

Alien kept in a freezer.

23rd January 2013

*MET*EORITES

ALIEN LIFE FOUND IN SPACE ROCK

A top British scientist claims he has found proof that extraterrestrials exist after cracking open a meteorite. Instead of finding an alien like Hollywood favourite ET, Professor Chandra Wickramasinghe discovered the two-inch wide rock was pitted with tiny fossils of algae, similar to the kind found in seaweed. The respected professor believes it proves we are not alone in the universe.

He said: "These finds are crushing evidence that human life started outside earth."

The rock was one of several fragments of a meteorite which crash landed in central Sri Lanka in December.

They fell to earth in a spectacular fireball and were still smoking when villagers living near the city of Polonnaruwa picked them up.

The fossils were discovered when the rocks were examined under a powerful scanning electron microscope in a British laboratory.

They are similar to micro-organisms found in fossils from the dinosaur age 55 million years ago. Critics say the rock had probably become contaminated with algae fossils from Earth.

But Prof Wickramasinghe insists they are the remnants of extraterrestrial life.

He said: "The algae organisms are similar to ones found in Earth fossils, but the rock also has other organisms we have not identified."

The scientist is a well-known champion of the "panspermia hypothesis" – which suggests the first seeds of life were deposited on our planet from outer space 3,800 million years ago. The professor believes these microbes came from comets, which then "multiplied and seeded" to form life on Earth.

He said: "We are all aliens – we share a cosmic ancestry. Each time a new planetary system forms, a few surviving microbes find their way into comets. These then multiply and seed other planets.

"These latest finds are just more evidence to point to the overwhelming fact that life on Earth began on other worlds."

The professor, an expert on interstellar dust, spent decades working with Sir Fred Hoyle – a British astronomer and mathematician who was well known for rejecting the Big Bang theory.

The pair set out on a mission to try to prove their "life from outer space" theory back in the 60s.

Prof Wickramasinghe said: "Evidence from astronomy overwhelmingly supports the view that life did not start on Earth but was seeded from outside."

24 M Daily Mirror
WEDNESDAY 23.01.2013

DMLI

MET

BY ADAM ASPINALL
adam.aspinall@mirror.co.uk

A TOP British scientist cl he has found proof that ex terrestrials exist after crac open a meteorite.

Instead of finding an alien Hollywood favourite ET, Prof Chandra Wickramasinghe di ered the two-inch wide rock pitted with tiny fossils of a similar to the found in seaw The respe profes believes proves we not alone in universe.

He said: "T finds are crus evidence that huma started outside Eart

The rock was on several fragments

▲ **SPACE MISSION** Professor Wickramasinghe and, left, ET

Magnification of meteorite fossils.

:ORITES

Alien life found in space rock

ıeteorite which crash landed in ɘntral Sri Lanka in December.

They fell to earth in a spectacular reball and were still smoking hen villagers living near the city f Polonnaruwa picked them up.

The fossils were discovered when ıe rocks were examined under a owerful scanning electron microcope in a British laboratory.

They are similar to micro-organms found in fossils from the inosaur age 55 million years ago. ritics say the rock had probably become contaminated with algae fossils from Earth.

But Prof Wickramasinghe insists they are the remnants of extraterrestrial life.

He said: "The algae organisms are similar to ones found in Earth fossils, but the rock also has other organisms we have not identified."

The scientist is a well known champion of the "panspermia hypothesis" – which suggests the first seeds of life were deposited on our planet from outer space 3,800 million years ago. The professor believes these microbes came from comets, which then "multiplied and seeded" to form life on Earth.

He said: "We are all aliens – we share a cosmic ancestry. Each time a new planetary system forms, a few surviving microbes find their way into comets. These then multiply and seed other planets.

"These latest finds are just more evidence to point to the overwhelming fact that life on Earth began on other worlds."

The professor, an expert on interstellar dust, spent decades working with Sir Fred Hoyle – a British astronomer and mathematician who was well known for rejecting the Big Bang theory.

The pair set out on a mission to try to prove their "life from outer space" theory back in the 60s.

Prof Wickramasinghe said: "Evidence from astronomy overwhelmingly supports the view that life did not start on Earth but was seeded from outside."

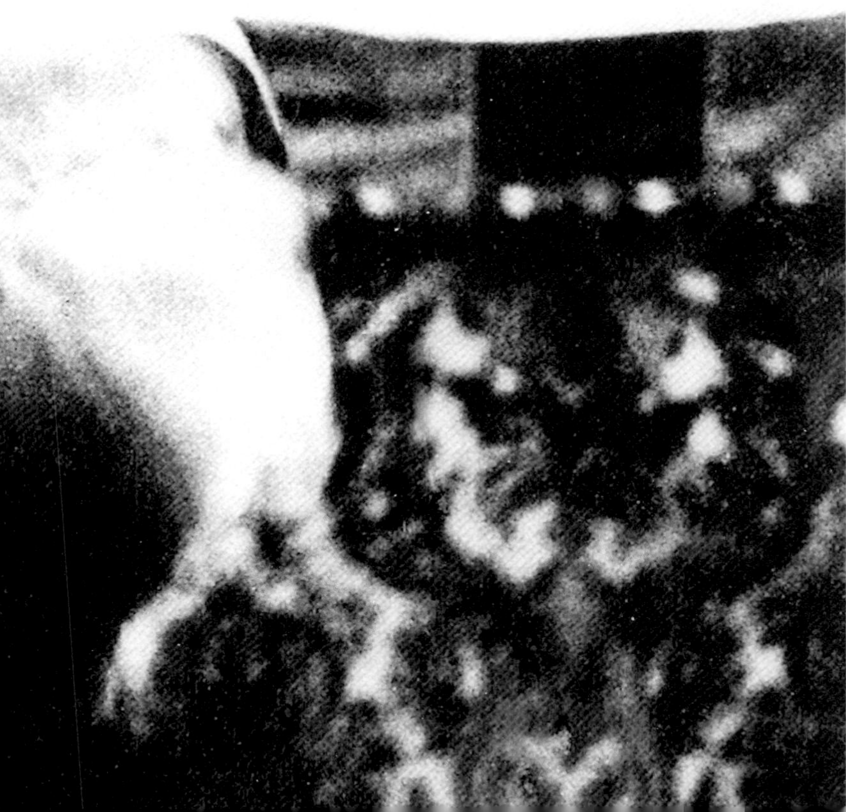

Ghosts – Neighbours from Hell

◀ The Reverend Christopher Neil Smith exorcising one of his patients.

Before William Friedkin made it into "the scariest film of all time", *The Exorcist* had started out as a novel by William Peter Blatty (who, contrastingly, also co-wrote the screenplay for Blake Edwards' comedy *A Shot in the Dark*, starring Peter Sellers). Blatty based the idea on the real-life exorcism of a boy in St Louis, who is reported to have experienced many of the symptoms of possession famously portrayed in the movie, except for the head-spinning! However, levitation, welts on his body, guttural speech and violence, as well as poltergeist-like paranormal activity, did all occur. Of course, the film was made all the better for its evocatively eerie soundtrack provided by Mike Oldfield's 'Tubular Bells'.

17th August **1981**

A FAMILY IN FEAR FLEE HAUNTED HOME

A family whose seaside home has been wrecked by a spooky intruder decided to move out yesterday in search of peace and quiet.

For two days Charles and Catherine Burden were under onslaught from a spirit that smashed crockery and sent a TV set, a table and ornaments flying around their living room.

They arranged seances and exorcisms.

But still the poltergeist pestered the couple and their daughter Deborah, 17, and foster son Bradley, eight.

Then a medium suggested they should move out for a few days.

Mr Burden, a 63-year-old window cleaner, said yesterday: "We've got to keep the ghost happy."

Colin Barker, the Burdens' next-door neighbour in Abbott Road, Bournemouth, said: "They came round to us and told us the trouble had started again.

"Mrs. Burden was very upset and has had to be sedated.

"She and her husband and daughter will be staying with me for the next few days and Bradley will stay with a friend until this is all over."

The Burdens believe the mischievous spirit is that of a nine-year-old boy called Ian.

It was last Friday when strange things first happened in their home. Furniture started whizzing around.

After a police chief saw what had been going on, an exorcism was carried out by a retired priest.

But on Saturday the spook was back.

Mr. Burden said: "This time the settee was overturned and a cabinet was thrown at me.

"A heavy door leaning against a wall in the garden was pushed over, narrowly missing my wife and daughter."

25th November 1981

Holding a seance.

GHOSTS PREFER COUNCIL HOUSES

TENANTS GET THE KEY TO TERROR

Ghosts have moved out of their haunted castles and into council houses.

A survey has found that 86 per cent of all reported poltergeists prefer to go bump in the night in council homes.

Most start their tricks within six months of new tenants moving in. The reason, a report out today suggests, is that tenants are more affected by the stresses of moving into strange surroundings than home owners, and this can result in poltergeist symptoms.

Ghost hunter Andrew Green, who wrote the report in the *British Association of Social Workers'* magazine, says most poltergeist activities can be put down to perfectly normal causes.

But he warns social workers to be careful if they are called in to help.

Often, he says, they make things worse. One social worker called in a vicar to exorcise a ghost and then held a seance. She was so upset by it that she needed psychiatric help. In fact there was no ghost. The tenant had just imagined it because she had been taking drugs.

9th May 1983

THE UNKNOWN FACTOR

You feel a sudden urge to call a friend. At that moment, your phone rings … and it is your friend calling you.

You dream about a strange-looking house you've never seen before … and next day you find yourself outside it.

You wake in the middle of the night and hear footsteps in the passage … but the passage is empty.

There may be a natural explanation for these and other similar events.

Often there is coincidence, a faulty memory or an overheated imagination. But if you are "psychic" and these things are continually happening to you – or even if you are not, but the circumstances of a particular case convince you that there is no natural explanation – you will be inclined to accept that they are paranormal.

DAILY MIRROR, *Monday, May 9 1983* PAGE 9

CONCENTRATING deeply, psychic Zak Martin (above) pressed a table-tennis ball to his forehead. Seconds later, he placed it on a transparent table and apparently willed it to move from side to side, across the table and in circles, as if of its own volition. The experiment was one of several witnessed by Daily Mirror writers and photographers in their inquiry into the paranormal, the unexplained, The Unknown Factor. The series—with a full report on the table-tennis ball test—begins tomorrow. Today, Brian Inglis, the author and broadcaster who has made a long study of the paranormal and who advised on the inquiry, introduces the series.

Picture: BILL ROWNTREE

Psychic Zak Martin demonstrates his psychokinetic powers.

FORCES

They are simply, The Unexplained. The Unknown Factor. That's not to imply that they are "supernatural" in the traditional sense of the word.

Most psychical researchers assume they are the product of natural forces – but of forces which have yet to be discovered.

During the past few years there has been a big increase in the number of people who believe in the paranormal.

According to recent opinion polls, nearly three out of four adults in Britain accept ESP – extrasensory perception which covers the obtaining of information other than through the normal senses.

A mass of material from psychical research – well-documented and well-attested – also lends support to the claim that ESP exists.

As it does with PK – or psychokinesis – which covers the action of mind, or unexplained forces, on matter. It includes: Psychic metal-bending, Levitation, Hauntings, Poltergeists, Apparitions. There is a mass of material which lends support to the existence of such things.

So why do most orthodox academics continue to ignore, or angrily reject, the evidence?

They cannot accept it because it conflicts with old, and now discredited, dogmas which lay down the laws of nature.

But these laws have been blown to smithereens by nuclear physicists who have found that nuclear particles indulge in most "illegal" behaviour, breaking all the old laws.

Orthodox scientists have been forced back on the argument that what happens at the nuclear level doesn't necessarily happen in real life.

Paranormal phenomena, they point out, have yet to be conclusively demonstrated in laboratory-type trials.

TRIALS

Yet this is hardly surprising, as the phenomena are spontaneous.

The across-a-crowded-room symptom – love at first sight – has yet to be demonstrated in laboratory-type trials.

But we do not, for that reason, deny that it can, and does happen.

A better case can be made out for the familiar plea that it can be dangerous to dabble in the occult.

Highly-strung people are ill-advised to fool around with witchcraft or even the ouija board, on which an upturned glass can spell out words and messages.

But there are many features of the paranormal which, if they were better understood, could be of inestimable value.

If mind can communicate with mind at a distance, the implications are profound.

The importance of psychic metal-bending to industry could be immense.

Premonitions – flashes of precognition – have saved many people from injury or death.

Dowsers demonstrate how their technique of finding answers from a metal object attached to a piece of string or thread can be used not only to find underground water.

It can also save time and temper around the house – in finding missing keys, for example!

And, potentially the most valuable, some healers have achieved miraculous cures with the sick.

24th November **1983**

BEDSIT GIRL FLEES 'GHOSTS'

A teenaged girl has been forced out of her bedsitter – by a plague of ghosts.

The girl, Mary Bell, 18, claims that evil spirits terrified her over a period of three months.

She says that she wrestled with a wraith while praying, was dragged by her hair by an unseen force and saw a woman's head float through the air.

Other tenants at the house in Maryhill, Glasgow, also claim to have seen strange things, including the ghost of an old woman.

Mary said yesterday: "It was terrifying. I have been on sleeping tablets since I moved out."

Glasgow University Professor Archie Roy, an expert in the supernatural, said: "The happenings seem typical of poltergeist activity."

28th July **1986**

PRIEST FLEES GHOST HOME

A mother and daughter were forced to quit their council home after terrifying ghostly goings-on sent a priest fleeing.

Furniture was mysteriously hurled about in the air and a flying umbrella almost hit a policewoman. The priest fled in shock after he was called to exorcise the house in Speke, Liverpool.

The tenant, 38-year-old Shirley Kane, and her teenage daughter Elizabeth left the house to stay with relatives.

Priest Paul Montgomery said: "Whether something evil was present I just couldn't say. But I wouldn't like to use the word 'poltergeist' myself."

23rd September **1994**

POLTERGEIST FRENZY HIT MY HOME

A woman watched in amazement as an electrical breakdown sent her household gadgets crazy.

"The radio came on, the dishwasher started and the video was clicking on and off," saleswoman Claudia Stokes, 35, said yesterday. "It was just like a Poltergeist film."

Old overhead power cables had snapped and sent electricity surging through her home in Adderbury, Oxfordshire.

The cables, which sparked and sizzled until earthed, will be replaced by underground lines.

28th February **1996**

GHOST THREW CARVING KNIFE

Sting has been plagued by ghosts at his historic house in Highgate, North London. He even called in a spiritualist to investigate.

"Ever since I moved there, other people have said things happen," he says. "They might be lying in bed and people start talking to them, or things go missing. I was very sceptical until the night after my daughter Mickey was born. She was disturbed and I went to see her.

"Her room is full of mobiles and they were going berserk. I thought a window must be open, but they were shut."

Another night, Sting woke and saw the figures of a mother and child standing in the corner of the bedroom. Later Trudie saw them, too.

The singer says: "I heard Trudie say: 'Sting, what's that in the corner?' I just went totally cold, icy cold."

There was an even more frightening incident when a poltergeist sent a carving-knife flying across the kitchen, where it stuck in a wall.

A few nights later Sting and Trudie woke to see a ghostly woman in Victorian dress, this time without a child. They never saw her again.

1st November **2001**

DON'T GIVE UP ON GHOSTS

Are you frightened of ghosts? Some people, if you ask them that, laugh cheerfully and say they never think of such things. But I wonder if they would be so bold at night time alone in a spooky old house, when footsteps are heard in the creaking of the staircase. As a child during the War, I lived with grandparents in a Hampshire village. Their house was old and cranky with many dark nooks and corners. In these, I imagined, nasty creatures were waiting to jump out, and I ran quickly past them.

Then I started reading ghost stories. They were so terrifying that I could not sleep, but lay tense in bed, expecting something dreadful to appear. Yet I loved those ghost stories and went on reading them.

But is it right to scare children with stories about ghosts and monsters? Yes, it is, said old Lord Halifax. He was a writer and collector of ghost stories, and on dark winter nights he would read them to his family. When his wife complained that the children were trembling with fear, he replied that it was good for their

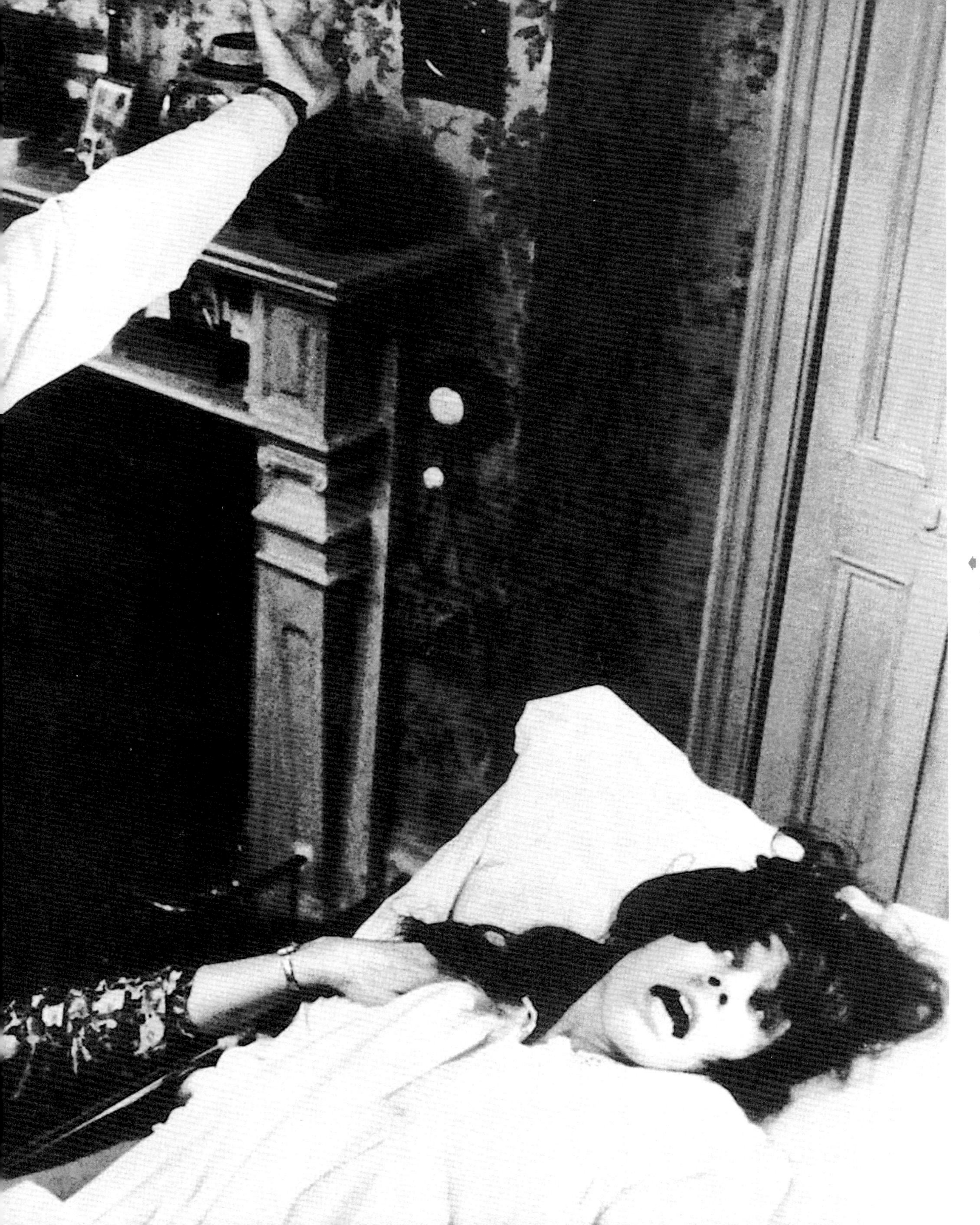

Sting, looking like he's seen a ghost, in Dennis Potter's *Brimstone and Treacle*.

imaginations. *Lord Halifax's Ghost Book* was later published by his eldest son.

The stories were terrifying, he admitted, but it was "a delicious terror", and he hoped other children would enjoy the feeling as much as he had. I am glad now to have been through those terrors. You cannot altogether avoid them, because they occur naturally in dreams, and in the minds of children. At that age ghosts and monsters are active realities. You long to hear about them, from older people who are not afraid of them. Then you grow up and realise there are no such things as ghosts.

But you can never be quite sure. Many people think they have seen ghosts and some have been frightened to death by the experience. Leap Castle in County Offaly used to be called the most haunted building in Ireland. An old lady I met, who knew it before it was burned in 1923, said that she had often seen ghosts there. They were harmless and the family had become used to them. But one of them was nasty. It looked like a sheep and it stank like a corpse. The man who described it had jumped out of a tower window to escape it – and had survived.

I have long given up being frightened of ghosts, and I do not even read the stories. But if you offered me £100 to spend a night in a haunted house, with just a candle, in a room where there had been a horrible murder, I would ask you to find someone else for the job. I couldn't trust my imagination.

5th December **2002**

MYSTERIES

You often hear of people or houses that are troubled by a poltergeist.

That is the German name for a noisy, disruptive "geist", or spirit. But what actually is it? Traditionally, the poltergeist is only known by what it does.

Often it behaves like a naughty child, throwing things around, making sudden noises or playing all sorts of tricks. But sometimes it is nasty and dangerous.

Sharp objects are thrown, fires break out and there is often damage to people and property. There was a case about 20 years ago, in Italy, that almost ended in tragedy. A young Scottish girl, Carole Compton, was working for an Italian family, looking after their child. Weird things happened around her.

Things moved about and pictures fell down. There were several small fires, and the child was nearly burned in its cot.

Carole was accused of arson and attempted murder. She was brought to court but the locals decided she was a witch, and there was a move to lynch her. She was found guilty but released immediately and sent back home.

It is often like that. An adolescent girl or youth, lonely or passionate, attracts poltergeist phenomena. Many examples are recorded through the centuries.

The Society for Psychical Research has investigated hundreds of cases. They agree that many turn out to be attached to a disturbed young person but say there are more where no such link seems to exist.

They say the poltergeist is best seen as "a form of uncontrolled energy" and if we want to learn more about what truly causes it, we should keep an open mind.

28th October **2005**

OUR GYM IS FIT FOR A GHOST

When Michelle and Jay opened their gym three years ago they didn't expect to sign up members from the other side …

As they set eyes on its spacious rooms and lovely wooden floors, Michelle and Jay Young knew the old church in Winsford, Cheshire, was the perfect spot for their new fitness centre.

Within weeks the couple were hard at work transforming the 1822 building into a modern gym.

But almost immediately Michelle, 27, noticed strange goings-on. "Nothing big at first – just little things like pens going missing or objects being moved," she says.

"With all the chaos, I thought I was just being absent-minded."

But it wasn't long before events had taken a more sinister turn.

"I felt I had a woman standing behind me all the time," says Jay, the 34-year-old ex-commando. "She even came with me into the loo. I had to say, 'I'm having a pee, go away.'

"I didn't tell Michelle because I didn't want to scare her. And besides, I didn't really believe it. I was a sceptic before all this started so it didn't make sense to me."

As they put the finishing touches to their new business ready for opening, the couple slept in the staff room. They were woken in the morning by a loud banging on the front door.

"I thought we'd overslept and the staff were waiting to get in," says Michelle. "But when we dashed downstairs no one was outside.

"There are gates to the gym. There's no way anyone could have got past them to the door without a key. We were baffled."

It was then that Jay told Michelle about his ghostly experiences.

Shortly afterwards came the event which persuaded the couple to call in a medium. One night as Jay was leaving after completing his closing-up routine of unplugging the treadmills, he heard a machine

bleep back into life.

"As I watched the treadmill started running. Then it went faster and faster and the heart monitor came on. I double-checked and the power was off. It freaked me out and I just bolted."

Michelle remembers: "The presences didn't seem malevolent but I wanted to know who our uninvited members were."

They got in touch with medium, Jacky Dennison, 48, from Northwich, Cheshire, and she agreed to hold a seance in the gym. As soon as Jacky walked in she said: "I can sense activity."

During the seance she made contact with the spirit of a woman named Miriam. She'd been a schoolteacher in 1907 and had lost her true love, Robert.

Jay reminded her of him which is why she'd been following him around.

She was also curious about what the couple were doing in the chapel.

The next spirit Jacky identified was a fair-haired six-year-old boy called Thomas wearing grey trousers and a dark jacket.

"As soon as she described Thomas I started to cry," says Michelle. "I felt so frightened."

The medium explained that Michelle could sense the boy's loneliness. He'd been the one causing all the noise.

"He'd got stuck in this plane when he had died and didn't know how to go over to the other side," adds Michelle.

"The medium then directed the boy towards the light." Jacky later checked chapel records at the local library and found a reference to a Miriam Heath who worked there in 1907.

"We were both gobsmacked when she came up with the proof," adds Jay.

"Now eight months on, the fitness centre, called The Gym Works, has a calm atmosphere.

"Miriam doesn't follow me around so much but she's still here and she helps us make our business decisions. When she disapproves of something she finds a way of letting us know.

"Thankfully, it hasn't put off any customers. Some even like the idea of being watched – it means they do their exercises right."

30th December **2005**

WE LIVE IN BRITAIN'S MOST HAUNTED HOUSE

This year Jayne and Tom Hayes are having a quiet New Year's Eve in their mansion. Just the two of them … and 26 ghosts.

The priest couldn't take his eyes off the old mansion. "This is the most haunted house I've ever seen," he told an astonished Jayne Hayes. "And I've done a few exorcisms in my time."

A shiver ran down Jayne's spine as she recalled the spooky noises she'd heard in the 34-room mansion in Nottinghamshire she and her husband Tim had chosen as their new home.

Living in a cramped two-bedroom flat in London, Jayne and Tim, 46, had dreamed of moving into the countryside and setting up a pet detective business.

Jayne, 46, says: "When I walked into the mansion I just knew we had to buy it, especially as it was the same price we'd paid for our small flat in London."

But she didn't realise the house had sitting tenants.

Weeks after moving into the mansion – parts of which date from 1590 – strange things began happening in the old hall.

The servants' bells began ringing on their own. Jayne also heard children laughing downstairs. "I didn't bother telling Tim, I just thought I was imagining things," she explains.

The couple finally succeeded in setting up their firm, Doglost, and, as a sideline, Jayne hired out the house for weddings.

A few weeks after the visiting priest made his spooky claim, Rachel Hughes, 33, who helped with the company's website, came running out of the house as Jayne and Tim were popping into town.

"I saw a ghost – a woman in a brown housecoat," Rachel stammered. She was hysterical and Jayne had to calm her down.

"Rachel was shaking as she recalled what she'd seen in the study. I thought she'd imagined it because she was tired, I didn't believe in ghosts back then," says Jayne.

But not long after that initial sighting Rachel began hearing shuffling footsteps, children laughing and even a piano playing by itself.

"It was so spooky," said Rachel. "I even saw a man in a black top hat and tails in the cloakroom. He was totally solid and then vanished into thin air.

"A little spirit girl has also pulled my hair when I was sitting working on the computer. I didn't see her but I heard her giggling. It was terrifying."

Jayne couldn't ignore the ghostly goings-on any longer. In January 2005 she called in a team of paranormal investigators for an overnight vigil.

As the medium walked into the hall, he shocked Jayne by announcing: "My God, they're all coming out to meet us."

The psychic began to identify the ghosts. He saw a woman in a brown housecoat, a housekeeper, a little girl called Emily, a man in a top hat, a painter, a Roman soldier … the list went on.

Page 42 **DAILY MIRROR**, *Friday, December 30, 2005*

Your LIFE *SPIRIT & FATE*

THIS YEAR JAYNE AND TIM HAYES ARE HAVING A QUIET NEW YEAR'S EVE IN THEIR MANSION. JUST THE TWO OF THEM... AND 26 GHOSTS

SPOOKSVILLE: Jayne in front of her haunted mansion with her pet bulldogs

We live in Britain's most haunted house

THE priest couldn't take his eyes off the old mansion. "This the most haunted house I've ever seen," he told an astonished Jayne Hayes. "And I've done a few exorcisms in my time."

A shiver ran down Jayne's spine as she recalled the spooky noises she'd heard in the 34-room mansion in Nottinghamshire she and her husband Tim had chosen as their new home.

Living in a cramped two-bedroom flat in London, Jayne and Tim, 46, had dreamed of moving into the countryside and setting up a pet detective business.

Jayne, 46, says: "When I walked into the mansion I just knew we had to buy it, especially as it was the same price we'd paid for our small flat in London."

But she didn't realise the house had sitting tenants.

Weeks after moving into the mansion – parts of which date from 1590 – strange things began happening in the old hall.

The servants' bells began ringing on their own. Jayne also heard children laughing downstairs. "I didn't bother telling Tim, I just thought I was imagining things," she explains.

The couple finally succeeded in setting up their firm, Doglost, and, as a sideline, Jayne hired out the house for weddings.

A few weeks after the visiting priest made his spooky claim, Rachel Hughes, 33, who helped with the company's website, came running out of the house as Jayne and Tim were popping into town.

"I saw a ghost – a woman in a brown housecoat," Rachel stammered. She was hysterical and Jayne had to calm her down.

"Rachel was shaking as she recalled what she'd seen in the study. I thought she'd imagined it because was tired, I didn't believe in ghosts back then," says Jayne.

But not long after that initial sighting Rachel began hearing shuffling footsteps, children laughing and even a piano playing by itself.

This house is spooksville Piccadilly Circus

"It was so spooky," said Rachel. "I even saw a man in a black top hat and tails in the cloakroom. He was totally solid and then vanished into thin air.

"A little spirit girl has also pulled my hair when I was sitting working on the computer. I didn't see her but I heard her giggling. It was terrifying."

Jayne couldn't ignore the ghostly goings-on any longer. In January 2005 she called in a team of paranormal investigators for an overnight vigil.

As the medium walked into the hall, he shocked Jayne by announcing: "My God, they're all coming out to meet us."

The psychic began to identify the ghosts. He saw a woman in a brown housecoat, a housekeeper, a little girl called Emily, a man in a top hat, a painter, a Roman soldier… the list went on.

"This is spooksville Piccadilly Circus," says Jayne. "The medium told me it was the most haunted house in Britain.

"I don't blame Rachel now for refusing to be left on her own. It was like the set of a horror movie."

Jayne believes the clairvoyant because she'd not given him any details. "He told me there were at least 26 ghosts in residence. But he said they weren't trapped. They all love visiting the house and invite their mates over at the weekend!

"I can't believe I haven't seen one of them yet," laughs Jayne.

"But as Tim and I toast in the New Year we won't be alone, which is fine. There's room enough for all of us."

BY MONICA CAFFERKY

Britain's most haunted house.

“This is spooksville Piccadilly Circus,” says Jayne. “The medium told me it was the most haunted house in Britain.

“I don’t blame Rachel now for refusing to be left on her own. It was like the set of a horror movie.”

Jayne believes the clairvoyant because she’d not given him any details. “He told me there were at least 26 ghosts in residence. But he said they weren’t trapped. They all love visiting the house and invite their mates over at the weekend!

“I can’t believe I haven’t seen one of them yet,” laughs Jayne. “But as Tim and I toast in the New Year we won’t be alone, which is fine. There’s room enough for all of us.”

“Okay! It’s all clear.”

HOME: Singer Robin

Robin house 'haunted'

By CAMERON ROBERTSON

THERE'S a strange noise coming from Robin Gibb's home – and it's not one of his old records...it's a ghost.

The 57-year-old Bee Gees singer claims his 12th-century house is haunted by a spook who likes to play pranks on him and his family.

Robin said: "There's a resident ghost who mysteriously fills up the water in the old font in the chapel which we converted into a dining room.

"This was a place where monks would be trained for their vocation."

Robin, who sang lead vocals for Giving Up The Ghost on the band's 1987 album ESP, said he has been a keen historian since the age of eight.

He added: "I love visiting old churches and reading about historical characters. I've always had at least one history book on the go, even on tour."

No doubt the poltergeist plaguing his home in Thame, Berks, will be shifting a few of his history book around.

And if it's a really good ghost, it'll hide his Bee Gees albums, too.

Voice of the Mirror: Page 6

c.robertson@mirror.co.uk

30th March 2006

Robin Gibb and his haunted home.

THE HEE BEE BEE GEES

ROBIN HOUSE 'HAUNTED'

There's a strange noise coming from Robin Gibb's home – and it's not one of his old records … it's a ghost.

The 57-year-old Bee Gees singer claims his 12th-century house is haunted by a spook who likes to play pranks on him and his family.

Robin said: "There's a resident ghost who mysteriously fills up the water in the old font in the chapel which we converted into a dining room.

"This was a place where monks would be trained for their vocation."

Robin sang lead vocals for 'Giving Up the Ghost' on the band's 1987 album *ESP*.

21st July 2006

GHOSTS CAME AFTER MY BABY

As a little girl Natalie Miller was plagued by spirits. But when they threatened her son, she took action …

Helping little Zack into his pyjamas, his mum Natalie suddenly felt the hairs on the back of her neck stand on end. A pot of cream flew across the room and a dark apparition appeared in the corner.

Natalie grabbed her baby son and ran into her bedroom. The single mum managed to hold back her own tears enough to soothe the distressed baby.

"'When will this ever end?' I cried. Since the age of four I had been seeing things in my parents' house," says Natalie, now 22.

"No one believed me when I told them that a little girl with black ringlets ran around my room then disappeared through the wall. Or that I felt cold spots in the house and heard people calling my name.

"Mum and Dad told me to stop being silly. But the psychic activity really picked up when I hit my teens. That's when I saw black apparitions.

"They would appear on the stairs. I hated having a shower because I felt I was being watched."

Then, when Natalie was 19, the nightmares began. "I saw black holes in the walls and evil entities appeared to be coming in to attack me. I felt terrified.

"Once I woke up pinned to the bed by something black with gaping jaws. I screamed 'Get off me!' It sounds daft but when I said the Lord's Prayer, it vanished.

"I sometimes felt like I was going mad. I tried to confide in school friends but got bullied for being a weirdo so kept my mouth shut.

"I felt so alone. Mum and Dad didn't believe me, my brothers took the mickey so I bottled up my fear."

When she got pregnant Natalie had another shocking experience at the house, in Tipton, West Midlands.

"I felt a pair of male hands pushing me hard off the top of the stairs. I stumbled and had to hang on to the banisters. I was terrified of falling and losing my baby.

"But after a cup of sweet tea I convinced myself that it must have been my imagination. The alternative was too frightening to contemplate – a ghost had tried to kill my unborn baby."

Luckily, after Zack was born things went quiet and it seemed as if the hauntings had finally stopped.

But then she felt the presences again – even stronger than before.

"The TV switched itself on and off and I had nightmares. I felt like I was being watched all the time."

When Zack was 18 months he began to get very distressed and Natalie would find him screaming.

"Pots of cream and toy boxes were thrown about and it was getting dangerous.

"I realized they were after my baby. Something snapped and I searched out a local medium."

The medium, Alan, found a total of 83 entities in the house, including a man on the stairs who had murdered his wife there and a woman in the bathroom who had been strangled by her husband.

"It's near Dudley Castle and the ground has soaked up the negative energy of battles and death," says Alan. "The area attracted villains, prostitutes and murderers and terrible crimes were committed."

But who was scaring little Zack?

Alan found the spirit of a woman who had lost her baby in childbirth and had become attached to him.

"She was peering over the cot and making him cry. Alan saw it."

Now thankfully the house is peaceful and Natalie has moved out.

"I just want to focus on being a mum now," she says. "Alan told me I have a gift and I'll develop it when I feel ready. I don't want to face ghosts again until I know how to send them into the light myself."

23rd March 2007

I was haunted by Robin Hood's killer.

I WAS HAUNTED BY ROBIN HOOD'S KILLER

As a child, Barbara Green had been a big fan of Robin Hood. So, when she discovered where the real man was supposed to be buried, her curiosity got the better of her.

But after trudging through the countryside to the grave she had a nasty surprise – a run-in with the outlaw's killer.

Despite legend associating him with Nottingham, the grave of the real-life Robin is believed to be near Huddersfield, West Yorkshire.

Retired district nurse Barbara, 61, says: "I set out late evening when the sun was starting to set. I had discovered the grave's location in the local reference library and knew vaguely where I was going.

"I parked the car, scrambled over a wall and began walking up a hillside. Within minutes I stumbled upon the mysterious 'tower' – a Victorian shooting lodge built on the site of a Roman fort and now buried in rhododendron bushes.

"Robin's grave was on the map as being nearby in a small clearing and I soon found it, all green and mossy, surrounded by twisted railings. There was an ominous silence there, and I felt like something was watching me."

Barbara's instincts were right. Seconds later she says she felt streams of evil energy coming out of the woods towards her.

"It was like a rush of air and it felt like I was being wrapped in blackness. The sensation was weird and unlike anything I've ever experienced. I grabbed the railings to steady myself."

Barbara, from Brighouse, West Yorks, was so frightened she started having trouble breathing. Then suddenly, she saw the ghost of a man with red hair appear from behind the trees.

"His face was contorted in anger, it was horrible, and he came rushing towards me. He was wearing a black cloak and was about

PAGE 46 **DAILY MIRROR**, *Friday, March 23, 2007*

YourLIFE SPIRIT & FA

FRIGHTENED: Barbara with her dog

Pictures: ROSS PARRY AGENCY

As a child, Barbara Green had been a big fan of Robin Hood. So, when she discovered where the real man was supposed to be buried, her curiosity got the better of her.

But after trudging through the countryside to the grave she had a nasty surprise – a run-in with the outlaw's killer.

Despite legend associating him with Nottingham, the grave of the real-life Robin is believed to be near Huddersfield, West Yorkshire.

Retired district nurse Barbara, 61, says: "I set out late evening when the sun was starting to set. I had discovered the grave's location in the local reference library and knew vaguely where I was going.

"I parked the car, scrambled over a wall and began walking up a hillside. Within minutes I stumbled upon the mysterious 'tower' – a Victorian shooting lodge built on the site of a Roman fort and now buried in rhododendron bushes,

"Robin's grave was on the map as being nearby in a small clearing and I soon found it, all green and mossy, surrounded by twisted railings. There was an ominous silence there, and I felt like something was watching me."

Barbara's instincts were right. Seconds later she says she felt streams of evil energy coming out of the woods towards her.

"It was like a rush of air and it felt like I was being wrapped in blackness. The sensation was weird and unlike anything I've ever experienced. I grabbed the railings to steady myself."

EERIE: Robin Hood's grave

Barbara, from Brighouse, West Yorks, was so frightened she started having trouble breathing. Then suddenly, she saw the ghost of a man with red hair appear from behind the trees.

"His face was contorted in anger, it was horrible, and he came rushing towards me. He was wearing a black cloak and was about 5ft 11 and his feet weren't touching the ground!

"Then a black shape appeared behind him, it had an outline of a woman. By now I was terrified. I was so scared I thought I was going to die on the spot.

"But I came to my senses and stumbled through the trees back to my car before the apparitions reached me."

The evil energy came out of the woods at me

Once home, Barbara became determined to solve the mystery surrounding the two ghosts. She delved into history books and unearthed the gruesome theory behind Robin's death.

She soon believed the man was Red Roger of Doncaster and the ghostly woman was his supposed lover, Sister Mary Startin, head nun at Kirklees Priory, which was founded in the 12th century.

"Robin Hood was reputedly murdered by Sister Mary in the 14th century," explains Barbara.

"When he turned up at her priory, in Huddersfield, injured and needing help she realised that he was the infamous Robin Hood. She bled him purposely to death in revenge for his preying on the clergy and robbing them while they travelled in the area.

"Bleeding was a common treatment in those times. Mary's zeal and skill has earned her the nickname in this part of the world as 'the Vampire of Kirklees'."

Over the past few years, other reports of ghostly goings on at Robin Hood's grave have been reported to the Yorkshire Robin Hood Society, set up by Barbara.

"People have seen ghosts of monks, nuns in the wood and one elderly woman says she often heard Robin calling for Marian."

The society has also discovered that the grave lies on ancient leylines of mystical power.

Barbara adds: "I've been back to the grave a few times in the daylight with friends who are curious to see where the Yorkshire hero is buried.

"But there's no way you would catch me there at night.

"This is no Blair Witch hoax – Robin Hood's grave and its surroundings are haunted for real."

BY MONICA CAFFERKY

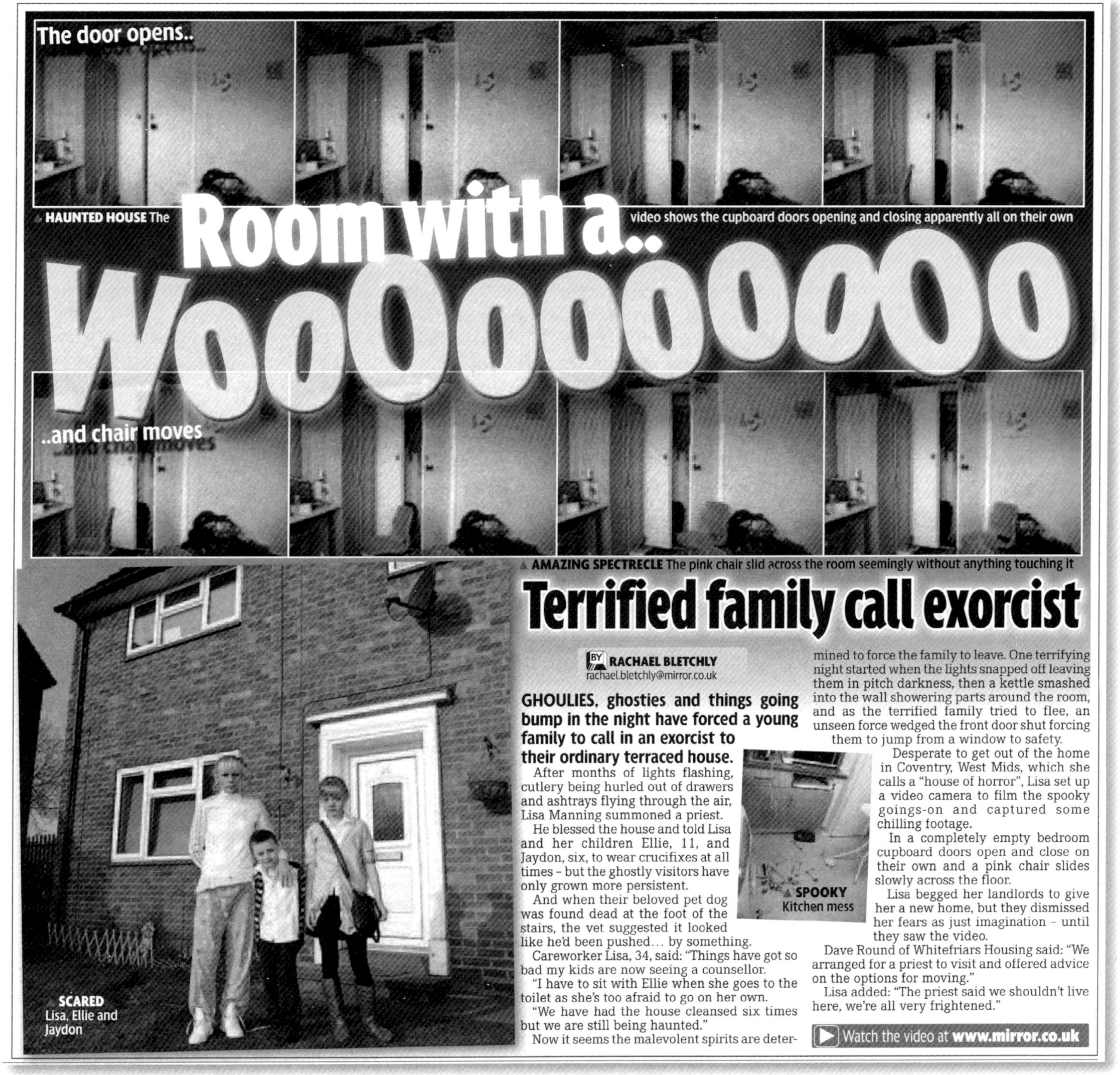

The door opens..

HAUNTED HOUSE The video shows the cupboard doors opening and closing apparently all on their own

Room with a.. WooOOOOOOOo

..and chair moves

AMAZING SPECTRECLE The pink chair slid across the room seemingly without anything touching it

SCARED Lisa, Ellie and Jaydon

Terrified family call exorcist

BY RACHAEL BLETCHLY
rachael.bletchly@mirror.co.uk

GHOULIES, ghosties and things going bump in the night have forced a young family to call in an exorcist to their ordinary terraced house.

After months of lights flashing, cutlery being hurled out of drawers and ashtrays flying through the air, Lisa Manning summoned a priest.

He blessed the house and told Lisa and her children Ellie, 11, and Jaydon, six, to wear crucifixes at all times – but the ghostly visitors have only grown more persistent.

And when their beloved pet dog was found dead at the foot of the stairs, the vet suggested it looked like he'd been pushed… by something.

Careworker Lisa, 34, said: "Things have got so bad my kids are now seeing a counsellor.

"I have to sit with Ellie when she goes to the toilet as she's too afraid to go on her own.

"We have had the house cleansed six times but we are still being haunted."

Now it seems the malevolent spirits are determined to force the family to leave. One terrifying night started when the lights snapped off leaving them in pitch darkness, then a kettle smashed into the wall showering parts around the room, and as the terrified family tried to flee, an unseen force wedged the front door shut forcing them to jump from a window to safety.

SPOOKY Kitchen mess

Desperate to get out of the home in Coventry, West Mids, which she calls a "house of horror", Lisa set up a video camera to film the spooky goings-on and captured some chilling footage.

In a completely empty bedroom cupboard doors open and close on their own and a pink chair slides slowly across the floor.

Lisa begged her landlords to give her a new home, but they dismissed her fears as just imagination – until they saw the video.

Dave Round of Whitefriars Housing said: "We arranged for a priest to visit and offered advice on the options for moving."

Lisa added: "The priest said we shouldn't live here, we're all very frightened."

Watch the video at **www.mirror.co.uk**

A video captures a poltergeist opening a door and sliding a pink chair across a room.

5ft 11 and his feet weren't touching the ground!

"Then a black shape appeared behind him, it had an outline of a woman. By now I was terrified. I was so scared I thought I was going to die on the spot.

"But I came to my senses and stumbled through the trees back to my car before the apparitions reached me."

Once home, Barbara became determined to solve the mystery surrounding the two ghosts. She delved into history books and unearthed the gruesome theory behind Robin's death.

She soon believed the man was Red Roger of Doncaster and the ghostly woman was his supposed lover, Sister Mary Startin, head nun at Kirklees Priory, which was founded in the 12th century.

"Robin Hood was reputedly murdered by Sister Mary in the 14th century," explains Barbara.

"When he turned up at her priory, in Huddersfield, injured and needing help she realized that he was the infamous Robin Hood. She bled him purposely to death in revenge for his preying on the clergy and robbing them while they travelled in the area.

"Bleeding was a common treatment in those times. Mary's zeal and skill has earned her the nickname in this part of the world as 'the Vampire of Kirklees'."

Over the past few years, other reports of ghostly goings on at Robin Hood's grave have been reported to the Yorkshire Robin Hood Society, set up by Barbara.

"People have seen ghosts of monks, nuns in the wood and one elderly woman says she often heard Robin calling for Marian."

The society has also discovered that the grave lies on ancient leylines of mystical power.

Barbara adds: "I've been back to the grave a few times in the daylight with friends who are curious to see where the Yorkshire hero is buried.

"But there's no way you would catch me there at night.

"This is no Blair Witch hoax – Robin Hood's grave and its surroundings are haunted for real."

29th March **2011**

ROOM WITH A WOOOOOOOOOO

TERRIFIED FAMILY CALL EXORCIST

Ghoulies, ghosties and things going bump in the night have forced a young family to call in an exorcist to their ordinary terraced house.

After months of lights flashing, cutlery being hurled out of drawers and ashtrays flying through the air, Lisa Manning summoned a priest.

He blessed the house and told Lisa and her children Ellie, 11, and Jaydon, six, to wear crucifixes at all times – but the ghostly visitors have only grown more persistent.

And when their beloved pet dog was found dead at the foot of the stairs, the vet suggested it looked like he'd been pushed … by something.

Careworker Lisa, 34, said: "Things have got so bad my kids are now seeing a counsellor.

"I have to sit with Ellie when she goes to the toilet as she's too afraid to go on her own.

"We have had the house cleansed six times but we are still being haunted."

Now it seems the malevolent spirits are determined to force the family to leave. One terrifying night started when the lights snapped off leaving them in pitch darkness, then a kettle smashed into the wall showering parts around the room, and as the terrified family tried to flee, an unseen force wedged the front door shut forcing them to jump from a window to safety.

Desperate to get out of the home in Coventry, West Mids, which she calls a "house of horror", Lisa set up a video camera to film the spooky goings-on and captured some chilling footage.

In a completely empty bedroom cupboard doors open and close on their own and a pink chair slides slowly across the floor.

Lisa begged her landlords to give her a new home, but they dismissed her fears as just imagination – until they saw the video.

Dave Round of Whitefriars Housing said: "We arranged for a priest to visit and offered advice on the options for moving."

Lisa added: "The priest said we shouldn't live here, we're all very frightened."

21st December **2012**

MY HUBBY'S THE GHOST OF CHRISTENING PRESENT

WIDOW'S SPOOKY PICTURE

A gran was stunned after a family christening photo seemed to show the ghostly image of her late husband.

Heather Sewell, 50, spotted the spooky black-and-white face hovering over the font.

She said: "I couldn't believe the likeness to my Terry and was completely amazed to see him at the christening.

"It knocked me back when I saw the picture. It looks so much like him. It was actually a bit upsetting to see his face.

"I tried to convince myself it was not Terry but it is so convincing that I believe it is." Heather was at the christening of granddaughter Mia-Bella when the baby's uncle, Jamie Sewell, 29, snapped the phantom face on his mobile.

It was not until later, when the family was in the pub looking at the day's pictures on Facebook, that Heather spotted her late husband's likeness.

The taxi driver from Petham, Kent, said: "Terry had a long face and so does the ghost. It has the same hairstyle and is the same height – about 5ft 8 in.

"I am quite a superstitious person but not over the top.

"I do believe there is something out there – there are too many things in the world we cannot explain. I know there has been no photo trickery so it is all very spooky and perhaps not what you want to see at a christening.

"When we first saw the Facebook page everyone was stunned because the image is so clear."

Heather's labourer husband committed suicide 17 years ago by hanging himself. He was 41.

DMIST

Daily Mirror FRIDAY 21.12.2012 M 15

My hubby's the Ghost of Christening Present

HOLY SPIRIT Facebook pic of 'ghost' at font

ALIKE Terry and 'phantom'

WIDOW'S SPOOKY PICTURE

BY EUAN STRETCH
euan.stretch@mirror.co.uk

A GRAN was stunned after a family christening photo seemed to show the ghostly image of her late husband.

Heather Sewell, 50, spotted the spooky black-and-white face hovering over the font.

She said: "I couldn't believe the likeness to my Terry and was completely amazed to see him at the christening.

"It knocked me back when I saw the picture. It looks so much like him. It was actually a bit upsetting to see his face.

"I tried to convince myself it was not Terry but it is so convincing that I believe it is." Heather was at the christening of granddaughter Mia-Bella when the baby's uncle, Jamie Sewell, 29, snapped the phantom face on his mobile.

It was not until later, when the family was in the pub looking at the day's pictures on Facebook, that Heather, spotted her late husband's likeness.

The taxi driver from Petham, Kent, said: "Terry had a long face and so does the ghost. It has the same hairstyle and is the same height - about 5ft 8 in.

"I am quite a superstitious person but not over the top.

"I do believe there is something out there - there are too many things in the world we cannot explain. I know there has been no photo trickery so it is all very spooky and perhaps not what you want to see at a christening.

"When we first saw the Facebook page everyone was stunned because the image is so clear."

Heather's labourer husband committed suicide 17 years ago by hanging himself. He was 41.

Baby Mia-Bella's christening was in St Martin's, Canterbury - England's oldest parish church in continuous use.

Services have been conducted there since 1668 but there have been no previous reports of any ghostly sightings.

Heather's daughter Gemma Sewell, 27, and her partner were joined by older daughter Jaiden, five, for their baby's service.

AMAZED Gran Heather

HAUNT OF THE LOST SOLE

BRITAIN'S most haunted church is said to be St Bartholomew's in Smithfield, London. Its most notable apparition is a monk hunting a sandal stolen from his tomb. Other regulars are the Duke of Argyll and 18th century cartoonist William Hogarth.

Ghost attends christening in church.

Loch Ness Monster – It's a Family Affair

◆ Humps of a great lake monster, or waves?

Descriptions of lake monsters and sea serpents are remarkably consistent. Small heads, long necks and tails, scaly skin, humps and flippers. There are exceptions, but considering the range of geographies and cultures where sightings of these creatures are reported, there are more similarities than differences. Does this suggest a pattern in their shape and form, or a universal tendency for humans to misinterpret other animals or inert objects for mythical beasts?

5th November **1937**

LOCH NESS MONSTER'S BROTHER

CAMEL FACE AND GOLF BALL EYES

The Loch Ness monster's "brother" is down in Devon.

Head gardener to Mr. Cyril Maude, the actor, of Redlap, Dartmouth, Mr. Harold Groves, met him while fishing in Redlap Cove.

This is the story Mr. Groves told me when I called on him to-day: –

"I was fishing in Redlap Cove in the evening when, looking out to sea, I saw about fifty yards away a creature swimming in the water.

"It had three humps, and there was at least 12ft. of its body above the surface.

"I drew in my fishing gear to climb to the cliff top for a better view, but when I raised my head again I was startled to see right in front of me the head of the monster.

"It had a face like a camel, the head was about 2ft. long, and a tuft of hair on the top of the skull was quite thick.

"Otherwise the head was entirely hairless and the skin almost white. It had large, unblinking eyes, bigger than golf balls."

And Mr. Maude is greatly impressed by Mr. Groves's story.

"My gardener is a very steady and respectable fellow who has had a lot of experience of the sea. I am certain he saw the monster."

23rd August **1969**

THE LOCH NESS MONSTER LOSES HER STAR BILLING

That's what comes of being a prima donna. Nessie, who has had a record-breaking run at Loch Ness these past thirty years, has played hard-to-get once too often. All that now-you-see-me, now-you-don't stuff. You can't treat monster fans like that.

Now she is just being severely up-staged by an immodest monster over the hills.

Nessie's fickle fans snatched up their cameras and binoculars and left Loch Ness to take up front row seats forty miles away here at Loch Morar, in Inverness-shire, where a new monster was putting on a line turn.

That's show biz, Nessie. Bright lights one day, forgotten for a newcomer in a lousy provincial loch the next.

Monsters are big business in this part of the world. Loch Ness has a quiet look about it now.

But along the road to Loch Morar, a forty-mile single track into the mountains beyond Fort William, police reported traffic jams.

Every bed in the village of one hotel, two shops, about forty houses and a tea van, is taken: visitors sleep in their cars.

Morag, as they've dubbed the monster who this week became an overnight star, is packing them in.

Loyal Ness men try to keep a brave face. Nessie has been pretty good to them over the years. She's their major industry.

And they say they have grave doubts about these fly-by-night monsters who never so much as smile at a passing camera.

"Nessie has put us on the map," says William Grant, 49, who serves teas to thousands of monster spotters at Drumnadrochit. "People come from all over the world to see her. Or not to see her.

"She's been with us for years. Her attraction won't be diminished by any distant relative. And she'll be here when they're all forgotten.

"Mind you, if this new, so-called monster was to keep on popping up ..."

A worried look crossed his face. You see that look a lot on Loch Ness side these days.

DEBUT

They speak of Morag as though she is some vulgar, little hoofer from the chorus, trying to oust the Callas of the monster world.

Jealousy? Well, certainly Morag made a fine debut. None of those blurred photographs for her. She almost jumped out of the water, and set about two local fishermen.

Cynics at Loch Ness say that people are always trying to get into the monster business.

It's true that every well-appointed tourist place wants a nice frisky monster. But Morar have had theirs for years.

Foxy the taxi man has seen it. So has Hanratty on the boats. And McVarish, the barman.

Anyway, they've got enough legends among the mossy mountains that surround the dull silver loch to shut down Ness, Lomond and Stratford-on-Avon overnight. They just don't shout

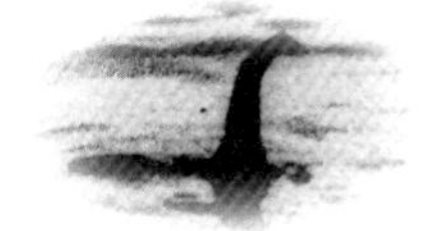

about them, that's all.

What about the ancient barge that slides empty and sinister across the loch whenever a member of a local family dies? "'Tis just a Gillies going home," they say.

And the grey dog that stalks the hills? That signifies another imminent death.

And they do say that fishermen who once dredged the bottom of the 1,000ft. deep loch screamed in horror at the vile sight in their nets and threw it back.

Very strong on doom and horror, the Morar people.

HARM

"There's plenty of strange happenings here," says Mrs. Julie Parks whose guest house at Bracara stands among the whispering trees on the loch-side. "We don't make the fuss they do at Loch Ness, that's the difference.

"Anyway, it will do more harm than good mark my words," she said glancing around for another evil omen.

"We used to get select people. But this will attract all sorts. People who are only bothered by their noses, if you know what I mean."

It was Mrs. Parks's brother who saw the monster the other night. All a bit embarrassing really for the monster's curse (and no monster is complete without one) says that whenever it appears it foretells the death of a McDonnel.

They are McDonnels. Their father, Donald McDonnel, is eighty-one and, while not superstitious, it would have been all the same to him if the monster had kept its head down.

Mrs. Parks believes in the monster. She has actually seen the barge.

But the curse, she says, is pure superstition. "Just the same," she added, "my father is taking it very carefully lately."

You can see his point.

The Morar monster may not do much for the gift shops.

But the curse, the barge and the dog are enough to put a glint in any undertaker's eyes.

9th July 1970

MONSTER HUNT FOR SISTER OF NESSIE

A big hunt for the "sister" of the Loch Ness monster will begin on Monday.

She is called Morag, and is reputed to live in lonely Loch Morar in Inverness-shire – the deepest lake in Western Europe.

A team of twenty-five scientists and biologists, mainly from London and Liverpool Universities, have staked their savings and their summer holidays on trying to find Nessie's sister.

Using the latest scientific equipment begged or borrowed from universities and leading firms, they intend to probe to the bottom of the 1,017-ft. deep loch.

25th November 1970

MIGHTY MORAG MAY EVEN HAVE A FAMILY

Morag the monster emerged clearly yesterday as a serious rival to her better-known "cousin" Nessie.

For scientists came up with new evidence, suggesting that not only does Morag exist, but that she has also probably got a family in tow deep down in Loch Morar.

Twenty-seven "sightings" of Morag were revealed by the scientists in a report on a survey of the Inverness loch, presented at a London Press conference.

One of them was by two Edinburgh men who told the survey team that they saw "three large, black, hump-shaped objects" near their boat.

They estimated that the "monster was travelling about twelve miles per hour". They "beached the boat and walked home in a state of considerable shock," says the report.

Another sighting was in the late 1950s by a Mr Alexander MacDonell.

He said it was the size of an elephant. It "plunged off rocks into the water with a terrific splash".

According to the survey team, the "monster" has an eel or snake-like head and neck, with several humps. Seven sightings were reported this year, they say.

Marine biologist Dr. Neil Bass was one of the investigating team.

He said: "I entered this inquiry with an open mind. I am neither a monster maniac nor a sceptic.

"All I can say is that, with two other members of the survey team I saw, on July 14, a black, smooth, hump-shaped object in the water about 300 yards from me.

"The only species known to inhabit the loch that could produce such a hump would be an eel. It would have to be an enormous eel to fit what I saw – whatever it was."

Dr. Bass said he believed that the team had "put together something which was getting very feasible".

23rd June **1980**

SON OF NESSIE SURFACES AGAIN

Son of Nessie has reared its head again in America. A farmer and five friends have reported seeing a water monster, about 14ft. long, in the Potomac River in Virginia.

It was the first sighting since 1978, when more than thirty people said they had spotted a creature like the Loch Ness monster. Local people have christened it "Chessie".

17th February **1983**

SWEETHEART FOR NESSIE

Nessie, the Loch Ness monster, may not only exist but have a boyfriend, scientists claimed yesterday.

They said sophisticated sonar equipment had picked up strong contacts.

Adrian Shine, 34, field leader of a research team which has spent eight summers on the 23-mile loch, said: "The latest findings are very exciting.

"We have had very strong contacts on sonar equipment working at great depths. On occasions two objects have been recorded."

He added: "If there are Loch Ness monsters, this is precisely how they would appear on sonar."

He said the expedition's next job would be to try to use mobile underwater cameras to film the objects once they had been spotted by sonar.

After news of the sonar sightings, bookmakers William Hill cut its odds against the monster's existence from 50-1 to 25-1.

5th November **2007**

SEA 'SISTER OF NESSIE'

The Loch Ness monster may have an ancestor – a mysterious sea creature washed up in the Orkney Islands 200 years ago.

The carcass of the 55ft tailed "serpentine with a 10ft neck and a head like a sheep" was found on Stronsay in 1808.

The backbone and a "bristle" are still in storage at the Royal Museum of Scotland in Edinburgh.

Now geneticist Dr Yvonne Simpson will present research linking the so-called Stronsay Beast to descriptions of Nessie at the first Highland Science Festival this month.

She says: "They are strikingly-similar massive aquatic creatures."

26 Daily Mirror FRIDAY 18.02.2011

For breaking news go to: www.mirror.co.uk RELATED LINKS

Is this Bownessie?

▼ BEAUTY Tranquil Lake Windermere

BY PAUL BYRNE paul.byrne@mirror.co.uk

EERIE SIGHT AT THE LAKE

THESE four humps floating on the gloomy surface of a lake could be the first photograph of the Beast of Bowness.

The bizarre shape - the length of three cars - emerged from the mists of Lake Windermere and was captured by Tom Pickles, 24. "It was petrifying," said Mr Pickles, who was out kayaking. "I paddled back to the shore straight away. Its skin was like a seal's but its shape was not like any animal I've ever seen before." Reports date back to the 1950s of a strange creature living in the waters of Windermere - the Lake District's answer to the Loch Ness Monster.

But Dr Ian Winfield, a lake ecologist at the University of Lancaster, said it was highly unlikely that an animal as long as three cars could survive in Windermere.

He said: "It's possible that it's a catfish from Eastern Europe."

18th February **2011**

▲ Sighting of humps at Lake Windermere in 2011.

IS THIS BOWNESSIE?

EERIE SIGHT AT THE LAKE

These four humps floating on the gloomy surface of a lake could be the first photograph of the Beast of Bowness.

The bizarre shape – the length of three cars – emerged from the mists of Lake Windermere and was captured by Tom Pickles, 24. "It was petrifying," said Mr Pickles, who was out kayaking. "I paddled back to the shore straight away. Its skin was like a seal's but its shape was not like any animal I've ever seen before." Reports date back to the 1950s of a strange creature living in the waters of Windermere – the Lake District's answer to the Loch Ness Monster.

But Dr Ian Winfield, a lake ecologist at the University of Lancaster, said it was highly unlikely that an animal as long as three cars could survive in Windermere.

He said: "It's possible that it's a catfish from Eastern Europe."

7th March **2011**

LAKE NESS PUNCTURE

The mystery of the "Lake Ness" Monster may have been solved – with the discovery of an old tyre.

Two canoeists claimed to have recently snapped an English version of Nessie in Windermere. But Bowness tourist John Phillips, 36, of Solihull, West Mids, reckons the split tyre he found nearby could hold a clue.

He said: "I don't want to spoil anyone's fun, but when we threw it in the water it looked very similar."

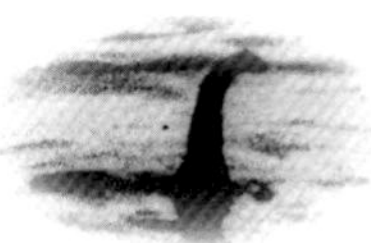

▼ **CAUGHT**
'Nessie' pic

BLOW OUT
The burst tyre

Lake Ness Puncture

THE mystery of the "Lake Ness" Monster may have been solved – with the discovery of an old tyre.

Two canoeists claimed to have recently snapped an English version of Nessie in Windermere. But Bowness tourist John Phillips, 36, of Solihull, West Mids, reckons the split tyre he found nearby could hold a clue.

He said: "I don't want to spoil anyone's fun, but when we threw it in the water it looked very similar."

Was this the Lake Windermere monster?

CRAIG'S COURT HOUSE
THE NATIONAL BANK
ISLE of SKYE
FOR PEACE
Easter MARCH
Easter MARCH
BRITAIN'S UNILATERAL ACTION ENDED THE ATLANTIC SLAVE TRADE
EBBW VALE CONSTITUENCY

British Big Cats – Cat Among the Pigeons

Trafalgar Square, London, 1964.

Panthers are not a distinct species, just the general name used to refer to any black big cat, for example, black leopards and black jaguars, occurring in the same litter of two to four cubs as their more usual spotted siblings. It is the combination of recessive genes from both parents that makes a cub black, the same for blondness in humans. There are 30 subspecies of leopard distributed across Asia and sub-Saharan Africa, while jaguars are found throughout Central and South America and parts of the USA. This means that panthers are incredibly adaptable to a great range of habitats and climates. They are solitary and nocturnal, which doesn't make spotting them easy. Their natural prey consists of deer, warthogs, wild boar, tapir and antelope, along with smaller species like birds and rabbits when larger prey is scarce. Like all big cats, when driven to desperation, they may attack humans.

13th January **1995**

PROBE INTO KILLER BEAST OF THE MOOR

The Government is launching an investigation into the Beast of Bodmin Moor.

Experts have been called in to examine evidence of big cats blamed for killing dozens of sheep and calves.

After years of ridiculing claims that pumas or black panthers are living wild in Britain, the Agriculture ministry have finally decided to take them seriously.

Up to a dozen "beasts" are thought to be at large.

6th January **1998**

KILLER WILD CATS SET TO STRIKE IN BRITAIN

Leopards and pumas living wild in Britain could kill people, an expert warned yesterday.

Zoologist and trapper Quentin Rose said that in the last six years he had identified 27 reliable reports of leopards and 32 of pumas, along with 18 smaller members of the cat family – jungle cats, leopard cats and ocelots. There had been sightings in the West Country, the Midlands, Wales, East Anglia and Scotland.

Mr Rose, who has worked with the Zoological Society of London, said the problem went far beyond the legend of the Beast of Bodmin Moor.

He said numbers could be out of control in 20 years, and warned: "People are going to be killed sooner or later.

"The threat to human life is greatest when an animal has been wounded, maimed and unable to hunt its normal prey."

The big cats are thought to be descended from exotic pets released into the wild after a clampdown more than 10 years ago. DNA tests are now being carried out on droppings thought to have been left by a puma or leopard in north Devon.

Mr Rose wants a national Government investigation.

Other experts back an inquiry but have played down the threat to humans.

26th August **2000**

THE BEAST OF TRELLECH

ITS FACE WAS COVERED IN BLOOD AND ITS BREATH SMELLED OF RABBIT GUTS. I THOUGHT IT WAS GOING TO KILL ME ...

Shocked Josh Hopkins told last night how he was savaged by the wild Beast of Trellech.

Josh, 11, was clawed and bitten by the panther in a field near his home.

He said: "The animal had blood on its jaws and its breath smelled as if it had just eaten something like a rabbit.

"Then it got my head in its jaws and bit me. I was terrified and I thought it was going to kill me.

"I started screaming and ran. The animal ran away as well into some nearby-fields.

"It was a really big cat, it would have ripped my face off, I don't feel safe to go out and play anymore."

Police marksmen were on standby last night as helicopters with heat-seeking equipment hunted the big cat. The public were warned to be on guard.

Josh's mother Rosemary Hopkins, 42, said: "I hope they get to it soon.

"Everyone is panicking around here. There's no way we can let our children go out and play on their own after this."

Josh was playing with his 15-year-old brother Jeremy in a field near their home at Trellech in South Wales when he was confronted by the 5ft long panther.

"I was on my way home after playing in my den in the woods when I saw a black tail and I thought it was my pet cat Sylvester," he said.

"I was just about to reach down when I suddenly realized it was a much bigger cat than I'd ever seen before. It turned and made a horrible hissing sound.

"Then it reared up and lashed at me with its paw holding my cheek for a second."

Bleeding from the cheek and head, Josh staggered back home.

He told his mother: "I've been attacked by a big black cat."

Mrs Hopkins said: "I thought he meant an ordinary cat but when I saw the wounds I realized it was a wild animal he was talking about.

"He described it as a big cat the size of a dog."

Josh's claw wounds and bites were treated with antibiotics at a nearby medical centre.

Mother-of-three Mrs Hopkins said: "It's a miracle he survived such an attack by a wild animal that belongs in the African bush. It's frightening that this happened just a few yards from the houses."

Last night, police warned villagers to be on the lookout for the black panther.

Chief Inspector Nigel Russell said: "We are taking this very seriously – it's the first time we've heard of anyone being attacked.

"There have been sightings locally of one or more of these large black cats. They have been seen walking across country roads by motorists late at night.

"We don't want to panic people but we are asking them to be very careful and vigilant."

Police said zoo keepers with stun guns would try to catch the beast humanely.

But snipers would be called in if it attacked again.

Chief Inspector Russell said: "It will be our last resort but we have marksmen if there is any danger to the public."

The chief inspector added that there had been no reports of a panther escaping from a zoo or wildlife park.

Neighbours of the Hopkins family revealed that they have lost chickens in recent weeks.

Big-cat expert Danny Nineham, who is helping the hunt, said: "Josh is extremely lucky to be alive.

"I'm baffled that the creature backed off when it did – but it was so lucky for the little lad that it did.

"They are quite capable of killing a small child even though they try to keep away from human beings."

Danny, 39, from Lydney, Gloucestershire, has been keeping track of the sightings of the cats throughout Britain for 15 years.

He believes the panther is not fully grown and was drawn to the village by the sound of children playing.

He added: "Since the Dangerous Wild Animals Act of 1976 private owners have been releasing animals into the countryside and they have just bred and bred.

"I see them frequently near my home and I'm sure there are a lot out there.

"They are very adaptable to our climate but they tend to steer clear of towns and villages and are no real threat if they are left alone."

The Act made it illegal to keep exotic pets without a licence. Some owners released animals into the wild rather than pay up to £3,000 to keep them. Britain's leading big cat expert, zoologist Quentin Rose, warned that at least 100 of the beasts could be on the loose.

Quentin, who has tracked black panthers and pumas for more than eight years, said: "There have been many reliable sightings of these creatures in South Wales including Newport, Swansea and the Gower.

"Some black panthers have even been spotted with cubs."

Black panthers or leopards, originally from Africa and Asia, can grow to up to 7ft from nose to the tip of the tail. Quentin, 45, had this advice for anyone who comes across one: "Never scream or run away – this could instigate an attack.

"Stand stone still, keep eye contact and don't bend down – that asserts your dominance.

"Allow the animal to wander away. Remember, it doesn't want to hurt you, it wants to escape."

Quentin added: "All cats, whether moggies or lions, have the flight-or-fight response. They can't do anything else.

"When a panther can't hunt for his usual prey of rabbits, badgers and foxes, he will try to kill a human."

26th August **2000**

WHERE THEY ARE ON LOOSE

There have been hundreds of sightings of feral big cats prowling the British countryside terrifying rural communities.

Out of focus snatched photos and the unexplained slaughter of sheep and chickens have added fuel to the reports.

But despite numerous investigations, nobody has managed to prove their existence beyond doubt.

It is thought they may be former pets released into the wild after new laws in 1976 made it illegal to keep exotic animals without a licence.

Former lion tamer Leslie Maiden, of Cradley Heath, West Midlands, claimed in January that he set a cougar and panther free in the Peak District, Derbyshire, in the 1970s.

He said: "I've always been an animal lover. But people came to me, saying they would have to put my animals down. I had no option."

It only became illegal to release wild animals into the countryside in the early 1980s.

Experts believe there could be 100 panthers and pumas roaming free – the offspring of creatures released.

Last week Betty Stephen, 51, spotted a panther-like beast in bushes in Kirkcaldy, Fife, as she walked her dog.

There have been several similar sightings between Kirkcaldy and Glenrothes.

Also this month the Beast of Malvern showed itself again in Worcestershire.

In July police were hunting a big cat which slaughtered sheep in Boblainy Forest, near Inverness.

Toolmaker Roger Kordas, 40, from Leigh Sinton, heard strange noises in a wheat field.

He said: "I shouted to see what the noise was and right before my eyes a black, muscular animal, bigger than a Labrador, with cat-like movements appeared."

His report follows other recent sightings of a feline creature in the area near the River Severn.

In March the Peak Panther appeared in the back garden of a house in Simmondley, near Glossop, Derbyshire.

None of these creatures is as notorious as the Beast of Bodmin which roams the Cornish countryside.

But they haunt suburban communities too. The Big Cat of Barnet is on the loose in South Mimms, Herts.

28th August **2002**

BIG CATS STALK EVERY COUNTY

Sightings of big cats roaming Britain have reached record levels, with more than 800 reported in a year.

New evidence released yesterday, including photographs of paw prints, sheep kills and hair samples, proves creatures including black panthers, lynx and pumas are loose, claim experts.

Daniel Bamping, of The British Big Cats Society, said: "We have had reports from every county. During the first six months of 2002 we have seen an incredible amount of big cat activity."

The society now plans to set up cameras to film the beasts.

"Big cats in Britain are real," Mr Bamping added. "They are breeding, and there are more of them."

In January this year Michael Cole was clawed by what he believed to be a lynx in Gravesham, Kent.

"It was about the size of a Labrador with tufts of fur on its ears," he said.

20th April **2004**

HUGE RISE IN BIG CATS

Sightings of big cats are soaring, with around 137 seen each month, according to a new survey of Britain's farmers.

There were 2,052 claimed sightings since the start of 2003, compared with 1,082 seen in 2002 and 679 in 2001.

Most are in Scotland, Wales, Kent, Yorkshire, Devon and Cornwall, with two-thirds of them black.

Danny Bamping of the British Big Cats Society said 17 exotic cats have been trapped, shot or run over in the last 20 years.

Mr Bamping, who wants an official study, said they may be breeding.

He added: "We have had calls from people saying they have a big cat with cubs on their land."

He believes they are likely to be large cats, lynx or black panthers.

23rd March **2005**

➧ Pinned to the ground by a hissing, snarling black beast.

THE BEAST OF SYDENHAM

'BIG CAT' HUNT AFTER ATTACK

Armed police were yesterday hunting a "big cat" in a London suburb after a man was mauled in his garden.

Anthony Holder, who is 6ft and weighs 15 stone, was pinned to the ground by the "hissing, snarling" black beast in the early hours.

He suffered a six-inch wound down one cheek and several scratches, but believes he could have been killed.

"I thought my life was in danger," said the 36-year-old DJ. "But all I was worried about was my family."

The animal could be a panther – usually a leopard or a jaguar with dark colouring. But experts have no idea where it could have come from.

Mr Holder went out into his garden in Sydenham, South East London, after he heard his pet cat – Kit-Kat – crying.

He said: "I saw a big black cat about 3ft tall and 5ft long on top of it.

"It let Kit-Kat go and jumped at me. I could see these huge teeth and the whites of its eyes just inches from my face."

The animal sank its claws into Mr Holder's finger and swiped at his face and arm before he beat it away.

His 11-year-old daughter Ashleigh watched in terror from her bedroom window. She said: "I saw dad flying backwards. I was

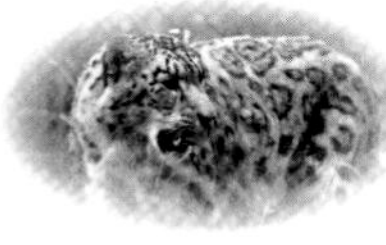

BEAST: Hunt is on for a huge black cat

The beast of Sydenham

'BIG CAT' HUNT AFTER ATTACK

ARMED police were yesterday hunting a "big cat" in a London suburb after a man was mauled in his garden.

By PAUL GALLAGHER

Anthony Holder, who is 6ft and weighs 15 stone, was pinned to the ground by the "hissing, snarling" black beast in the early hours.

He suffered a six-inch wound down one cheek and several scratches, but believes he could have been killed.

"I thought my life was in danger," said the 36-year-old DJ. "But all I was worried about was my family."

The animal could be a panther – usually a leopard or a jaguar with dark colouring. But experts have no idea where it could have come from.

Mr Holder went out into his garden in Sydenham, South East London, after he heard his pet cat – Kit-Kat – crying.

He said: "I saw a big black cat about 3ft tall and 5ft long on top of it.

"It let Kit-Kat go and jumped at me. I could see these huge teeth and the whites of its eyes just inches from my face."

The animal sank its claws into Mr Holder's finger and swiped at his face and arm before he beat it away.

His 11-year-old daughter Ashleigh watched in terror from her bedroom window. She said: "I saw dad flying backwards. I was really scared."

Wife Joy, 32, kept Ashleigh and her sisters Jamie, three, and Jorja, 18 months, inside and raised the alarm.

Police officers armed with tranquiliser guns combed the area yesterday.

Sydenham Girls School kept their pupils in at lunchtime and gates locked.

One sixth former said: "We were told to be vigilant."

Plasterer Billy Rich, 44, saw "something" run to a park.

"It was the size of a labrador, but definitely not a dog," he said.

The RSPCA warned: "It has potential to be extremely dangerous."

paul.gallagher@mirror.co.uk

SAFE: Anthony with his own cat

really scared."

Wife Joy, 32, kept Ashleigh and her sisters Jamie, three, and Jorja, 18 months, inside and raised the alarm. Police officers armed with tranquiliser guns combed the area yesterday.

Sydenham Girls School kept their pupils in at lunchtime and gates locked.

One sixth former said: "We were told to be vigilant."

Plasterer Billy Rich, 44, saw "something" run to a park.

"It was the size of a labrador, but definitely not a dog," he said.

The RSPCA warned: "It has potential to be extremely dangerous."

16th April **2005**

THE BEAST OF CWMBRAN

SNAPPER CLAIMS PANTHER IS ON LOOSE

A huge black cat gorges on a pigeon in a snap the photographer claims proves a wild panther is on the loose in a forest.

Norman Evans said he came face to face with the beast near a track three miles from his home.

The 43-year-old divorced dad-of-nine told how he feared the cat would attack him after taking the shots in Cwmbran, South Wales.

Norman said: "I couldn't believe my eyes. I was in utter shock.

"I had a heart attack three years ago and this nearly sparked another.

"My nerve went, I was shaking like a leaf. I was just worried about being attacked.

"It looked like a black panther from straight out of *The Jungle Book*.

"It was fully grown and really healthy, eating its lunch about 30ft away.

"I walked away quickly. People have been taking the mickey out of me. But I know what I saw. I won't be going for a walk in those woods again while he's on the loose.

"There have been several reported sightings of big cats in the area. I'm in no doubt it's true."

Norman was in the forest above Henllys village looking for a location to take photos of model Hayley Evans when he claims he spotted the animal.

He added: "I walked back to Hayley and said, 'Don't say a word, just grab your things and jump in the Jeep.' Once inside I showed her the picture."

Hayley, 23, said: "Norman looked white as a sheet. It's scary to think a panther's wandering around in an area where kids play." Norman told police of the sighting. He returned to the spot with

DAILY MIRROR, *Saturday, April 16, 2005* PAGE 15

MEAL: Big cat tucks in

THE BEAST OF CWMBRAN

Snapper claims panther is on loose

A HUGE black cat gorges on a pigeon in a snap the photographer claims proves a wild panther is on the loose in a forest.

Norman Evans said he came face to face with the beast near a track three miles from his home.

The 43-year-old divorced dad-of-nine told how he feared the cat would attack him after taking the shots in Cwmbran, South Wales.

Norman said: "I couldn't believe my eyes. I was in utter shock.

"I had a heart attack three years ago and this nearly sparked another.

"My nerve went. I was shaking like a leaf. I was just worried about being attacked.

"It looked like a black panther from straight out of the jungle book.

"It was fully grown and really healthy, eating its lunch about 30ft away.

"I walked away quickly. People have been taking the mickey out of

By RICHARD SMITH

me. But I know what I saw. I won't be going for a walk in those woods again while he's on the loose.

"There have been several reported sightings of big cats in the area. I'm in no doubt it's true."

Norman was in the forest above Henllys village looking for a location to take photos of model Hayley Evans when he claims he spotted the animal.

He added: "I walked back to Hayley and said, 'Don't say a word, just grab your things and jump in the Jeep'. Once inside I showed her the picture."

Hayley, 23, said: "Norman looked white as a sheet. It's scary to think a panther's wandering around in an area where kids play." Norman told police of the sighting. He returned to the spot with brother John later and found pigeon feathers but no big cat footprints.

John Partridge of Bristol Zoo said of the picture: "The image suggests this is a black panther. Fully grown."

Cwmbran police confirmed there have been reports of big cats roaming the area "over the last couple of years".

Last month Tony Holder, 36, claimed he was attacked by a black panther in his back garden at Sydenham, South East London.

KILL: Feathers lie at site where "panther ate bird"

richard.smith@mirror.co.uk

brother John later and found pigeon feathers but no big cat footprints.

John Partridge of Bristol Zoo said of the picture: "The image suggests this is a black panther. Fully grown."

Cwmbran police confirmed there have been reports of big cats roaming the area "over the last couple of years".

Last month Tony Holder, 36, claimed he was attacked by a black panther in his back garden at Sydenham, South East London.

♦ Huge black cat gorges on a pigeon.

31st July 2007

THE DEVIL OF DARTMOOR

MYSTERY OF HUGE BEAR-LIKE ANIMAL

A scary-looking beast has been spotted skulking around scrubland on Dartmoor.

Stunned walkers came across the mysterious muscular creature on a moorland track.

It is the size of a bear and moved like a wild cat as children rock-climbed nearby.

Witnesses said it was massive – but did not look like any animal they had ever seen.

Falconer Martin Whitley, who photographed the monster, said: "It was black and grey and comparable in size to a miniature pony.

"It had very thick shoulders, a long, thick tail with a blunt end and small round ears.

"Its movements appeared feline, then bear-like. There was a party climbing opposite making a racket but it ignored them completely."

Big cat expert Mark Fraser said the creature is baffling. He added: "It looks like a wolverine or a bear in some shots and a big wild dog in others. It is a very strange animal." Mr Whitley said: "I have worked with dogs all my life and it was definitely not that. I have seen a collie-sized black cat in the area about 10 years ago and this was a lot bigger.

"You would be surprised at the number of people who have seen black big cats and something resembling a small bear in the area over the course of the years."

Farmers fear the animal will prey on their stock. But the mystery beast is most likely a large and hairy wild boar. More than 100 escaped from Al Dedames North Devon farm two years ago and the survivors are believed to have bred.

According to local folklore, a wild dog pack known as the Hounds of Hell roam the tor in Dartmoor, Devon. The area, known as Hound Tor, is said to have inspired Sir Arthur Conan Doyle's *The Hound of the Baskervilles*.

27th November **2008**

FELINE DAFT OVER PHOTO

A student was feeling foolish yesterday after his photograph of the legendary Beast of Bodmin turned out to be a fat pet cat.

Paul Dennys took a snap of a black creature running across Bodmin Moor in Cornwall as part of his wildlife degree.

The 21-year-old, of Exeter, Devon, said: "It was quite a distance away but it was clearly a very large cat. I was convinced we saw the beast."

But zoologist Chris Moiser said: "With the best will in the world it is not a wild creature. I have no doubt it's a large domestic cat."

28th January **2009**

OSTRICH KILL BY 'BIG CAT'

An ostrich found with her head bitten off may have been the victim of a big cat.

The 7ft bird, kept behind a 4ft fence, also had internal bleeding caused by a blow to her abdomen.

Owner Anthony Bush, of Noah's Ark Zoo Farm, in Clevedon, Somerset, said: "It's possibly a big cat because we've had several sightings in the area."

Wildlife expert Nick Hammond said it was unlikely to be a fox: "It would have to be something much bigger and more violent."

DAILY MIRROR, Tuesday, July 31, 2007 PAGE 19

MASSIVE: The muscular creature is the size of a bear

THE DEVIL OF DARTMOOR

Mystery of huge bear-like animal

By RICHARD SMITH

THIS scary-looking beast has been spotted skulking around scrubland on Dartmoor.

Stunned walkers came across the mysterious muscular creature on a moorland track.

It is the size of a bear and moved like a wild cat as children rock-climbed nearby.

Witnesses said it was massive – but did not look like any animal they had ever seen.

Falconer Martin Whitley, who photographed the monster, said: "It was black and grey and comparable in size to a miniature pony.

"It had very thick shoulders, a long, thick tail with a blunt end and small round ears.

"Its movements appeared feline, then bear-like. There was a party climbing opposite making a racket but it ignored them completely."

Big cat expert Mark Fraser said the creature is baffling. He added: "It looks like a wolverine or a bear in some shots and a big wild dog in others. It is a very strange animal." Mr Whitley said: "I have worked with dogs all my life and it was definitely not that. I have seen a collie-sized black cat in the area about 10 years ago and this was a lot bigger.

"You would be surprised at the number of people who have seen black big cats and something resembling a small bear in the area over the course of the years."

Farmers fear the animal will prey on their stock. But the mystery beast is most likely a large and hairy wild boar. More than 100 escaped from Al Dedames North Devon farm two years ago and the survivors are believed to have bred.

According to local folklore, a wild dog pack known as the Hounds of Hell roam the tor in Dartmoor, Devon. The area, known as Hound Tor, is said to have inspired Sir Arthur Conan Doyle's The Hound of the Baskervilles.

richard.smith@mirror.co.uk

◀ Muscular creature the size of a bear is roaming Dartmoor.

21st May 2010

GIRLS CHASED BY 'BIG CAT'

A big black cat pursued two schoolgirls after they saw it by a tree in woods, scared 15-year-old Kim Howells said yesterday.

The "Great Dane-sized" animal followed her and cousin Sophie Gwynne, eight, home to Ruspidge in the Forest of Dean, Glos – where puma-like beasts have been sighted before.

29th January 2011

EX-COP'S BIG CAT SIGHTING

A former policeman claims his sighting of a big cat is proof the beasts exist.

Michael Disney says a large black "puma-like animal" crossed in front of him.

He said: "It had a cat-like head, muscular build and was 3ft tall."

The council public protection officer was driving down a narrow country track near Haverfordwest in Pembrokeshire.

His bosses at Pembrokeshire council are treating his sighting as authentic and want the public to report anything similar.

23rd May 2011

In what distant deeps or skies, burnt the fire of thine eyes?

TIGER: IN A CAT FLAP

Police scrambled armed officers and a helicopter after an "escaped tiger" was spotted in a field – but it turned out to be a life-size cuddly toy.

The public were told to stay inside after reports of the animal on the loose in Hedge End, Hants. Trevor Haywood, who was at a cricket match, said: "We were told to go to our cars and stay there.

"I saw two officers go off on a golf buggy with a rifle. It looked like they were going on safari."

17th December 2011

Sheep mutilated by a puma in Hertfordshire field.

FARMER FINDS SHEEP KILLED BY A 'BIG CAT'

A sheep has been found mutilated by a puma – in a Hertfordshire field.

WILDLIFE

▲ **MAULED** Sheep's remains

Farmer finds sheep killed by a 'big cat'

By ALUN PALMER

A SHEEP has been found mutilated by a puma - in a Hertfordshire field.

Farmer Johanna Collings, 40, who discovered the dismembered remains, said: "One of his front legs was gone and his rib cage was completely exposed.

"All the insides had been cleaned out perfectly, which is a typical trait of a cat."

The find in Loudwater, near Rickmansworth, follows 24 reported sightings of a big cat since January 2010 in the area. It has been dubbed the Beast of Buckinghamshire.

It comes after experts confirmed paw prints found on Wycombe Heights golf course, Bucks, were those of a puma. And Thames Valley Police wildlife officer PC Simon Towers recently found a big cat paw print in woodland in Oxfordshire.

He said: "We are not just getting reports from members of the public, but also from gamekeepers. They are coming from professionals."

Farmer Johanna Collings, 40, who discovered the dismembered remains, said: "One of his front legs was gone and his rib cage was completely exposed.

"All the insides had been cleaned out perfectly, which is a typical trait of a cat."

The find in Loudwater, near Rickmansworth, follows 24 reported sightings of a big cat since January 2010 in the area. It has been dubbed the Beast of Buckinghamshire.

It comes after experts confirmed paw prints found on Wycombe Heights golf course, Bucks, were those of a puma. And Thames Valley Police wildlife officer PC Simon Towers recently found a big cat paw print in woodland in Oxfordshire.

He said: "We are not just getting reports from members of the public, but also from gamekeepers. They are coming from professionals."

12th January 2012

KILLER BIG CAT SAVAGES DEER IN TRUST PARK

A big cat is believed to have viciously savaged to death a deer at a public park.

Dog walkers found the mutilated carcass, which experts say was "almost certainly" the result of an attack by a puma, panther, jaguar or leopard.

BEAST

▲ **DEADLY** A black panther

Killer big cat savages deer in Trust park

By MARTIN FRICKER

A BIG cat is believed to have viciously savaged to death a deer at a public park.

Dog walkers found the mutilated carcass, which experts say was "almost certainly" the result of an attack by a puma, panther, jaguar or leopard.

Its abdomen had been torn open and major organs including the heart, kidneys and liver were missing.

The deer's snout was also severed, as would happen if a big cat clamped its mouth shut to suffocate it.

National Trust staff at Woodchester Park, Glos, called in specialists Frank Tunbridge and Rick Minter who said it had been eaten by a "large predator".

Big cat author Mr Minter said: "It's hard to think of anything indigenous that could have done this."

National Trust spokesman David Armstrong said: "There is plenty of space for a big cat to live relatively undisturbed in 300 acres of woodland nearby."

Its abdomen had been torn open and major organs including the heart, kidneys and liver were missing.

The deer's snout was also severed, as would happen if a big cat clamped its mouth shut to suffocate it.

National Trust staff at Woodchester Park, Glos, called in specialists Frank Tunbridge and Rick Minter who said it had been eaten by a "large predator".

Big cat author Mr Minter said: "It's hard to think of anything indigenous that could have done this."

National Trust spokesman David Armstrong said: "There is plenty of space for a big cat to live relatively undisturbed in 300 acres of woodland nearby."

◆ A black panther.

17th January 2012

BEAST OF STROUD

FEARS OF BIG CAT ON LOOSE AS SECOND DEER IS SAVAGED

A killer big cat is believed to be on the rampage in the Cotswolds after a second deer was found mutilated.

The carcass was in a field 10 miles from where the first deer had been ripped apart a fortnight ago in Woodchester Park, near Stroud.

Experts fear the animals were brought down and devoured by a powerful predator such as a puma, jaguar or leopard.

Big cat expert Frank Tunbridge, 65, said yesterday about the latest kill: "I believe it could be the same cat that attacked in Woodchester because these animals usually have a territory of 100 square miles. Big cats could be thriving because there are plenty of deer and winter weather creates cover for hunting."

The second body was found by a woman walking her dog between Whiteway and Rendcomb, Glos. When she returned to take photos, the roe deer had been stripped out with just its spine left.

Experts say the first body had been ripped open and the heart, kidneys and liver were gone.

Dr Robin Allaby, of Warwick University, is studying DNA samples from this deer to see if it was killed by a panther-like cat.

He said: "I'm prepared to believe in the existence of big cats in the UK and we have a decent chance of finding out if it was there."

BEAST OF S

BY **RICHARD SMITH**
richard.smith@mirror.co.uk

Fears of big cat on loo
as 2nd deer is savage

A KILLER big cat is believed to be on the rampage in the Cotswolds after a second deer was found mutilated.

The carcass was in a field 10 miles from where the first deer had been ripped apart a fortnight ago in Woodchester Park, near Stroud.

Experts fear the animals were brought down and devoured by a powerful predator such as a puma, jaguar or leopard.

Big cat expert Frank Tunbridge, 65, said yesterday about the latest kill: "I believe it could be the same cat that attacked in Woodchester because these animals usually have a territory of 100 square mile cats could be thriving because are plenty of deer and weather creates cover for hun

The second body was foun woman walking her dog be Whiteway and Rendcomb,

◆ A puma.

20th January 2012

THIRD DEER IS MAULED

The Beast of Stroud may have struck for a third time after a mutilated roe deer was yesterday found 10 miles from the scene of the first killing.

Worker Mike Gorry, who spotted it on a building site while moving fencing, said: "It was big so something large must have

ROUD

she returned to take photos, e deer had been stripped out ust its spine left.

erts say the first body had ripped open and the heart, ys and liver were gone.

Robin Allaby, of Warwick rsity, is studying DNA samples his deer to see if it was killed anther-like cat.

said: "I'm prepared to believe existence of big cats in the d we have a decent chance of g out if it was there."

▲ **POWER** Puma may be culprit

killed it, although I'm no expert."

Big cat hunter Frank Tunbridge, 65, believes the animal was mauled by the beast, thought to have killed two other deer in the past two weeks. He said: "With these carcasses the prey's nose was bitten off, which is something lions and other big cats do. There also seems to be a few quarries near where the latest one was found.

"Big cats love to hide in places like that. It could have hunted all night and then killed the animal, maybe going back for seconds afterwards."

Experts believe a panther-like predator is behind the deaths in the Cotswolds. The first carcass was found in a National Trust park in Stroud, Glos, two weeks ago with a large paw print just 70 yards away. A dog walker discovered the second body near Cirencester and the latest corpse was found at Cooper's Edge, not far from Gloucester.

There have also been three separate sightings of a large creature in nearby South Woodchester and Nailsworth during the past eight days. Results from DNA swabs from each of the dead animals are due back next week.

26th January 2012

THE BEAST OF STROUD KILLS 3 WALLABIES

Three wallabies have been found mauled to death just weeks after a puma-like creature is believed to have killed three deer.

The mutilated bodies were found in the same area where it is thought a big cat – dubbed the Beast of Stroud – savaged three roe deer.

Wildlife expert Frank Tunbridge, 65, said yesterday: "No creature other than a big cat could bring down and kill these wallabies.

"The field was surrounded by a 7ft fence and there was no apparent entry sign. It must have leapt over it."

The animals, part of a private collection, were kept in a farmer's field in the Cotswolds, just 12 miles from where the first deer's body was found in Stroud, Glos. Warwick University experts are studying DNA samples from its carcass.

28th August 2012

BIG CAT TALES DOG OFFICERS

The hunt for the St Osyth lion is the latest in a series of reports of beasts on the loose to have caused cops major headaches.

West Yorks Police scrambled a helicopter and rail passengers were prevented from leaving a train after a driver reported seeing a lion in Shepley, West Yorks, last November. A hunt found nothing.

In May 2011, another helicopter was scrambled and a golf course cleared after a "white tiger was spotted in a field near Hedge End, Southampton".

But as officers approached the animal they realized it was not moving and a helicopter crew, using thermal imaging equipment, discovered there was no heat from it.

The "creature" was, in fact, a stuffed toy. But the Beast of Bodmin is still Britain's most famous big cat. After years of sightings around Cornwall it was declared a phantom in 1995 by the Ministry of Agriculture, Fisheries and Food.

In 2009, what appeared to be a black, panther-sized cat was filmed prowling along a railway line in Helensburgh, Argyll. And in 2007, a large black cat was photographed in Derbyshire. Experts calculated it was at least 18in tall and 3ft long.

28th August 2012

DEAR KITTY, KITTY

COPS SPEND £25,000 ON HUNT FOR 'ESSEX LION' … A GINGER TOM CALLED TOM

Police called off a huge lion hunt yesterday after deciding the alert was sparked by a large domestic cat.

And the *Daily Mirror* can reveal that the £25,000 operation involving more than 30 officers, specialist marksmen, and two police helicopters equipped with heat-seeking cameras, was most likely caused by 12-year-old ginger tomcat, Tom.

The dramatic two-day search left tens of thousands of residents in panic after they and thousands more Bank Holiday tourists were warned to stay indoors for their own safety.

While officers and zoo workers searched St Osyth, near Clacton, Essex, chief suspect Tom – who lives at an old people's home less than 200 metres from the original sighting – was said to have been

TOP RIGHT + INSET: Was it a lion in Essex, or Tom the cat? BOTTOM LEFT: Taking no chances. Police marksman called out in hunt for Essex lion. Bottom RIGHT: Hoax photos of the Essex lion were circulated on social media.

6 M Daily Mirror TUESDAY 28.8.2012

BIG CAT TALES DOG OFFICERS

By ANDREW GREGORY THE hunt for the St Osyth lion is the latest in a series of reports of beasts on the loose to have caused cops major headaches.

West Yorks Police scrambled a helicopter and rail passengers were prevented from leaving a train after a driver reported seeing a lion in Shepley, West Yorks, last November. A hunt found nothing.

In May 2011, another helicopter was scrambled and a golf course cleared after a "white tiger" was spotted in a field near Hedge End, Southampton.

But as officers approached the animal they realised it was not moving and a helicopter crew, using thermal imaging equipment, discovered there was no heat from it.

The "creature" was, in fact, a stuffed toy. But the Beast of Bodmin is still Britain's most famous big cat. After years of sightings around Cornwall it was declared a phantom in 1995 by the Ministry of Agriculture, Fisheries and Food.

▲ **PHANTOM** Bodmin beast

In 2009, what appeared to be a black, panther-sized cat was filmed prowling along a railway line in Helensburgh, Argyll. And in 2007, a large black cat was photographed in Derbyshire. Experts calculated it was at least 18in tall and 3ft long.

GUARD Police on lion watch

Dear ki

COPS SPEND £25,000 ON HUNT FOR 'ESSEX LION'.. A GINGER TOM CALLED TOM

EXCLUSIVE

BY LOUIE SMITH and ANDREW GREGORY
louie.smith@mirror.co.uk

POLICE called off a huge lion hunt yesterday after deciding the alert was sparked by a large domestic cat.

And the Daily Mirror can reveal that the £25,000 operation involving more than 30 officers, specialist marksmen, and two police helicopters equipped with heat-seeking cameras, was most likely caused by 12-year-old ginger tomcat, Tom.

The dramatic two-day search left tens of thousands of residents in panic after they and thousands more Bank Holiday tourists were warned to stay indoors for their own safety.

While officers and zoo workers searched St Osyth, near Clacton, Essex, chief suspect Tom – who lives at an old people's home less than 200 metres from the original sighting – was said to have been out and about on the prowl.

A carer at the home said: "He's always out in the fields hunting for mice, rats and even hares.

"I was working here on Sunday and he was definitely out then, so it certainly could have been him. His colouring means he does look a bit like a lion, but he's not dangerous.

"He's quite a large, mean-looking tom, but beneath all that he's an affectionate cat who just likes the odd stroke. The residents love having him around the place."

The scare began when holidaymaker Sue Wright, 58, took a grainy picture of a "lion" near a caravan park in St Osyth at around 7pm on Sunday.

She showed the image to police who decided to launch a full-scale search. Fake sightings and pictures posted on Facebook and Twitter only added to the panic.

And fuzzy long-range pictures taken by holidaymakers Stephen and Gill Atkin also appeared to show a big cat lazing in a field.

The hunt continued overnight, even after a witness rubbished the lion claims early Sunday evening. It was only halted yesterday afternoon.

Farmer Roger Lord, who co-owns the caravan site, watched the animal through his binoculars.

He said: "I had a look and said, 'That's a cat. It was sitting in stubble that was six to eight inches high and you could just see its head sticking out of the top.

"In my opinion it was a cat. I don't think it was large enough to be a lion but probably a big ginger cat. It was pale and I suppose a bit lion-coloured."

Pub landlord Dave Sparks, who runs the Red Lion pub in St Osyth, described the police hunt as "surreal". He said: "You don't really expect to be told there's a lion wandering around the area." In the ensuing panic, local residents reported further sightings and even claimed to have heard lions roaring.

Eyewitness Rich Baker, 39, said: "A man started running towards us yelling, 'It's a f***ing lion'. He looked so panicked you knew it was not a joke."

The van driver, from Romford, Essex, added: 'I grabbed my children's hands and we ran towards our caravan. It was one million per cent a lion. It was a tan colour with a big mane, it was definitely a lion." And mum-of-three Sue, from Dagenham, Essex, whose picture started the scare, last night insisted she had seen a lion.

"We watched it for a good half-an-hour before it disappeared. There is no doubt in my mind that we were looking at a lion." Her sister-in-law Denise Martin, 52, added: "I could see this shape in the field, so I got the binoculars out. It looked like a lion."

Building maintenance inspector Stephen, 52, from Louth, Lincs, who was staying at the caravan site, said he and wife Gill were eating when there was a knock on the window of their caravan.

Stephen said: "A gentleman was asking if we could confirm to the police that we were witnessing a lion across the other side of the field." Stephen added he took a phone from the gentleman and spoke to the police and told them: "Yes, what the gentleman has just told you is definitely a very large animal, and possibly a lion, definitely a large cat." He also said the animal was the length of two sheep "put together". Hospital administrator Gill, 51, then gave her pictures to the police.

St Osyth has a population of 4,000 but it swells to over 20,000 in the summer with the influx of holidaymakers. After the shock sighting on Sunday, everyone in the area was warned to stay i[...] Police advised residents to dial 999 if the[...] the animal.

During the night helicopters searched [...] creature's hideout using infrared cameras [...] were backed up on the ground by [...] marksmen. Keepers from Colchester Zoo [...] the hunt with tranquiliser guns. But n[...]

PUSSPECT Hunted 'beast' out hunting

MANE EVENT Stephen and Gill's picture which added to lion fears

◀ **BIG CAT** But it was probably only Tom

▲ **SIGHTING** Stephen and Gill Atkin took snap

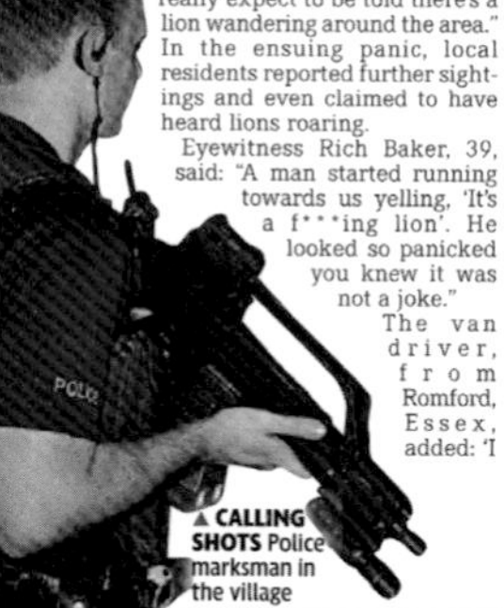

▲ **CALLING SHOTS** Police marksman in the village

YOU CAN'T HIDE YOU[...]

THE TWITTER FAKE

EXCLUSIVE BY ANDREW GREGORY A PICT[...] of a lion on the loose in Essex share[...] thousands online was yesterday expo[...] by the Daily Mirror as a fake.

Twitter user @tylerpittaway posted [...] image on Sunday and added: "I saw [...] lion like half an hour ago in #Basild[...]

Basildon is 50 miles from the orig[...] sighting in St Osyth which sparke[...] police hunt, but the photo re-tweeted [...] appeared on other papers' websites.

We discovered it was a doctored vers[...] of a red-eye photograph of a lion wh[...] we found by searching for "lion at ni[...] on Google. The Twitter user failed [...] respond to our calls yesterday.

Daily Mirror TUESDAY 28.8.2012 M 7

ty, kitty

▲ **GOT A FELINE** Mirror's Steve picks up predator's trail in Essex

Safari so good as I track down beast

STEVE MYALL Daily Mirror Big Game hunter

WHEN I heard there was a big cat on the prowl near Clacton I knew I was the mane man for the job.

I've hunted cougars in Faces Nightclub and feel at home among the leopard skins of Brentwood.

So, kitted out with camouflage hat, green and khaki shorts and shirt, desert boots and binoculars, I headed off to the, er, sun-baked plains of Essex.

Colchester Zoo's Anthony Tropeano has warned the public to "stay away from large, open and quiet spaces and, if confronted by the beast, to keep very still or risk encouraging it to chase them".

I just hoped I'd be able to fend it off with cat food and Lion bars.

Arriving in St Osyth I stopped by a pub – the Red Lion – to tap local wildlife experts for advice.

One man was convinced the sighting was genuine, and said: "Huge mouth and orange in colour, you say? Definitely from Essex; I think she was in last night."

Back out in the wild, a man walking his dog told me the lion had been staying in a caravan park.

Before I could approach its lair, I was intercepted by an over-zealous police community support officer. I bet that never happens to Sir David Attenborough.

It seems the police, after looking for signs of kills and scat (poo to you and me) have decided the "lion" is a domestic or wild household cat.

Village wags are joking that it might be a snow leopard with fake tan and hair extensions.

Then I spotted Tom, the ginger cat who's in the frame for lion impersonation. I thought it was a fur cop but as I grabbed him he swiped me with his paw and fled.

I'd been warned to keep very still if I saw the lion..or risk being chased

▲ **CLAW OF THE JUNGLE** Ginger Tom slashes me and scarpers

uch as paw prints or a lair, was found. Colchester Zoo, 15 miles away, were ccount for their lions.

Great British Circus, which recently area, was also asked if there had escapees.

cus, owned by Martin Lacey, had Rochford, Essex, over 50 miles away, two weeks previously. Mr Lacey, 70, said: "A female police officer came around on Sunday night and asked if we had lost any lions.

"We haven't got any lions at all. I gave them away three years ago to my sons. They use them for breeding programmes in Germany and America. The staff reassured her by showing her our tigers, which were all fast asleep, and she left." The intensive hunt is believed to have cost up to £25,000 with the bill for flying the police helicopters coming to at least £8,000 alone.

Wages for the 30 police officers involved in the search are expected to run to around £10,000.

Essex Police last night defended their investigation, saying their aim was to protect the public.

A spokesman said: "We believe what was seen on Sunday evening was either a large domestic cat or a wildcat.

"Extensive searches have been carried out, areas examined and witnesses spoken to, yet nothing has been found to suggest that a lion was in the area.

"We would like to thank the local community and holidaymakers for their patience and support."

Voice of the Mirror: Page 10

ON EYES

out and about on the prowl.

A carer at the home said: "He's always out in the fields hunting for mice, rats and even hares.

"I was working here on Sunday and he was definitely out then, so it certainly could have been him. His colouring means he does look a bit like a lion, but he's not dangerous.

"He's quite a large, mean-looking tom, but beneath all that he's an affectionate cat who just likes the odd stroke. The residents love having him around the place."

The scare began when holidaymaker Sue Wright, 58, took a grainy picture of a "lion" near a caravan park in St Osyth at around 7pm on Sunday.

She showed the image to police who decided to launch a full-scale search. Fake sightings and pictures posted on Facebook and Twitter only added to the panic.

And fuzzy long-range pictures taken by holidaymakers Stephen and Gill Atkin also appeared to show a big cat lazing in a field.

The hunt continued overnight, even after a witness rubbished the lion claims early Sunday evening. It was only halted yesterday afternoon.

Farmer Roger Lord, who co-owns the caravan site, watched the animal through his binoculars.

He said: "I had a look and said, 'That's a cat.' It was sitting in stubble that was six to eight inches high and you could just see its head sticking out of the top.

"In my opinion it was a cat. I don't think it was large enough to be a lion but probably a big ginger cat. It was pale and I suppose a bit lion-coloured."

Pub landlord Dave Sparks, who runs the Red Lion pub in St Osyth, described the police hunt as "surreal". He said: "You don't really expect to be told there's a lion wandering around the area." In the ensuing panic, local residents reported further sightings and even claimed to have heard lions roaring.

Eyewitness Rich Baker, 39, said: "A man started running towards us yelling, 'It's a f***ing lion.' He looked so panicked you knew it was not a joke."

The van driver, from Romford, Essex, added: "I grabbed my children's hands and we ran towards our caravan. It was one million per cent a lion. It was a tan colour with a big mane, it was definitely a lion." And mum-of-three Sue, from Dagenham, Essex, whose picture started the scare, last night insisted she had seen a lion.

"We watched it for a good half-an-hour before it disappeared. There is no doubt in my mind that we were looking at a lion." Her sister-in-law Denise Martin, 52, added: "I could see this shape in

Sullivan the lion with his mane in curlers before appearing in a television commercial for hair-care.

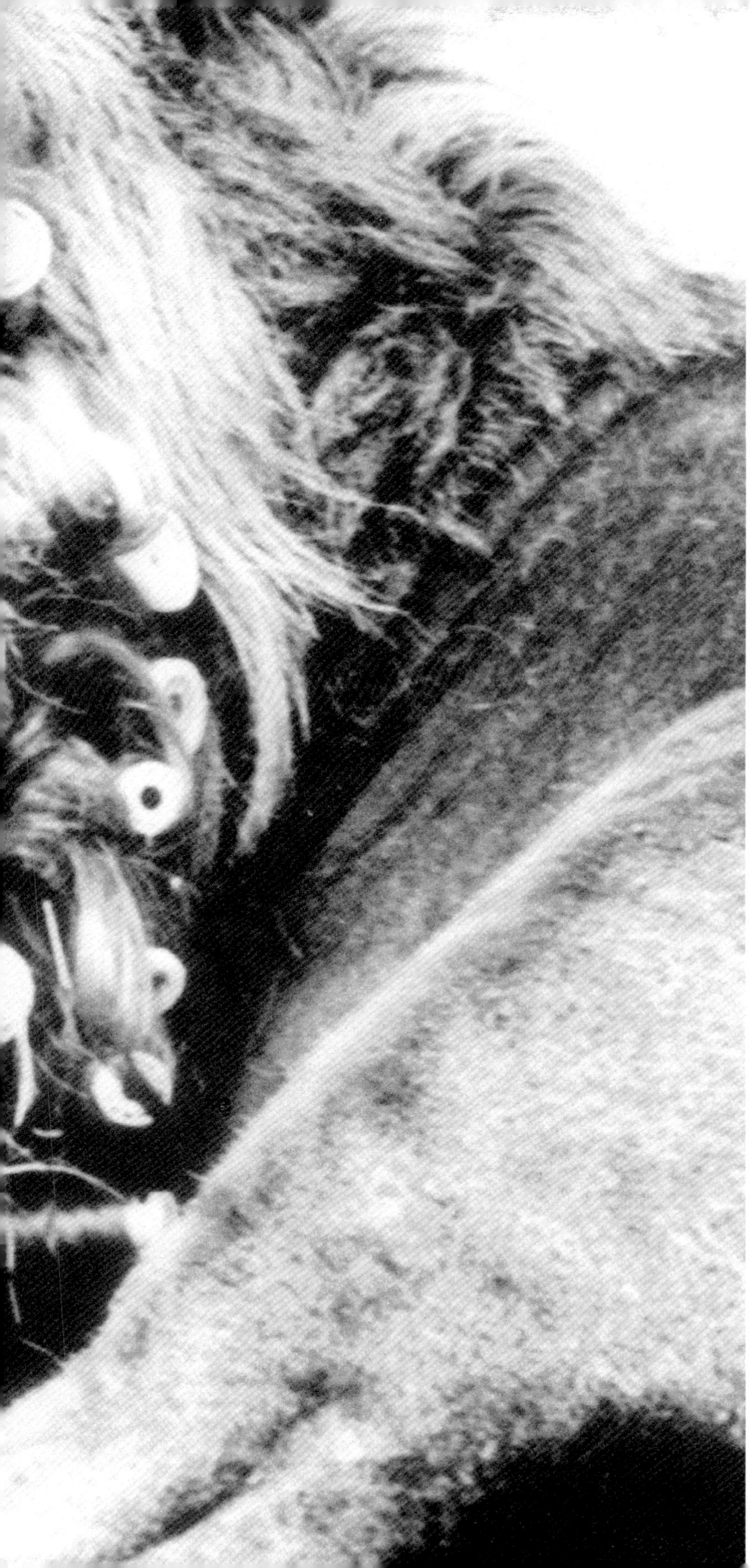

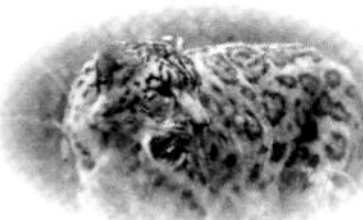

the field, so I got the binoculars out. It looked like a lion."

Building maintenance inspector Stephen, 52, from Louth, Lincs, who was staying at the caravan site, said he and wife Gill were eating when there was a knock on the window of their caravan. Stephen said: "A gentleman was asking if we could confirm to the police that we were witnessing a lion across the other side of the field." Stephen added he took a phone from the gentleman and spoke to the police and told them: "Yes, what the gentleman has just told you is definitely a very large animal, and possibly a lion, definitely a large cat." He also said the animal was the length of two sheep "put together". Hospital administrator Gill, 51, then gave her pictures to the police.

St Osyth has a population of 4,000 but it swells to over 20,000 in the summer with the influx of holidaymakers. After the shock sighting on Sunday, everyone in the area was warned to stay inside. Police advised residents to dial 999 if they saw the animal.

During the night helicopters searched for the creature's hideout using infrared cameras. They were backed up on the ground by police marksmen. Keepers from Colchester Zoo joined the hunt with tranquiliser guns. But no new evidence, such as paw prints or a lair, was found. Officials at Colchester Zoo, 15 miles away, were asked to account for their lions.

And the Great British Circus, which recently toured the area, was also asked if there had been any escapees.

The circus, owned by Martin Lacey, had moved to Rochford, Essex, over 50 miles away, two weeks previously. Mr Lacey, 70, said: "A female police officer came around on Sunday night and asked if we had lost any lions.

"We haven't got any lions at all. I gave them away three years ago to my sons. They use them for breeding programmes in Germany and America. The staff reassured her by showing her our tigers, which were all fast asleep, and she left." The intensive hunt is believed to have cost up to £25,000 with the bill for flying the police helicopters coming to at least £8,000 alone.

Wages for the 30 police officers involved in the search are expected to run to around £10,000.

Essex Police last night defended their investigation, saying their aim was to protect the public.

A spokesman said: "We believe what was seen on Sunday evening was either a large domestic cat or a wildcat.

"Extensive searches have been carried out, areas examined and witnesses spoken to, yet nothing has been found to suggest that a lion was in the area.

"We would like to thank the local community and holidaymakers for their patience and support."

Epilogue – The Wonder Years

Watch this space...

The reason that the mysteries throughout this book persist is that they are exactly that, unexplained phenomena about which we cannot help but wonder. Such wondering stretches our minds and our imagination, and creates a less mundane reality yet we still like to think of ourselves as intelligent and rational, and therefore highly advanced. Even so, the reason that mythical creatures and phantoms evade explanation may be because our technologies are still insufficient to detect them.

As we push back the boundaries to advance our understanding of the universe, we may also begin to reveal the realm of the unexplained.

8th September **1995**

... AND SOME ALIENS CLOSER TO HOME

We all want to believe in crop circles and flying saucers, myths and monsters.

We were intrigued by the idea of the Beast of Bodmin, the puma-like creature that terrorized Cornish sheep, enraged farmers and titillated binocular-clutching explorers.

There have been countless sightings of big, hairy creatures in Russia, South America and the Himalayas. Some leave no footprints, some seem immune to gunfire. The sea, too, is full of fabulous monsters, such as the huge 100ft eel seen speeding along at 50mph off San Francisco by a builder in 1983. It reared out of the sea to gaze balefully at the shore with deep, ruby-red eyes.

The Loch Ness monster has been talked about so much that it seems inconceivable that it doesn't exist. But there have also been sightings of a similar creature off the Cornwall coast – about 18ft long with its head perched on the end of a trunk.

And lots of people have seen a 10ft monster off the coast of Barmouth in North Wales with a head like ET and a big, baggy, turtle-shaped body.

1st May **2003**

THE NEW WAVE OF MONSTERS

Science is meant to explain mysteries. But often it creates more than it solves. Look at crypto-zoology, the study of monsters and unknown creatures.

One of its main subjects is the yeti or Bigfoot – the large, hairy, ape-like being that haunts the mountain wildernesses of Asia and North America.

These things are just fantasies or folklore. That is the scientific view. But it does not explain why monsters keep appearing, sometimes leaving footprints and other traces. Since the 1920s, when explorers first reported strange creatures in the lonely mountains, there have been literally thousands of sightings.

In the United States alone, more than 500 are recorded each year.

2002 was a peak year for Bigfoot sightings, most of them in the forests of the Pacific Northwest. The media paid no attention until a professor of psychology, hiking with his family, saw a tall, hairy monster in the Oregon woods. He heard its grunts and smelt its disgusting odour.

There is no real mystery about these apparitions. The American Indians and other native people have always known them.

You will never catch one, they say, because they are not flesh-and-blood animals but more like phantoms or demons. Their appearance is ominous. It warns of troubles to come. That, I think, is a better explanation for Bigfoot than science will ever come up with. But it means you have to accept the reality of spirits.